DATE DUE

NOV 26 1975			
D.37' 2-7-76			
D-362 3-20-76			
APR 1 0 AUG. 1 6 1976			
A UG. 30 - 1976			
NOV 9 1977			
APR 1 - 1980			
MAY 4 1981			
OCT 2 0 1983			
GAYLORD			PRINTED IN U.S.A.

Rudy Vallée

Stackpole Books

LET THE CHIPS FALL . . .

Published by
STACKPOLE BOOKS
Cameron and Kelker Streets
Harrisburg, Pa. 17105

Printed in the U.S.A.

Library of Congress Cataloging in Publication Data

Vallée, Rudy, 1901–
  Let the chips fall.

  1. Vallée, Rudy, 1901–   2. Musicians—Corre-
spondence, reminiscences, etc. I. Title.
ML419.V2A28   784'.092'4 [B]   75–17629
ISBN 0–8117–0947–7

To the denizens of New York City
and all its boroughs,
who in 1927 took me to their hearts
and never let me go!

Contents

PART III   Offstage

I Contend!

When I awoke on the morning of July 28, 1975, I looked at my wristwatch and closed my eyes as I leaned back on my pillow to contemplate the fact I had been *inhaling and exhaling* for the past seventy-four years on a planet of the universe!

On other birthdays I had usually reflected on the main events of the past year. But on this—my seventy-fourth birthday—I ruminated on the priceless gifts that had come to be in me, not through any mythical God or deity, nor the environment, nor the sun, nor the air, nor the food and water of which I had partaken throughout those long years, but from the stream of my ancestry —my French, Irish, and English forebears—to whom I bow in deep gratitude every day of my life!

It is repugnant to most human beings to credit their ancestors with all they are or ever hope to be, because to do this denies them the privilege of enjoying the satisfaction of vanity! To credit someone or anything else but one's self simply means that the individual may not honestly proclaim that "I did this . . . I accomplished this . . . I, and I alone, achieved this modicum of success!" Most human beings could not live with themselves if denied this privilege.

Just which ancestor caused me to "see red" when Aimée Boisaneau put the chocolate syrup in the lime juice jug without changing the label, I'll never know. I became choleric, whereas a boy of Scandinavian extraction would probably have shrugged his shoulders on seeing the chocolate syrup pouring out of a lime juice jug and gone about his chores, thinking nothing of the incredible mistake. Some ancestor or combination of them implanted in my genes an almost pathological angry intolerance of any stupid act, and since so many stupid acts, statements, and happenings occur every day, it is a wonder we're not in a worse mess than we are.

No matter what other traits, abilities, perceptions, understandings, emotions, wishes, desires, and talents one inherits, they mean nothing, if one lacks a sound and healthy body, or, if you prefer, constitution! When I think of how I might have emerged from my mother's womb—deaf, blind, with all the horrors of epilepsy, consumption, rickets, deformity of the limbs, idiocy, a hare lip or the inability to speak at all—I am deeply grateful, not to a deity *but to my ancestors!* In all of those seventy-four years, I emulate my father, who never really knew a day's serious illness!

And when I think of those great men of art and science who were plagued throughout their lives with crippling physical ailments but who in spite of these torturous handicaps were still able to contribute so much to mankind, I am more than ever beholden to my ancestors, who gave me not only the physical and mental gifts themselves, *but the awareness that I possessed them, the desire, the purposefulness, the stick-to-it-tiveness not only to develop and maintain these gifts but to put them to their best uses and to make them a contribution to the enjoyment and pleasure of others.*

The gift of recognizing latent greatness in others was in me from the age of nineteen when I first saw Rudolph Valentino in the *Four Horsemen of the Apocalypse*. Most instinctively, I pegged him for a star. Years later, on a small TV amateur show in San Francisco in 1949, I said to a young man named Johnny Mathis, after hearing him sing: "You are going to go a long way!"

—a prophecy of which he was to remind me on a TV program in Los Angeles four years later when he was already well on his way to his second million dollars.

It was this same gift of recognizing some intangible outstanding worthwhileness in persons, scripts, songs, plays, books, sports (years and years ago I saw tennis as the most popular sport of all for the personal enjoyment of the individual), dress and attire, and architecture and decoration of the home! Yes, even medicine, and, more importantly, surgery. Finally, in the enjoyment of good food and beverages, the ability to recognize the best of Don the Beachcomber's rum creations, and the outstanding delicacies of the kitchen as epitomized by George Mardikian and a chef named Langlois of Laguna Beach who has created a delicious morsel that is indeed heavenly in gastronomic ecstasy—his smoked epicure's delight, the "Winglet."

I can remember the day when, at the age of twelve, I sampled my first Shredded Wheat biscuit and said to myself, "This is a most satisfying and delicious food creation."

I pleaded with the makers of the new corn flake-type cereal, Buc Wheats, which I consider one of the most delicious concoctions of its kind (it could be my Vermont background that causes me to enjoy the maple syrup flavor of Buc Wheats), to let me do a commercial in which I could honestly say that "sometimes as I'm driving along *I begin to dream* about the bowls of Buc Wheats I am going to enjoy on arriving home." They were just not interested!

I knew long ago that American products such as wines, champagnes, and particularly soda pop would come into their own; and they have—they are doing spectacularly!

I am sure I would have recognized the superiority of Folger's coffee without the aid of Mrs. Olsen!

But there is a gift, which, next to good health, is the most priceless gift of them all and one which is practically nonexistent in the average person: namely, that elusive and little understood faculty—*the gift of an unusually good memory!*

My lovely wife is so bereft of this gift that if I suddenly ask her what her name is, she blurts out "Jane Smith"! My lovely Ellie has no memory at all! But in this lack she is joined by too many millions to attempt to summarize, even by computer. I became aware of this important gift in my youth when I had to memorize something during my school days. I found it was as simple as adding two and two! That is why this writing is not going to be so much about Rudy Vallée as it is my recollections of my association with other persons and situations.

Soon after radio catapulted me to great fame, I found myself associating with persons whom I had worshipped from afar (and still do!). I still have stardust in my eyes and will always be excited at the thought of being in the presence of those whom I used to bring to life on the screen when in 1917 I cranked that old projector in the Star Theatre for one dollar a day! My worship extends beyond the "show world" to include anyone who has achieved mightily in whatever the field might be, whether art, science, literature, or what have you.

Along with the gift of recognition of greatness in persons and things came an inordinate desire *to understand why it is as it is or was!*

Since in these forty-seven years in the fascinating yet sometimes murderous, cruel, shabby, and completely disillusioning world of "show business" it has been my fortune to meet almost everyone of importance, I have set down here some experiences, analyses, and happy and unhappy results of these associations which I have (in my cups after dinner) reeled off to fascinated friends, only to have them beg me to "put them in a book!"

For years I have evaded doing this—not for fear of the results of such revelations, but because I, in my strict New England upbringing (oh, yes! I admit that environment may have an effect, providing there are the inherited traits, seeds, and characteristics for the environment to bring out or try to suppress!) felt that one just does not "kiss and tell"!

Don't take credit for that great drive which enables you to work fifteen hours a day, that unquenchable urge to perfect yourself or the situation at hand, the inexhaustible energy that makes you the top sportsman of the day, or that all-consuming wish to better yourself and the world! Where do you think it came from? From the potatoes and meat you ate last night? From the air you breathe?

My kid brother William was brought up by the same mother as I, ate the same foods and inhaled the same air as I breathed in and out; yet William was as reluctant to labor manually—or, in plain English, as thoroughly lazy—as I was energetic not only in my youth, but throughout my life! In the drugstore, I chopped twenty pails of ice in the morning and twenty at night, then lugged them up a flight of slippery stairs to be packed around seven flavors of ice cream. By the time William was old enough to perform this chore seven days a week, father had installed electric refrigeration! I took the coals out of the furnace after they had been shaken down through, supposedly burned out; then, spreading them in the snow, I picked out for reburning those coals which somehow had failed to ignite. By the time this could have been William's happy chore, we had an oil burner in the furnace!

Even when success enabled me to have a chauffeur, I have always driven my own car and carried my own heavy bags and served myself in a cafeteria. I am a compulsive and tireless slave-worker and perhaps stupidly exert myself at times when I should let others do it for me, but so far I have escaped the curse of the hernia and will probably go on lifting heavy cases of wines and liquors to our storerooms and wine racks. William, for all of his retreat from exertion, has always been plagued by poor health. Recently he almost expired and in his post office work is now forbidden to even lift a mail sack!

What most persons fail to realize is that we inherit very little from our parents. As we go back into the stream of our ancestry, it is that ancestor of maybe fifty years back who pops out in us giving us either the blessing of a fully developed trait or skill or maybe the tendency or susceptibility to some horrible disease or affliction.

My sister Kathleen, who taught piano, could never extemporize or play really well any composition *unless the music was in front of her.* I, on the other hand, was always able to "fake" or play from memory almost any tune I had heard a few times. Conversely, I have always been a *slow and poor reader of the printed notes.* The re-creation from *memory* of anything in music or writing has always been my forte.

The host of a TV talk show, who has gone back into the obscurity from which he should never have emerged, on the single occasion of my guesting on his show, declared in his opening remarks to me that I was supposed to be very opinionated. He caught me completely off guard and before I could ask him to define the word or give me his interpretation of it, I found myself aimlessly stammering some sort of excuse or explanation of why I didn't think that I was the victim of this horrendous affliction. Actually, I wouldn't give a damn for a person who didn't have strong beliefs or ideas about something which he had learned or studied or about which he had read.

It is very possible that when I express an opinion about a subject about which I believe I am an expert or by virtue of much application and study I am qualified to speak, I may seem to be overbearing and slightly pompous. This is because in my enthusiasm for the subject I speak with force and conviction, just as I *italicize* when I write in an effort to impress the listener or reader with my thoughts on the subject. I make no apology for this trait as all too often in life, I have found too many persons extremely wishy-washy in their statements about subjects concerning which they should be more explicit and authoritative.

But one trait—the love of applause—is entirely lacking in me. I was totally ignorant of this until a laughable yet very vivid portrayal of this lack was forcibly shown to me on a stage before four thousand persons!

My band and I were performing on the stage of the New York Paramount Theatre. After bursting out into our great radio popularity, which meant that we had to show ourselves in the flesh to the millions in and around New York City who had come to worship our modest radio broadcasts because they were different from all the other orchestras of the day, we had played in thirteen RKO Vaudeville Theatres, including the famed Palace Theatre. We were then enjoying a very lucrative contract with the Paramount Publix Theatres which was to endure for almost two years.

This was our second show of six shows we were doing daily at the flagship of the Publix Theatres chain, the New York Paramount. On the unit bill that week was a brilliant comedic wit, Jack Osterman, who on the nightclub floor was unmatched for his ability to destroy with his rapier wit any heckler or adversary who dared challenge him. We had become friends and it was Osterman who introduced me to Mamma Leone's, which along with Manny Wolfe's Steak House on the lower East Side, was to become my favorite eating house. Osterman had evidently studied the manner in which I led my little group of seven musicians and also, *the way I personally performed while singing and my reaction to the audience when I finished singing!* On this afternoon as he passed me after doing his spot in the show, I could detect that he had been drinking!

I then proceeded to place my hand on my head to be sure the hair was in place, pick up the megaphone, spread my legs apart, and sing a chorus of a popular tune titled "My Sin." After singing a chorus, I put the megaphone down and looked at the pianist while he played one-half the chorus, and then at my two violinists, while they played the second half, and then picking up the megaphone, sang another chorus of the song.

I had just finished doing my rendition of "My Sin" when Osterman abruptly strode out on the stage, took the megaphone away from me, and, after feeling the part in his hair, picked up the megaphone and then stood with legs spread apart and sang the song looking at the musicians exactly as I had done. But at the conclusion of the number, as the audience began to applaud, he turned around, bent over, and *stuck his rear end out at the audience!* My boys, who had observed the fact that I *ignored the audience's applause and appreciation* of my performance, fell off their chairs when Osterman portrayed this trait of mine!

I apparently have always been like the great surgeon who is too busy performing his superb and skillful operations to take any bows for what he does so easily and naturally; in other words, he is the last person in the world to realize that he is almost a genius and is too busy doing what he is doing to *think about it!* Yes, I am very much like this great surgeon except that I do not feel that I am anything remotely resembling a true genius. I use that word very sparingly.

I have always lost myself too much in the pleasure of singing or playing a fine composition to care whether or not anyone else was likewise enjoying it. I have *never,* but *never,* been spurred by the monetary reward or the applause of a receptive audience, but have always lost myself in the enjoyment of doing something that to me is the breath of life and that I was destined to do! Even today, in my delivery of humor, I rarely wait until the laughter at the last bit of humor has ended before I am on to the next one-liner or anecdote. But likewise, I do not mentally or under-the-breath curse the audience if they fail to react, or recall how it went before a more enthusiastic audience. Nor do I say, as Fred Allen used to, "Forgive me for *laughing,* I *know* what's coming!"

Most persons who essay comedy—especially Milton Berle—wait until the last small titter or handclap has stopped before going on. Berle waits for hours, *savoring the triumph he has just achieved in bringing forth from the innards of his audience that precious phenomenon which the world needs so badly and which we call laughter.* I, on the other hand, am enjoying myself *even more than my audience* and I just don't really care whether you were able to rise to enjoy what I had to offer. When I know that what I have shown to you is a *fine something,* created by a very gifted someone and which has been delivered to you as well as I believe it could have been delivered, I am too impatient to get on to my next morsel, to wait for you *to tell me what I already know!*

I paraphrase this lack of vanity perhaps best in the phrase that there is no ham in me and that I don't pine for or greatly desire the spotlight. I have never had any illusions as to my personal appearance or the extent of my gifts first in music and later in the ability to make human beings laugh. I have been too busy *doing it* to wonder or worry whether you might enjoy what I had to offer!

The thousands of letters that greeted our early broadcasts told me so clearly that I had hit upon a magic formula for a little band with a simple small singing voice that was going to carry us to great heights that I did not need continued proof of it! When I first discovered that I possessed the gift of uttering words that could literally "fracture" an audience, again, I did not need to wait to read what one individual, *no matter how gifted in the art of criticism,* thought of my performance! Thus it is that I sometimes *do seem to patronize my audiences* in night clubs as one Miami critic so sagely observed. I assure you, I am vaguely aware of their enjoyment or lack of it, *but I still am not unhappy or deliriously happy as are most Berle-minded performers!*

If further proof were needed that there is little or no vanity in Rudy Vallée, I need only point out that throughout the course of four marriages over a period of forty-seven years, there has never been a single progeny to bear my name!

This is incomprehensible to many persons, especially my most devout fans who just cannot believe that I would not wish to see myself perpetuated. Others, after surveying all of the memorabilia that reposes in our lower museum-office-theater building, feel that all of this should be inherited by my own flesh and blood and not wind up in the halls or room of some college or the Smithsonian Institution.

The invariable question is "Don't you want to see another Rudy Vallée carrying on your life?"

To which I reply, completely demolishing these inquisitors, "Another Rudy Vallée? Heaven forbid!" I can only repeat that unlike some other men who live for that moment when they can proclaim themselves proud fathers, I have never deviated from this lack of interest in seeing myself perpetuated in this life, and in all my peregrinations into the enjoyment of the sexual act, I have never breathed more freely and happily than when the rabbit test proclaimed there would be no issue!

Please forgive me for this too long preamble, but I did want you to know me a little better since this writing is not a biography *per se*, but rather an attempt to acquaint the average person with what actually goes on in this fabulous world of entertainment, as I am thoroughly aware that very few of you "laymen" have any idea of the inner feelings, makeup, or real personality of the gifted immortals to whom you have given fame and fortune as you elevated them to stardom.

These chapters are confrontations with persons who made our association either happy or unpleasant. I have not attempted to "get even with" any of them—even poor Winchell, who was punished enough in his dying days—but I have merely set down the facts *as I vividly remember them for better or for worse* and I can only finally say, LET THE CHIPS FALL WHERE THEY MAY!

PART I

A WEAKNESS FOR BRUNETTES

Why I Can't

Ever Play a

I first became aware of my strong preference for brunettes in my early youth—Joan Crawford, Pola Negri, and Hedy Lamarr were my ideals.

One day in my junior year at Yale I was shaken as never before when I saw a beautiful brunette who epitomized in every way my concept of the ideal woman. There she was, totally devastating in her loveliness, staring at me from the cover of *College Humor* on a newsstand outside the Yale Post Office. I immediately wrote to H. N. Swanson, who was then editor of the popular *College Humor* magazine (Swanson is now an agent for writers in Hollywood and Los Angeles), and asked if I could meet the girl. Of course, he never replied. Eventually I met Rolf Armstrong, who did the crayon drawing of this fascinating girl; he offered to sell it to me for $3,000. I declined. But it all made one thing painfully clear to me: If a girl had a beautiful face in addition to brunette hair, I was a goner!

Then, in the fall of 1941 at a British war relief affair, I met Mary, a girl who might be likened to Jinx Falkenburg. She was tall, with golden auburn hair and a well-scrubbed complexion—a

Howard Hughes
Vegas Hotel

typical American beauty. Although not my ideal of earlier years, she soon became a truly passionate love of mine. By the time our country had entered the war I was more deeply involved with Mary than I had ever been with anyone else in my life. In fact, had she really loved me I would certainly have married her.

It was our custom to have dinner at Musso Franks—the first famous Hollywood restaurant—and then go to the newsreel theatre to watch scenes of the war in Europe. There we watched our forces being pounded by the Japanese in the Philippines, Guadalcanal, and the South Pacific. One night, though, the newsreel showed three young girls modeling the first WAC uniform on the steps of the Capitol in Washington. For the first time since meeting Mary I saw in the newsreel a brunette beauty with a captivating smile and Oriental eyes.

The next day I sensed the faint spark of a possible release from the torment that Mary had aroused in me, when I spotted a full-page shot of the three young ladies in *Life* magazine. I quickly contacted Max Lowe, who was in charge of music and entertainment at the Shoreham Hotel. Max had asked me to open at the

Rolf Armstrong and I stand before his drawing of the girl I fell in love with on the cover of *College Humor* magazine.

Shoreham in 1929, paying me $15,000 for fifteen minutes of music; after that he had asked me to play there several times. I wanted him to give me the name of the young lady in the *Life* photograph. I'm sure he must have known, but for some reason he failed to convey that *she had been working as a singer* with Enrique Madruguera's orchestra at the Shoreham!

"I'll send you her phone number," he told me, and he did.

I called her at once and as we talked I could sense the warm, friendly waves over the telephone. "I have an agency," I said. (This was true—Fay Emerson, Victor Borge, Slapsy Maxie were my clients.) "I'm interested in putting you into pictures, and," I added, "I have a *personal* interest in you."

She seemed to understand this immediately.

"Would it be possible for you to come to Hollywood?" I asked.

"Yes!" she replied very quickly.

"Without your mother?" I prompted.

She agreed, and I couldn't help feeling that I was "in like Flynn!"

In the next few weeks my golden auburn beauty was giving me

less and less trouble. She had always worn everything to please me, from false eyelashes and satin dresses to five-inch heels. And as far as sex was concerned she left nothing to be desired. But it was all destined to come to an end.

By this time I had enlisted in the Coast Guard as a Chief Petty Officer bandmaster. The Coast Guard had decided to let me continue my radio broadcasts for National Dairies, the "Sealtest Show," which by now had become very successful, mainly because John Barrymore had given it such a tremendous lift that our rating had climbed from a lowly four to twenty-two! It was decided that I could conduct the show, *provided that I turned over whatever monies I had coming to me for the broadcast* to the Coast Guard Welfare Fund, which I did.

Our broadcasts were very happy ones and the pleasure of working with John Barrymore was something I'll never experience again! We had the greatest writers in the world. Paul Henning— who created "Beverly Hillbillies," "Green Acres," and "Petticoat Junction"—was one of our first writers at $250 a week. Then we had Norman Panama and Mel Frank; a gifted creator, Jess Oppenheimer, who conceived the idea for radio of "I Love Lucy"; a newcomer, Charlie Isaacs; and a veteran, Frank Galen. The combined writing talents of these men sent our show on its way to the high-

I was paid $15,000 for providing fifteen minutes of music at the opening of the Hotel Shoreham in Washington, D.C. in 1929. The orchestra and I had Amelia Earhart's trimotored plane to take us from New York to Washington and a special train waiting at Penn Station in the event the plane couldn't go. The plane made it safely, although forced down at Camden. A special car took us back to New York.

Below mike and to left at piano is Walter Gross, piano genius and author of "Tenderly."

Here I am with Mary McBride in 1942.

est ratings. Abe Burrows was our head writer, and the show was supervised by Ed Gardner, one of the greatest directors and handlers of comedy writing the business would ever know. We did our broadcast from the old NBC studios at Sunset and Vine.

One particular Thursday evening my Coast Guard Band and I were playing a concert at Alhambra High School where admission was by war stamps and bonds. As I left the NBC radio studio by the backstage door after the broadcast there was the usual group of song pluggers, begging me to put their songs on our program, and down the street was a redhead whom I had picked up the night before at a party (taking her away from Mickey Rooney, in fact!). She was attractive enough, but very frankly, I wasn't overboard in my feelings about her. Then, as I was talking to the eight or ten song pluggers I heard a lovely, fluid voice speaking to me. I looked up and there was a vision of loveliness in a flowered dress, with a little black velvet bellboy cap on her head.

"Mr. Vallée?" she asked.

"Yes," I answered.

"I'm Bettejane Greer."

I was blank for a moment.

"You remember, you called me in Washington," she said.

"Oh, yes!" And then I quickly added, "Where may I phone you?"

She gave me her number, which was a very simple one—Hollywood 1241. In those days our phone numbers had only four digits. I jumped into my station wagon and drove to Alhambra with the redhead sitting beside me. But later I stopped at a service station to call Bettejane Greer, suggesting dinner at my home in the Hollywood Hills.

She readily assented, but added that it would be better if she didn't, because *Mr. Hughes* did not like her to go out! I subsequently discovered that Howard Hughes had heard her sing at the Shoreham Hotel in Washington with Madruguera's orchestra and had sent her to Hollywood to make pictures. Whether he had already proposed to her by the time we met at the NBC studios, I don't know. Later she told me that he had asked her to marry him on several occasions, but that she had no feeling for him, "although I liked him personally."

I drove home after the concert at the high school and dropped the redhead off without so much as a peck, leaving her to wonder what the hell was wrong with me (although I think she had witnessed my brief conversation with the song pluggers and Bettejane).

The next morning I awoke about 11:30 or 12:00 and placed the call to Bettejane. Apparently I had the right digits, *but not in the right order*—I tried several combinations of the four digits without any success. So I called RKO Studios, which Howard Hughes then owned.

"Oh, no, Mr. Vallée!" the girl said. "Mr. Hughes doesn't permit us to give *anyone's* number, *especially* a young lady's number."

By now it was 2:30 P.M. and I was in a panic because I was supposed to pick up Bettejane at 4:00! Stupidly, I had not given her my telephone number (which also was a very simple one—Hempstead 5555). Furthermore, she had no idea that I was in the book (although I always have been, in New York for three years in *How to Succeed*, and here).

About 3:15 P.M. the phone rang. It was the most elegant of all the song pluggers—a young man who wore $200 suits because he represented Chappelle, the music firm that had all the show business hits. He began out of left field discussing songs. Suddenly he said, "That young lady last night—."

"Yes?" I asked eagerly.

"Did you get her phone number?"

"No, did you?"

"Yes," he said, and generously gave it to me.

"You're 'in' on the next ten programs!" I announced happily, and quickly called Bettejane.

I picked her up at four o'clock, and within moments it became obvious that she had apparently conceived an affection for me before we had even met. It was very easy for me to become infatuated with her, too. She was beautiful, amorous, and intelligent—a wonderful, delightful companion, with a fabulous sense of humor!

To the consternation of some in the Coast Guard I had her dress in a Spars' uniform, and at some of our concerts she sang with the band. She did a wonderful impression of a drunk getting drunker by the moment, a routine that I had filmed when we were making a Coast Guard short and that I still have in my film collection.

As I continued to enjoy Bettejane's company we would occasionally have dinner at her mother's home and go to a movie. We were always required to leave the name of the theater with her mother in case Howard Hughes wished to reach Bettejane. Invariably, about ten o'clock the usher would come down the aisle to tell Bettejane that she was wanted on the phone. This was Hughes' way of breaking up our evening. I would drive her to one of his offices on Romaine just off LaBrea Avenue, where on the fourth floor he would be waiting for her. When she would enter his office, she says, he would be seated at his desk (I would wait in the car). He would sit there, drumming his fingers on the desk, and then would suddenly grab her hand to see if there was a ring on the engagement finger, flinging it back and telling her that she could leave. This happened at least six times before we were married.

In time Bettejane became acutely aware that I had once been deeply in love with my well-scrubbed, auburn-haired Mary, and that she was still very much in my system. In fact, one day as I was lying on my bed and Bettejane was seated on the couch opposite me, I received a call from Mary, and after I hung up Bettejane started to cry.

"You have no need to worry or be concerned." I tried to reassure her. "I'm going to stop seeing her." But I could see that Bettejane still felt it was something to be concerned about.

Finally a situation arose where she overheard me talking about a possible blind date in San Diego when my band and I would be playing there on a Sunday afternoon, a date that never materialized and wouldn't have meant anything anyway. But when I came to see Bettejane two nights later, she slammed the door in my face. Later, however, the world-famous photographer Paul Hessee informed me that Bettejane was very unhappy, and he suggested I call her. I did.

As we sat in the car after coming home that night, she suddenly cried out in a burst of emotion and tears: "I don't want any *career*. I don't want anything but to be your *wife!*" It reminded me of the time when my first wife, Leone Cauchois, and I were driving home the night of our wedding in 1928, crossing the 59th Street bridge, when she startled me by screaming to the stars: "I love Rudy Vallée! I love Rudy Vallée!"

Once again I found myself almost speechless, overwhelmed by Bettejane's outburst. Finally I said, "Mary is still in my system, but if you want to take the chance, so be it. We'll do it before Thanksgiving."

Our wedding was a military one under swords of my fellow officers at a little church on Wilshire Boulevard. Foolishly I took her to Palm Springs for a short honeymoon. I say "foolishly" because I had once taken Mary there with her mother, and had one of the most fabulous two weeks of sexual enjoyment that I probably have ever experienced.

It rained every day that Bettejane and I were in Palm Springs. I tried vainly to type a long letter exposing a sordid bit of chicanery that was being perpetrated by the head of an advertising agency. He was forcing stars like Victor Mature to appear on the Lux program for nothing, in return for which the program gave a short one-minute plug to that person's branch of the military, *which the show's sponsor had to do anyway!* But it was no use. I couldn't concentrate. There was so much of Mary in everything at Palm Springs, and with the rain keeping us indoors all of the time, I realized that she was still too much in my heart.

After arriving back in Hollywood I immediately phoned her.

"Will you meet me?" I asked, and she agreed. But as we talked in the car she made it clear that it was finis as far as she was concerned.

Every time Bettejane and I went to the Mocambo or some other place to dance, there would be Mary with her beautiful smile, in the arms of an air force captain or colonel, pretending to

Bettejane Greer and I are married under the swords of my fellow officers at a little church on Wilshire Boulevard.

be as happy as hell—as she probably was! But seeing her in the arms of another man was like a stab in the heart to me. Bettejane was aware of this as she knew who Mary was. As the months wore on we both realized that we must terminate a marriage that never should have been, and finally we agreed upon a separation.

After several weeks in which I had seen neither Mary nor Bettejane I began phoning Bettejane again. She refused to answer my calls. I finally tricked her into coming to the office supposedly to meet with a new executive at RKO Studios, who left the office as soon as he got her in. It took little pleading on my part for her to agree to another try, and I drove her to her mother's home where she had been staying during the separation. She was going to move back into our home again, and we planned a dinner with several friends. But the hour approached 8:00, then 8:30, and then 9:00. I knew something was wrong and phoned her mother.

"Bettejane's gone," she said. "Howard Hughes came and drove her away."

My heart sank. What was to have been a very happy dinner was now merely a means of satisfying hunger, what little I had at that point.

At eleven o'clock the telephone rang. It was Bettejane.

"Rudy? I'm calling from Balboa," she said, almost breathlessly. "Howard drove me here, but he let me make this call to you. He's bringing me back!"

I could hear a clicking sound. "What's that?" I asked.

"Oh, Howard has the habit of going around the car, hitting anything metal with the ring on his finger. He does it whenever I phone anyone."

I drove to her mother's house and parked on the hill, watching for their return. They appeared in a fairly small car with Hughes behind the wheel. Both of them got out and he talked to her for about a minute or two, but made no attempt to kiss her. She ran into the house then, and he drove away.

I picked her up and brought her back to the house where we had experienced so much unhappiness. For the next week or so, however, we were fairly happy. But on our first night out at the Cocoanut Grove in the Ambassador Hotel, there again was Mary with an officer, and again the misery in my heart! So after a few more weeks we decided to end it completely—once and for all. Still we remained good friends.

I'll never forget one night in New York in 1946 when I went to El Morocco with a very tall, horsey, raw-boned, titled English lady who was about a half foot taller than I. We had met at a party and she had persuaded me to take her there. As we danced, she towering above me, I looked around and there was Bettejane Greer with her new husband, Ed Lasker, son of the famous advertising executive who had left him many millions of dollars. Both of them wore smiles and Bettejane couldn't help but laugh at my predicament.

I didn't see her again until May 1953 when my present wife, Eleanor, and I were the guests of Tony Hullman at the 500-mile Indy speedway race. We attended a party at the Indianapolis Athletic Club the night before the race, and Bettejane was there with Earl Muntz. We exchanged pleasantries; I introduced Bettejane to my wife. The next day I watched Bettejane kiss Vukavitch, the Californian who won the race. She is divorced from Lasker, and at present, I understand, is enjoying the companionship of a very pleasant person. I sincerely hope she has found the happiness she richly deserves. I have never met a more charming, kind, and intelligent person than Bettejane Greer.

Why, then, can't I ever play a Howard Hughes' hotel in Las Vegas? The man who books all of the Hughes' hotels was my close buddy in our Coast Guard band—Walter Kane, a former vaudevillian himself, who became a lieutenant in the Coast Guard during the war and was assigned to handle our band bookings, and has long been associated with Howard Hughes. He has a telephone by his bedside that at any moment might summon him to do anything for Hughes.

Walter booked me (probably the first booking of a star) in Las Vegas in 1947 at The Last Frontier, for the unheard of sum of $4,000 as a single! At that time there were only two places on The Strip: The Last Frontier and The Rancho Vegas. The Flamingo had opened and then closed again for alterations. Now, several decades later, Walter Kane is booking all of the Hughes' hotels, but every time I mention a booking for me, he always gives me the evasive answer, "I'm working on it." Obviously, since it has been a number of years ago that I asked him to book me, there must have been word from the great master: "No bookings for Rudy Vallée!"

I have even written to Howard Hughes, trying to explain that I didn't mean to hurt Bettejane—that someone else was simply in my system and I just couldn't shake her off. But the Bettejane Greer incident could only have added insult to injury when Hughes later learned that I was going with another object of his attention—Pat Dane.

I missed a real chance to get a booking by not contacting Robert Mahew, the man who is now estranged from Howard Hughes but to whom Hughes paid the magnificent sum of $500,000 a year after giving him a beautiful $400,000 home in which to live. Back in 1969 I was amazed to receive an invitation from Mahew to the first Howard Hughes' tennis championship to be held in Las Vegas—a week of much tennis with room and food plus access to all the Hughes' hotels and shows!

All of the tennis celebrities had met on a Sunday afternoon for cocktails, when suddenly Frank Sennes, who did the entertainment booking at that time, grabbed me by the arm, and said, "I want you to meet the big man!"

I knew he didn't mean Howard Hughes. I had always pictured Mahew as a Jim Aubrey—tall, six-foot-two, Princeton man, beautifully attired, slim, very elegant; in short, a man of great distinction—but instead I met a roly-poly, short character who pumped my hand and started to speak Canadian French. To my great astonishment I learned that Mahew came from Waterville, Maine. "Why," I said, "that's only thirty miles from where the Vallée family used to live, and that's where Colby college is."

He nodded. "At one time I owned two grocery stores in Waterville."

I am sure Mahew did not know that I had previously taken out two of Howard Hughes' girls and married one of them, or he would never have invited me to the tennis championships. Of course, he is now in the doghouse himself, so that makes us two of a kind.

It has always been puzzling to me why none of those who wrote about Howard Hughes and who wanted to find out more about him never consulted Walter Kane or Bettejane Greer. These two people could have, if they wished, told much about the "invisible god."

The

Not long ago I stopped at the old Roosevelt Hotel on Hollywood Boulevard opposite Graumann's Chinese Theatre to pick up an airplane ticket. In the late twenties the Roosevelt was *the* hotel of Hollywood. I obeyed an irresistible urge and entered a door leading off the main entrance—the first door on your right as you come off the boulevard. As I had done many times before, I peeked into a room that now is just a simple banquet room. It was empty, as usual, with the same dirty yellow walls and one or two tables and a few chairs scattered around. But I was seeing another room and remembering other days.

In more recent years a number of banquets and dances have brought me to this room. About five or six years ago my wife, Ellie, and I were guests on the dais with our dear friend George Mardikian, who is rated as one of the world's greatest chefs. He made the wedding cake for our marriage in 1949, but I first met him in 1938 when he owned a small Omar Khayyam restaurant in Fresno, California. As a result of our meeting then, Mardikian spent four days preparing a gargantuan feast at my former home at Harold Way in 1940, where I entertained all the cast of Co-

2

Blossom Room

lumbia Pictures' *Time Out for Rhythm*, including Jimmy Roosevelt and his nurse whom he subsequently married. Then in 1941, when I moved into my present castle in the Hollywood Hills, I gave two banquets—one for all of the painters, electricians, plumbers, etc. who had helped renovate the castle, and their wives: approximately twenty-five to thirty persons; and the other for a group of my personal friends. For both parties Mardikian spent days preparing entrees, desserts, soup of the Armenian kings—food as only he can prepare it! Subsequently Mardikian moved to San Francisco and took over the old Coffee Dan's, where he had been a dishwasher when he first come to California, and made it into the Omar Khayyam of today—a restaurant that is the shrine of all lovers of good foods, especially Armenian foods.

However, it is not the banquets I have attended in the last fifteen years that flash into my memory, but a Monday night in 1929 when this room was known as the Blossom Room. On Monday nights all the elite—and only the elite—of the film colony met there to enjoy themselves.

I first came to know the Blossom Room when I arrived in Hollywood to make *The Vagabond Lover* in 1929. My mother and father had accompanied me on the trip, and we had taken the Santa Fe Chief, which lacked air conditioning, in the last hot days of August, stopping at various places along the way for me to say a few words from the back of the last car. Somehow word had reached Kansas City and a few other places along the route that I was on the train, and some of our radio fans were at the stations.

We arrived in Los Angeles' Union Station at eight o'clock. It was Saturday night in September—Labor Day weekend. The picture was to be made at RKO Studios, and we were met by six girls from a recently completed Wheeler and Woolsey RKO picture called *Rio Rita*. The mayor also appeared and presented me

A bevy of beautiful girls from the RKO picture *Rio Rita* was on hand to greet me when I arrived on the Santa Fe Chief in Union Station, Los Angeles on the Saturday before Labor Day in 1929. My parents had accompanied me on the train. They are shown descending the steps. The occasion of my visit was to make *The Vagabond Lover* at RKO Studios in Hollywood.

with a large key to the city. My parents and I then climbed into a white Rolls-Royce, that looked not unlike a funeral hearse, and we proceeded with sirens screaming from a police escort of eight or nine motorcycles. The people in Los Angeles were bewildered, wondering what in hell this cavalcade was all about!

We finally went all the way to the end of Pico Boulevard, past the famous Willard's Chicken Restaurant, that served a thousand dinners nightly, and back to the Roosevelt Hotel. In front of the hotel was one of the famous bands of that day—one I had watched perform in 1927 in a show called *Paris*, with Irene Bordoni at the Alvin Theatre in New York, at which the band performed not only in the pit but also on the stage with Miss Bordoni. This band, Irving Aaronson and his Commanders, was in front of the Roosevelt Hotel playing "The Vagabond Lover" as we alighted from the Rolls-Royce.

My father and mother stayed with me at the Roosevelt Hotel until the second week, when my father approached me on a Sunday morning. "Hubert," he said, "We are having lunch with a director from Maine. Would you like to join us?"

I didn't mean to be cross with him, but somewhat petulantly I said, "Dad, don't bother me with these little directors from Maine. Our picture is being directed by Marshall Neilan."

Marshall Neilan had indeed been one of the great directors along with Alan Dwan and others. He had directed several great feature pictures; mine was to be his last and, unfortunately, not a very good one. A few years later I discovered that the director whom Dad had met in Portland came from Lewiston, Maine, which is twenty or thirty miles from Portland and Westbrook, our home town. He was named O'Feeny—I think my father called him O'Fiernan. If I had gone to that luncheon I might have played the part that Wally Ford got in *Stagecoach* and become an important personality in motion pictures. Who knows? The little director from Maine—John Ford!

We had arrived in Hollywood on a Saturday night and by Monday I was asked to come to the studio to make a screen test to judge makeup and what type of lighting to use. "How far is it to RKO Studios?" I asked one of the Roosevelt bellboys.

He said, "Just a short walk."

But it turned out to be a walk of several miles in the blazing sun, and I was bareheaded. By nightfall I was suffering from sunstroke. It was so bad that when they made the test I looked as if I had strips of skin peeling from my face.

The second week I was approached by someone asking me if I would be the guest of honor at the Monday night Blossom Room soiree, where all of the film colony elite met. The film colony, learning that a radio personality named Rudy Vallée had come to make a picture, was curious to see what this "phenomenon" looked like. Certain film personalities who sang or performed in musicals were curious to see if I might be a threat to them. So I agreed to bring my little band and do a few numbers.

The now yellow-walled banquet room was in 1929 a beautiful room in shimmering green, with a profusion of flowers and foliage that made it a floral wonderland. I sat at my table, surveying the film personalities. There were Douglas Fairbanks, Jr. and Joan Crawford against the wall—how I envied them, particularly Fairbanks, who had won this wonderful, dark-haired creature who was very much my ideal. There was Ruth Roland, whom I used to bring to life as I cranked a motion picture projector in 1917, and who was known for her daredevil stunts of jumping from one moving freight car to another. On my left were Gary Cooper and Lupe Velez, apparently very much in love. Perhaps it would be simpler to say that everyone who was anyone in the film colony was there. I was tremendously flattered that they had deigned to turn out for our debut in the film capital.

Our offering was very simple. I used the megaphone, as amplifying sound had not yet come in, and I would assume that by the third or fourth number there were sighs of relief. I felt that we had acquitted ourselves well, however, and we relaxed to enjoy a delicious dinner while listening to Irving Aaronson and his Commanders.

Enter Mary Brian. In my senior year at Yale in the spring of 1927 I was performing on the saxophone with an orchestra owned by two Yale graduates, playing at Franklin Hall Fraternity house for the spring dances. I had played Franklin Hall many times during my four years at Yale and usually it was a fairly routine affair with the boys cutting in and out on the girls. The dances were held in the afternoon until early evening. On this particular afternoon, well, something different had been added.

We were told that we were to be honored by the presence of a movie star—Mary Brian, a young girl who had just made a Paramount picture called *The Poor Little Rich Girl*. She finally arrived and, of course, was the center of much attention. Suddenly I realized that she was staring at me. After an hour or so one of the Franklin Hall boys came over. "Would you like to dance with her?" he asked. Of course, I was tremendously flattered. Evi-

Mary Brian, a Paramount star from 1927 on

dently the boys had been instructed not to cut in, as we were able to have a four- or five-minute dance without interruption. For the life of me I can't remember what we discussed.

"I'm returning to Hollywood shortly," she said. "If ever you wish to write me, you may reach me at Paramount Studios."

Subsequently, in the fall of 1929, almost two and a half years later, I found myself working at RKO Studios next door to Paramount. I wasn't greatly surprised when one morning, as we were shooting our picture, Mary Brian walked onto the set and invited me to have lunch with her at the Paramount Commissary. (The Paramount publicists at that time were trying to build a romance between Mary Brian and Buddy Rogers, although actually there was no romance whatsoever, as Buddy had other ideas. I gather that Buddy was not Mary's type either.)

At lunch Mary made a suggestion. "Let's go to the Blossom Room Monday night."

I readily assented, and it was on that Monday night when I discovered the girl of my dreams. Back in my Yale days I had seen the perfect woman staring at me from the cover of *College Humor*—a gorgeous brunette beauty, with a pile of beautiful black hair falling around her shoulders, a sensuous mouth with parted lips, and beautiful eyes that promised limpid pools of sex and love. Now, on this September evening in the Blossom Room of the Roosevelt Hotel she had almost come to life, and I made no attempt to conceal my interest.

Mary calmly said to me, "Her name is Fay Webb and her father is chief of police in Santa Monica."

I replied with more forensic foresight than I realized. "I shouldn't want to meet her, but I know I'm going to, and I'll regret it."

I felt somewhat like a heel as I knew that I was making Mary unhappy, although I had never promised her anything; had never told her that I loved her; had never made passionate love to her when I held her in my arms. She simply was not the dark, exotic Arabian nights' beauty that was my ideal.

The following morning on the RKO set of *The Vagabond Lover* I approached Marie Dressler, who was really the star of our little opus. Marie had been loaned to us by MGM for our picture, and I had subsequently learned that Fay Webb was under contract to MGM for $50 a week, enabling Louis B. Mayer to look to Police Chief Webb for favors for anyone from MGM who got into trouble in Santa Monica.

"Will you get me Fay Webb's phone number," I asked Marie.

"Indeed, not!" she replied.

I could only assume her refusal stemmed from the fact that she wanted me to concentrate on her friend Frances Marion, who had a crush on me.

During our first week at the Roosevelt Hotel we all met one night in the suite where Marshall Neilan had a piano and where he used to play songs he had written, among them "My Wonderful One," which Paul Whiteman's band had recorded. On this particular evening Marie introduced me to Frances Marion, who was anything but my ideal, but who I knew was a very gifted writer and occasionally a producer and director for motion pictures. She asked me to go for a drive with her in the Hollywood Hills. We drove to a high point to admire the beauty of the lights of the Hollywood of that day, when suddenly she pulled me to her and began smothering me with kisses. As quickly as possible I made it clear to her that she didn't appeal to me, and we returned to the Roosevelt.

Finally Marie gave me Fay Webb's phone number. "You'll regret calling her," she said.

But I phoned Fay right away. Her first words were, "I *knew* you would call."

I replied, "I knew *you* knew I would call." I asked her if she would have dinner with me that night, and she agreed.

After that day's shooting she and I returned to my bungalow where I took her into my arms—not, however, before sharing three or four Alexanders, which I knew she liked—but it ended in a violent embrace, nothing more.

Meanwhile, Marshall Neilan, the director of our picture, had a sweetheart on the RKO lot—a girl named Sally O'Neil—who evidently had developed a crush on me, much to his annoyance, although at the time I was not aware of it. During the course of the picture Neilan's mother died and he, being inclined to drink anyway, went off the deep end and disappeared for a week while the assistant, who knew nothing about direction, took over. (These were the days when it took almost a half-hour to load the camera, as they had no way of muffling the sound of the motors, and it was necessary to put blankets and quilts around them to keep the sound of the motors from reaching the microphones into which we were talking.) The last night of shooting, a Friday night, in order to get Marie Dressler back to MGM Saturday morning for a picture that awaited her there, I was kept up all night before they finally got to me at 5:30 in the morning—something that, as a star of the picture, I resented bitterly and so expressed myself to the head of the studio.

We finished Saturday noon. I took Fay Webb to the Brown Derby on Vine Street, where I met George Raft. When I was a student at Yale I had watched him perform in the fall of 1927 at Tommy Guinan's Playground on Broadway, where Tommy's sister Texas greeted you with "Hello Suckers!" I had come from New Haven for a night on the town all alone. I sat there and watched Helen Morgan make her debut in the nightclub field, sitting on a piano and singing, and then had seen a fellow bearing a startling resemblance to Rudolph Valentino perform several dances. On several occasions I later saw this same person, whose name I learned was George Raft, standing in front of Ben Rock's clothing store on Broadway. I wondered why he didn't go West to capitalize on his amazing resemblance to Rudolph Valentino. I kidded him about this that Saturday at the Brown Derby.

"Well," he said, "I think maybe I've made it," which of course he had, as he was working on *Scarface* for Howard Hughes.

After leaving the Brown Derby Fay and I phoned her father. "May I take Fay to the Santa Barbara Biltmore to stay overnight?" I asked him, and then added reassuringly, "You'll have nothing to worry about."

Frankly, I think he rather hoped I would compromise her so I would have to marry her! We stayed overnight at the Biltmore, and, true to my word, nothing ever happened—until we were married, in fact.

The following Monday I invited all of the crew of *The Vagabond Lover* and the entire cast to be my guests at the Cocoanut Grove. These were the days of Prohibition, but I was able to secure enough gin, rye, and bourbon for everyone. My father and mother as well as Mary Brian were with me that evening. Although I had met Fay Webb, I still felt obligated to spend my last night in Hollywood with the girl I had met at Yale.

The band playing in the Cocoanut Grove was Gus Arnheim's, in whose orchestra were Jimmy Grier, Russ Columbo, and perhaps Bing Crosby—although I don't think Crosby had joined him at that time. As we sat eating and drinking the maitre d' came over to our table. "Florabelle Muir of the New York *Daily News* would like to interview you," he said.

I was really annoyed and felt like saying: This is a hell of a time for an interview—I'm playing host to fifty or sixty persons. Why didn't she come earlier? But being the stupe I am, I said, "All right, bring her over."

Florabelle Muir, whose face resembled that of a horse, approached our table with another woman. They enjoyed a $5 dinner and proceeded to gulp down the booze. She made note of the fact that my father and mother were on my left and Mary Brian on my right. She then asked me a few questions, among them, how did I feel about going back to New York?

I had known I would love Hollywood long before I went to California. My saxophone idol Rudy Weidoft had described California to me as a place where you have lovely sunshine and warm days and slept under blankets at night. I found it exactly as he had portrayed it, and resolved someday to make it my home. On our return to New York I knew I would go back to the daily grind of the Paramount Theatre, doing four and five shows a day, then to the Villa Vallée from twelve at night to four in the morning.

The *Daily News* came out a few days later. In her column Muir said *I had deigned* to let Mary Brian sit on my right. Hell! I was happy and thrilled to have as charming a person as Mary with me that evening. Muir also made fun of my father and mother, calling them cheap. Then came the blowoff—she quoted me as saying that the thought of returning to the Brooklyn Paramount Theatre "made me ill!" And on my return to New York I was supposed to go out on the stage of the theatre to tell them how thrilled I was to return to Brooklyn, where I had become known as "Brooklyn's boyfriend." The article did me no harm, however, as I remained at the Brooklyn Paramount until the fall of 1931, when I voluntarily terminated the engagement in order to go into *George White's Scandals.*

The morning after the night at the Cocoanut Grove dinner-dance for the crew and cast of *The Vagabond Lover,* as I was

Buddy Rogers (seated, sixth from left) and I having dinner together at a Jewish restaurant on Thirty-ninth Street off Broadway in 1929. Rogers was starring with me at the New York Paramount.

crossing the RKO lot one of the film editors stopped me, and said very simply, "Mr. Vallée, no one but no one has ever given a dinner and invited all of us in the crew and the cutting department. But I must tell you that we have been instructed in the cutting of this picture to give you the works!" Whether it was because of my display of temper at being asked to wait until five in the morning on the final day of shooting or because of Marshall Neilan's anger that his girl had a crush on me, I don't know—I only know what that editor told me.

Back in New York I was called one morning by RKO to be told that there had been a fire at Consolidated Film studios in Hollywood. This was the plant where films were developed for pictures for the studios. They were not sure but they thought that *The Vagabond Lover* negative had escaped the fire. Not having seen anything but rushes of the picture, I had no idea how really amateurish and stilted the filming of a very bad story could be by a director who had long gone over the hill. I had actually felt that this was a classic epic. I experienced a feeling of despair at the thought that this great opus might have been destroyed!

Actually, it's too bad it wasn't destroyed. It was made at a cost of $150,000, which in 1929 was considered a fortune, and the screwing I got from NBC and RKO, both sons of RCA, was that after making this picture, which damned near destroyed me, I wound up with less than $20,000—this for making a picture that we never mention in our family! They are still fumigating the theatres where it was shown; in fact, I think it was only shown in penitentiaries and comfort stations!

That was a long time ago, and I can't help but smile when I recall the things that happened then. You can imagine some of the thoughts that run through my mind whenever I look in at the empty yellow walls of the banquet room, which once knew the glory of Monday nights at the Blossom Room.

A-G-N-E-S . . .

Agnes,

I really believe I loved Agnes O'Laughlin, or at least I cared for her very much and very passionately. In physical appearance she personified more closely than anyone else the girl I fell in love with on the cover of *College Humor* back in my Yale days. And even though she was later to bring a breach of promise action against me, I have never regretted knowing her, as she gave me some of the most deliriously happy moments of my life.

I first saw her in early 1928 after we had finished an eight-hour stint at the Heigh Ho Club in New York. Several of us in the band had wandered into a nightclub speakeasy that stayed open all night. There I saw her seated against the wall. I'm sure she was not aware of me. As she was with a large party and particularly with one man who seemed interested in her, I made no attempt to try to find out who she was. I have always adopted the "hands off" policy toward any married woman or any woman who appears to belong to someone else. But as I left the club I must confess I hoped we would meet someday!

It happened about nine months later at the Heigh Ho Club

3

I Love Y-O-U!

one Sunday night. At that time, 1929, Sunday night was the Jewish night out—all of the restaurants and nightclubs were practically taken over by men and women of Jewish faith. Invariably the men wore blue shirts with grey or blue suits, and nine out of ten couples danced a peculiar dance called "The Balconade," in which the bodies were pressed very close together, particularly the middle portion of the anatomy. Each body moved in a wide arc, not unlike the movements of a hula dancer—only much closer, doubtless resulting in an orgasm as they danced. Unless you've experienced an orgasm while dancing, you've really missed something! Later, at college dances we collegians created our own style of dancing, in which again the middle portion of the body was pressed closely to the other; only it was the female of the duo who leaned way back, almost parallel to the floor—that is, from the waist up—again probably resulting in enough movement upon the male organ to produce an orgasm.

As we came back to start another set after a ten- or twelve-minute intermission at the Heigh Ho Club, I looked through the curtains at the wings of the small stage. (The owners of today's

Copacabana—formerly my Villa Vallée—later removed the entire stage and placed the band at the opposite end of the room, down on the floor.) As I looked out my gaze was riveted upon the beautiful dark-haired creature I had seen at the nightclub speakeasy in early 1928. I ran back to my dressing room, wrote a note, and then asked Fritz, a short German waiter (my favorite), to deliver it. I pointed out the young lady to whom he should take the note and watched as he gave it to her. I then went back to my dressing room.

I was totally unprepared for the reappearance of Fritz, highly agitated, ashen-faced, and trembling, as he told me, "That girl is with Larry Fay!" *Larry Fay was one of the top gangsters of that era!*

Hurriedly I ran to the wings and watched in horror as Larry Fay opened the note. Instead of being angry Fay looked up and saw me watching him. He laughed uproariously and waved for me to come over.

With great trepidation I approached him, but he stood up and put his arm around me, and said, "Rudy, she's all yours! Her name is Agnes O'Laughlin."

I don't remember if I saw her home that night, but at least I

The Brooklyn Paramount Theatre, where I played for nearly two years from 1929 to 1931, alternating with appearances at the New York Paramount

Crowds outside the New York Paramount during my opening week there in 1929

phoned her the next day. "Would you like to come over to the Brooklyn Paramount Theatre and have dinner with me between shows?" I asked.

She explained that she was in Ziegfeld's *Whoopee*, a show starring Eddie Cantor, and obviously would not be able to join me until she was through with her performance, which terminated each evening about the same time we were finishing our last show at the Brooklyn Paramount. However, she joined me at the Villa Vallée that night and many nights thereafter.

I was doing much recording at this time for RCA Victor; Mac Gordon and Harry Revel, who were to write so many hit songs for Twentieth Century pictures, had approached me with one of their first writings, a song called "M-A-R-Y . . . Mary, I Love Y-O-U!" I had recorded "M-A-R-Y," but each night at the Villa Vallée, I sang it "A-G-N-E-S . . . Agnes, I Love Y-O-U," which of course delighted her and brought an appreciative smile from her.

Since we worked Sundays at the Brooklyn Paramount Theatre, Agnes was free to join me. We spent the entire day together, driving across Manhattan Bridge in my car to have dinner at

Manny Wolfe's Steakhouse at Forsythe and Grand. Manny Wolfe, who became one of my closest and dearest friends, had one of the most fabulous restaurants in the heart of Manhattan's lower east side—sawdust on the floor and the most succulent steak, cooked by gas, with hashbrown potatoes for $1.25. The most fantastic aspect of Manny Wolfe's Steakhouse was a twenty-five-foot mahogany bar over which flowed every type of drink one could imagine to clientele who might be the governor of the state; the mayor of New York City; famous actors and actresses; the leading sports figures; or Lucky Luciano, Little Augie, and no doubt the great Capone himself! The most amazing and puzzling fact about Manny's twenty-five-foot bar is that, to my knowledge, he was never raided!

You have only to look at the photo of Agnes O'Laughlin to perceive that she was probably the most voluptuous and physically attractive woman any man could desire, that is, if he liked the dark, sultry, brunette type. I have known many attractive women, but Agnes was the most desirable from the standpoint of an armful of amorous, tantalizing sex. She was Irish, of course, not overly bright, and yet in no way was she a dumb-Dora. She made it clear from the outset that we could smooch to our heart's content, but there was to be no hankey-pankey, and there never was! My dressing room boasted a large, lovely leather couch and we were in each other's arms for hours in the most passionate and enjoyable embraces for which anyone could wish. I felt I had come to the end of my quest for the woman of my dreams. Although I actually never proposed to her, I did give her every reason to believe that marriage was not far off.

As we were driving back across the upper level of Manhattan Bridge to the Villa Vallée one Sunday night after my last show, I was suddenly pulled over by a burly traffic officer wearing large, dark goggles. He was the unfriendly type who had nothing to say and when I expostulated that I was going only a few miles over the thirty-mile speed limit, he quietly and silently wrote the ticket and departed.

Somehow the fact that I was cited for speeding found its way into the newspapers, along with the name of the officer who had given me the ticket. His name was James Oliffe, and apparently

Agnes O'Laughlin, whom I regarded as the physical embodiment of the attractive girl appearing on the front cover of *College Humor* magazine

he had complained to the press that a great many women had berated him for giving Rudy Vallée a ticket.

A few weeks before I received the ticket I had performed at a benefit in Brooklyn and the gentleman in charge of the affair, whose name was Shientag, gave me his card. "If there's ever anything I can do for you," he told me, "you are only to call on me!" I pulled out this card after receiving the ticket and discovered that the firm was Shientag and Liebowitz—yes, the same Liebowitz who was to become a famous judge and preside over the trial of *Quentin Reynolds* vs. *Westbrook Pegler*. I phoned Lawyer Shientag and told him about the ticket.

He called me back. "I've arranged a trial in Brooklyn on Friday morning before you begin your ten o'clock rehearsal."

I arrived at the Brooklyn court where an Italian judge presided, and there sat Officer Oliffe.

If ever there was a travesty in justice, this was it! They put Oliffe on the stand and questioned him as to the color of my car, the make of my car, and, of course, he could only say that he couldn't remember anything about the car. He was then questioned by Lawyer Shientag about his speedometer—when was it tested?

Oliffe replied, "The first of the month."

It seemed he had given me my ticket near the end of the month. Lawyer Shientag then asked, "Is it possible that bouncing around the curbstones your speedometer might be out of whack?"

Oliffe readily agreed that indeed it might be.

Case dismissed!

To my amazement, a few days later as I approached the end of Manhattan Bridge on my way to the theatre, there was Oliffe waiting with his motorcycle to speed me across the bridge at thirty miles over the speed limit! Then, a few weeks later, he informed me that a group of his buddies and cycle officers—all men who had been in the service—would like me to come to one of their dinners near to the Brooklyn Paramount Theatre. I not only attended the dinner but also sang a few songs for them. To prove his great affection for me poor Oliffe met me on a Sunday night, one of the coldest nights of the year, *and without any ear muffs* drove me all the way to a benefit in Long Island and back to the Villa Vallée, refusing any compensation. We became the best of friends.

In 1971, when I was playing *How to Succeed* in Florida, I discovered that Jimmy Oliffe had retired there. He called me and I invited him to be my guest with anyone he wished to bring at the Cocoanut Grove Playhouse in Coral Gables.

About this time—it was August 1929—Hollywood beckoned. I kissed Agnes good-bye and I left for Hollywood to make the unforgettable and unmentionable *Vagabond Lover* for RKO. There I met Fay Webb, and although she was not quite so precisely my girl of the magazine cover, she did indeed knock me for a loop. Before we returned to New York I sent a letter to Richard Himber, who was running my office while I was away, asking him to try to break the news gently to Agnes O'Laughlin that I had found someone else on the Coast to whom I had given my heart and hand completely.

Bert Lown, who had put me in charge of the Heigh Ho Club orchestra, but who had forfeited every right to my allegiance or partnership after having unsuccessfully sued me in court, was now doing everything possible to destroy me. Somehow he got this letter (which was sent special delivery) from under the door of our office and gave it to Mark Hellinger, one of the great columnists of that day. Unlike Walter Winchell, Hellinger was a fine gentleman, a man of great ethics and honesty. He mailed the letter to me saying he didn't stoop to this type of thing to attract attention to his column, and I've never forgotten this act of friendship. Hellinger and I became good friends and very often he and his wife, Gladys Gladd—one of the most beautiful of Ziegfeld's showgirls, and I would spend the weekend at his cabana at one of the exclusive beach clubs on Long Island.

As with Helen Morgan, brandy was Hellinger's undoing and his meteoric career as a successful movie producer was cut short by his addiction to the strongest of all liquors, the deadliest of the grape—brandy.

On my return to New York I was not surprised when I was served with a suit asking for the usual million dollars for breach of promise of Agnes' hand in marriage. I was fortunate in having an attorney who knew how to fight fire with fire, and although I

Clowning with one of the acts at the Brooklyn Paramount in 1929

felt guilty about the whole thing, I realized there was no other way but to terminate the action somehow.

My attorney, former Magistrate Hyman Bushel, had, before becoming a magistrate, represented many criminals. It took Hymie only a few days to learn that Agnes O'Laughlin had often associated with Kiki Roberts, who was the beautiful girl friend of the notorious Legs Diamond. It was a simple matter for Hymie to let the lawyer representing Agnes know that if Agnes were to be put on the stand he would extract from her the fact that she had associated with Kiki Roberts—and this would look very bad in the newspapers. Subsequently we settled out of court for $1,000.

Agnes' attorney, strangely enough, was a charming man who later became one of my friends. One day, however, for some unfathomable reason he committed suicide by jumping from a roof.

About twenty years ago I discovered that Agnes had moved to Hollywood. I don't remember whether she phoned me or how it happened, but I visited her and found her almost as attractive as ever and still as impracticable as ever, as far as going to bed is concerned. That was the one and last time I ever saw her. As I look at her photograph now, I wonder whether she is still alive, whether she is still beautiful, because she was indeed one of the most appealing, adorable, and voluptuous creatures ever to nestle in my arms.

There Will

Never Be

After meeting Fay Webb in Hollywood during the filming of *The Vagabond Lover* in 1929 I felt that I must bring her East to find out if she was the woman I should marry.

She made two trips to New York: The first was delayed by a short bout with incipient tuberculosis. Even though my mother completely disapproved of her, I still was so enamoured of her beautiful face and body that I threw all caution to the winds and proposed to her and she accepted. I say "all caution" because she had told the wife of an important music publisher that she was going to marry me and take me for everything I owned!

The wedding was all screwed up. It was a clandestine, justice of the peace, hurried affair in New Jersey, as we had hoped to keep it a secret, fearing that my being married might affect the popularity of my radio drawing power and hurt me with the sponsors of my new radio program. The justice of the peace was paid twice, due to the stupidity of my NBC agent, who also was already moving in on my wife. He and she immediately phoned all the New York press about the wedding and we celebrated it in the top speakeasy of the day—The Club Napoleon. Then our

4

Another Trial
Like This One

honeymoon in Atlantic City was interrupted by the death of my mother, to whose bedside we both flew.

As I became immersed in the rehearsals of *George White's Scandals*, Fay became restless, and I suggested a trip to California to show off her new ermine coat to her parents. But once there she refused to return. I was upset as I read stories about her going out with Pat DiCico, one of the more attractive wolves in Hollywood and a good friend of Joe Schenck, who I later learned always took the same train as Fay did so they could be together on the trip.

Enough things began to happen so that I knew I had married the wrong person. When I found her in the arms of my NBC agent one New Year's Eve, I resolved to record her phone conversations and really learn the truth.

Earlier I had walked out of three very important contracts and had flown to the Coast to spend two weeks with Fay, during which time we searched for a California home (I hoped to come back to live in California) and found one that was listed on the market for $50,000 but that cost me $90,000! Although she had been on the Coast almost two months, she refused to return to New York with me. Finally she agreed to return if I would give her a $7,500 mink coat!

Once back in New York I began recording her phone conversations, which I have since copied from the rough metal plates on which they were engraved to modern tape. I may someday release these conversations, as they would serve as a good deterrent to some of the young, hot-blooded idiots of today who rush into marriage!

One of Fay's conversations was with an old school sweetheart who had become an adagio dancer. His name was Gary Leon and he was not really tall, but was dark and quite handsome. He had visited her in our apartment the first night that I was in Atlantic City with the *Scandals* and had ripped the apartment to pieces in the orgy! He called her one day from the Plymouth Hotel, where small-time performers usually stayed when in New York. The conversation went something like this:

"This is Gary, darling. What are you doing?"

Fay replied: "I'm lying here on the bed in the nude with nothing but my mules on!"

Gary replied: "To hell with the mules, I'll take the body!"

My brother and another person worked with the recording

Fay Webb and I on the boardwalk at Atlantic City, where we spent our short-lived honeymoon in September 1931

machine, a very crude apparatus called a Speak-o-Phone, which made deep cuts by a stylus into a metal aluminum disc with only a fair quality of reproduction.

They had been at work for several weeks and had some real lulus. On one disk Fay and the daughter of a music publisher were ridiculing me and the other girl's husband and exchanging ideas on where to hide the booze they were drinking from their husbands who were trying to stop them from over-indulgence.

I returned home one Friday at four in the morning following an engagement at the Black Cat Ballroom in New Jersey. Tired as I was I listened to an hour of her phone conversations and then took the elevator to our apartment. I pushed her from my arms as she tried to embrace me and told her that our marriage was finished and that I had recorded her phone conversations for the last five weeks. She screamed, "Tear the phones out of the house!" Of course, she didn't realize how stupid this grand gesture of repentance was, and I left the apartment to go over to the Essex House to the apartment of my attorney, who was only vaguely aware of our wire-tapping—which he frowned on, even though he knew I had no other choice.

I called Fay's father, the Santa Monica police chief, and told him to come and take his daughter home. The first question her mother had asked Fay was, "What have *you* done?" Suffice it to say that when her father came to get her she was more than content with the weekly settlement that our crazy laws demanded I should provide for her.

We had come to a parting of the ways once before, and had agreed that she was to go to Reno, Nevada for the usual termination of a marriage. A few days before her departure for Reno, Irving Berlin's manager, Max Winslow, had sent for me to ask if I would listen to a song that Berlin had written. Berlin was in the doldrums of his song-writing career, and, according to Max, felt that he had "written himself out." So you see, even Irving Berlin had his bad days! Whether this was a subterfuge or whether Berlin, who in my opinion was a true genius in the art of fashioning melody and lyric, had actually reached the conclusion that his gift of creative fantasy had indeed come to an end, I do not honestly know. But I did listen to him play a song for me, one which I intuitively and instinctively knew was a truly inspired melody and lyric. I agreed to do it on my next Thursday broadcast.

Thursday evening, as my wife and her father representing her sat in my attorney's office, my attorney turned on his radio to listen to my radio hour and the poignancy of Irving Berlin's lyric and melody, "Say It Isn't So." It hit all three of them with the impact of a bomb! Tears were in Fay's eyes as she listened, and yet she signed the separation agreement. It was I who was to weaken later and beg her to return from Reno. She did, and we made another vain but inglorious attempt to mend a marriage that had always been doomed to failure. I nearly weakened on several other occasions, such as when we met after the recorded phone conversations, but she returned to her home in California, and except for the times that we faced each other in a court, our companionship of marriage was over.

I think Fay Webb would have gone on accepting the terms of our separation agreement until she found or married someone else; but it was an innocuous item in the great Winchell's column that was to foretell a legal battle without parallel in matrimonial and judicial history. The Winchell item simply said that "Fay Webb is hitting the nightspots with Ben C. Cohen" (a California lawyer). Frankly, I thought nothing of it until I was suddenly served with papers in New York City—papers that claimed, in spite of the recorded phone conversations I had heard and her willingness to accept the more-than-fair settlement we had made (in the presence of her father), that this settlement had been obtained under duress and fraud!

My New York attorney, Hyman Bushel, warned me that if I went into California I would be completely hamstrung by the jurisprudence of that state. I have become a confirmed Californian as I write this today, but it is true, and I think any fair-minded California judge or lawyer will admit that of all the states in the union, California still lives in the shadow of the days when, in a California gold-mining town, a good woman was enshrined on high, and any man who looked askance or even dared accost any virtuous creature was liable to be strung up without due process of law. Therefore, when in 1933 I contemplated going to the Coast to make a picture, *George White's Scandals* at Fox studios, I was warned that to go into that state was to deliver

Walter Winchell strolling with Fay Webb and me past the stage door of Carnegie Hall on Fifty-sixth Street. The photograph was taken on the day after our marriage in September 1931.

Fay Webb and I in one of our happier moments

myself into the arms of my adversary. But I felt I *had* to wipe out the taste of the ill-fated *Vagabond Lover*, so I accepted the role and prepared for the worst.

Fay's attorney timed it beautifully. It was not until the last three days of the picture that I was served with sealed papers that threatened to destroy the career of Alice Faye. Her career in films was just beginning and they hinted that the contents of these papers, if revealed, would certainly wreck it. The accusations weren't true, but who cares about truth in a scandal-loving world? Alice Faye and I both knew we had nothing to hide, nothing of which to be ashamed. It was to her honesty, courage, and credit when I asked her if we should authorize the newspapers to open these papers that she replied "yes" without hesitation. The papers contained nothing of any consequence, however, and through the brilliant legal maneuvering of Hyman Bushel we forced our opponents to come to New York and fight us on our home ground!

The night before the trial in 1934 I had foolishly agreed to perform at the El Morocco in New York City, which kept me up until 3:00 in the morning. At 8:30 I was in the chambers of Judge Salvatore Cotillo to listen to his plea that we settle the case rather than drag our "dirty linen" before the public. Half-awake and trembling with emotion, I pointed out to the judge that I had done no wrong; that I could not see paying anyone to punish me.

I had been informed that the judge was going to "give me the works." Further than that, Ben Hartstein, the New York lawyer who had originally represented my wife, had engaged Tom Sheridan as his assistant counsel, a lawyer whose son had married the daughter of Judge Cotillo. As if to make matters worse my attorney Hyman Bushel, because he had occasionally escorted my wife to dinner on evenings when I had been working out of town, could not represent me in the courtroom. His partner, Sam Gottlieb, handled it beautifully.

The morning of the first day of the trial, the judge declared a recess. Feeling very low, I walked to a window that overlooked "the Bridge of Sighs." The judge walked by me, and muttered under his breath, "I see what they're trying to do to you, and I'll crucify them."

The trial wore on. We were privileged to introduce the recordings of the phone conversations. This would be impossible today, due to federal restrictions on the tapping of telephonic conversations. Actually, it was just as difficult in those days, but this judge knew, because of something I had told him earlier in his private chambers, that I had really tried to make a go of this marriage. He had but one course to pursue.

Unfortunately, the day of the acetate recording had not yet come into electronic invention, and the tape recorder was twenty-two years away. The aluminum discs that had been made could only be played with wooden needles and reproduced the voices so badly it was small wonder that both Fay and her father denied these were their voices. However, the *verisimilitude* of the telephone operators making the various calls to California on the morning I had called her father to come and take Fay home was too real to be the work of any sound-recording man from a radio studio.

One afternoon near the end of the trial, one of Fay's attorneys, Tom Sheridan, grilled my attorney. With all the wiles and tricks a learned attorney can use, he abused and vilified Hymie Bushel. This was too much for me. At the end of the trial, when the judge was leaving his bench, I glared at Ben Hartstein (who had engaged Sheridan) with obvious malevolence.

Hartstein, observing the disgust and anger in my features, stupidly said to me, "Stop acting! You're not in the movies now!"

With that I let fly a right that just missed him, and suddenly the court was in an uproar! The judge was back at his bench banging the gavel, calling for order; flashbulbs were popping as court officers sought to separate me from Hartstein.

Up to this time my wife's California playboy attorney Ben Cohen had been seated with her father, usually *outside* the rail of the inner sanctum of the court. (All three had come East at their own cost.) Since a California attorney is usually not allowed to practice in the state of New York, and vice versa, he had been a spectator, hoping that the two men they had chosen in New York would bring the case to victory. I had studied his pale, hawk-like features, and hated him with every ounce of intensity in my body. I felt that had he not come into the picture, this trial would never have taken place.

It dawned on me after I read the Winchell item that he had probably said to my wife one evening, "Let's bring an action against this jerk husband of yours; he loves the spotlight, the limelight, and his career too much to dare to fight us in court! We can accuse him of anything and everything. We can throw the book at him, and rather than risk the loss of his career he'll kick in for any amount we ask." They failed to reckon with my Irish temper. Nuts to my career! Who thinks of his career when he's being crucified?

The worst mistake Fay Webb could have made was to demand $90,000 a year. At the time I met her she was receiving $50 a week from MGM Studios, which was actually a sop to her father, the chief of police of Santa Monica, since MGM Studios is on the border of that city. Even some of the newspapers that previously had given me no quarter as a performer had boiled with indignation at her demand of $90,000 a year as a permanent settlement for a divorce. One paper in the South headed its editorial on this fantastic demand with: "Let Them Eat Cake!"

During the commotion, when I tried to knock out Hartstein, Fay's California attorney, Ben Cohen, for some unaccountable reason, had moved inside the rail and was sitting at the table next to Sheridan and Hartstein.

Hartstein was yelling to the judge, who was banging his gavel on the bench, "He snuck up behind me, Your Honor, and tried to hit me when I wasn't looking!"

The judge leaned forward, and said, "He didn't sneak up behind you, and I don't think Mr. Vallée knew that the court was still in session!" (The court is in session as long as the judge is still in the courtroom.)

Then occurred one of the most amazing series of happenings that probably will ever occur within any courtroom. Judge Cotillo observed Ben C. Cohen, seated within the rail next to Tom Sheridan, the New York attorney whose son had married the judge's daughter. The judge pointed his finger at Cohen, and said, "I thought I told you to sit outside the railing!" To my amazement he went on further. "I understand they call you the Steuer of California. That is a libel on Steuer!" he cried. (During the thirties Max Steuer was considered one of the greatest trial lawyers in the United States. He had succeeded in getting Alexander Pantages, the great theater magnate, acquitted of rape in a sensational California trial.)

Cohen turned as white as $10,000 worth of skimmed milk. He

rose from his chair, moved toward the rail, turned, faced the judge, and said, "I would like to have *you* in California!"

From this judge came the most cataclysmic statement—that should have completely called for a retrial—as he answered, "I'll meet you in New Jersey or anywhere you say—name your weapon!"

At this point Hartstein jumped to his feet. "I heard that, Your Honor! I heard that!" he shouted.

The judge (bless him) very calmly fixed his pince-nez upon his nose, and said to the bailiff, "Swear this man in," and then said to the attorney now seated in the witness chair, "and now for the record, *what* did you hear?"

Hartstein completely lost his nerve, and replied very meekly, "I heard nothing."

To you, dear reader, this may be commonplace, and may not strike you as being fantastic or unusual. But let me assure you that on much less than this technicality of a judge challenging a lawyer to a duel, many a case has been declared a mistrial, and assigned to another judge. It has always been my belief that there is a justice, at least on some occasions, right here on earth. This was a clear case of this phenomenon. Not only did the case continue to its conclusion with the same judge, but he decided in our favor, and back to California at their own expense went my wife, her father, and her California attorney-lover.

Naturally the decision was appealed and went to the Appellate Division of New York City, where it remained for about one year after Fay was defeated in her attempt to set aside the separation agreement and have it nullified in our New York courts.

Late one night I was driving from the Brooklyn Paramount Theatre back to Manhattan to perform from midnight until two or three in the morning at the Villa Vallée (which has been for the past many years the Copacabana on 10 East 60th Street in New York). As I drove along Madison Avenue heading toward 60th Street I noticed a sleek black limousine lolling along at a very leisurely pace ahead of me just as we were passing Reuben's famous restaurant on 58th Street and Madison. The driver seemed to have all the time in the world and drove at a maddening pace of about twelve miles an hour. I had been working all day in the theatre, doing four or five shows and was eager to change into my tuxedo and step out on the stage of the Villa Vallée. The limousine turned left on 60th Street and slowly rolled to a stop a little back of the entrance to the Villa Vallée. By this time I was really boiling at the leisurely speed of this driver and I gave his car *a little bump* as I came in back of him.

The driver jumped out and came back with blood in his eyes. On recognizing me as I calmly stepped out of my little car, he screamed, "Judge! Oh, judge! It's Rudy Vallée!"

A short, stocky, gray-haired man stepped from the limousine and came back to give me hell for hitting the back of his car. I said something, and since I had had dinner at Manny Wolfe's and had partaken of a few glasses of sauterne, the odor of the wine was still evident on my breath, as the judge screamed, "Oh! You've been drinking . . . you've been drinking!" and then noting a policeman at the corner of 60th Street and Madison, he commanded this officer to approach us and ordered him to arrest me.

The officer, seeking to calm things, remonstrated with the judge, saying, "Well now, Judge Martin, I don't think I can arrest Mr. Vallée and I'd suggest that he apologize to you and just forget the incident."

I immediately apologized and the judge cooled off and went to his limousine and escorted his wife across to the swank Metropolitan Club directly opposite the Villa Vallée.

I asked someone who Judge Martin might be, and I was told that he was just an *unimportant little judge* from Brooklyn. I thought nothing more about it until a few weeks later when my attorney Judge Bushel suddenly asked me if I had ever met Judge Francis Martin. I thought for a moment and remembered the incident about the bumping of the limousine. I replied, "Yes, Hymie. I did bump into the car of a judge but I understand that he is an unimportant little judge from Brooklyn."

Hymie delivered the coup de grace, as he loftily informed me, "Little judge, hell! He is the *presiding* judge of Appellate Division—the fifth man whose vote to sustain or reject an appeal is all too powerful!"

I nearly died as I realized that at that very moment Fay Webb's appeal from Judge Cotillo's decision in our favor was before the Appellate Division! With a sinking heart, I asked Hymie, "Does he want my scalp?"

Hymie laughed and put an end to my fears, as he said, "No. He wants to bring his children to your broadcast some night and wants tickets for the show!"

Was I ever relieved!

A few days later Judge Francis Martin came backstage at the studio where we did our Thursday Night "Fleischmann Hour" and proudly introduced me to his two sons. We both had a good laugh about the car bumping and parted the best of friends.

In time the Appellate Division upheld the superior court decision and we all breathed a great sigh of relief. I should have remembered that Hyman Bushel was beloved of not only most of the legal profession but of many of the top jurists, and I knew that this meant a great deal in all judicial matters and that Hymie's friendships extended even to Albany, where the Court of Appeals would now review the case. I think here we would have won a resounding victory, but just before the three-man Court of Appeals in Albany was to hand down its decision, the brothers Warner—Harry, Jack, and Albert—asked me to step in to play the lead in a picture that Dick Powell had refused.

I was under contract to Warner Brothers at that time, and being a good soldier, I agreed to replace Powell. I sent my attorney to California to straighten out my marital situation by a settlement, something I had never wanted to do. I realized that any settlement would, regardless of the amount, accrue to the benefit of Ben Cohen, who had dared to take my wife dining and dancing and probably to bed and who had talked her into bringing this thoroughly unjustified action against me. Whatever the small amount involved, it would at least *repay him* for such treachery! It is my New England nature to rebel not only against waste, but to refuse, completely and at all costs, to ever in any way contribute money to pay anyone for a dishonest, diabolical, or cruel action.

The fact that Dick Powell decided after all to make the picture left me holding the bag for a $25,000 settlement, no portion of which could be charged off as a business cost, because, as they said to me at Warner Brothers, "We didn't marry the girl!"

Fay, between drugs, liquor, incipient TB, and three or four beach boys in an afternoon, completely disintegrated and left this world six months later—1934.

When

Ginger Rogers

She stood out like a rose in a brier patch as I walked into the brightly improvised picture studio down at the old RCA recording studios where I was later to make some of my early Victor records. She was on the set about to rehearse a dance with a young boy in a raccoon coat, she in her bobby socks and her dutch-cut hair. The same inherited instinct that had enabled me to see great promise in Alice Faye, Dorothy Lamour, Frances Langford, Lyda Roberti, Yvonne DeCarlo, and Helen Kane told me that Ginger Rogers was destined for fame.

I asked someone about her and was told that she was married to a fellow named Jack Pepper, who wrote comedy and played the piano. Having been hurt myself when the girl of my choice was stolen from me, I have always vowed never to interrupt a love affair, even when it was very obvious that the girl cared little or nothing for her escort. And I *never* have intruded into a marriage. So I made no attempt to speak to this attractive young girl.

The picture being made by RCA was an experiment to de-

5

Came Into

My Life

termine the value of a new type of lens invented by a scientist named Spoor. He had created what was called a *split lens,* to give some effect of three dimension. Whoever at RCA had determined to embark upon this test evidently had decided on a very modest budget; in fact, the two leads for the story were to be chosen from the ranks of RCA itself. The girl lead, a rather attractive blonde, not unlike Florence Henderson in facial appearance, had won the title of the most attractive young mother in a New Jersey contest. She was the wife of Bill McCaffrey, who today manages Art Carney (remember Carney's mention of him on the 1975 Academy Awards?) and who was originally a booker for RKO-Keith Vaudeville houses. In 1929 he reluctantly had offered me $400 for three days at the Keith 81st Street Theatre, where we made unforgettable show business history. McCaffrey had been persuaded to come over to the Heigh Ho Club to watch us play several dance sets. He failed to ignite, but was prodded by an old song plugger, a former baseball player named Sammy Smith. McCaffrey booked us only because all the girls on the floor of the booking office in the Keith Palace Building in New York were excited when he told them he was going to book us into the 81st Street Theatre.

For the male lead of this RCA picture, which was to be called *Campus Sweethearts,* someone had the bright idea to choose the son of the president of NBC, young Aylesworth. His father, Merlin Hall Aylesworth, was the same president who had asked me to come to NBC one morning shortly after I'd signed with them, to tell me how grateful he and all of NBC's hierarchy were for my showing to the world at large the tremendous power and possibilities of radio for anything or anyone who had anything to offer the medium.

Evidently young Aylesworth was quite unsatisfactory at playing the romantic lead in this picture. I was awakened at three o'clock one morning, having retired only an hour before after finishing our nightly stint at the Villa Vallée. The caller was Ed Schueing, who had been delegated by someone in NBC to be my manager for the agency that NBC was running at the time, known as the Artist's Service Management. Schueing explained to me the nature of the film, estimating that it would take about a week to complete it and that it would pay me $5,000 for that week's work. Thus, four hours later, roughly 7:30 a.m., found me on the set at the improvised studio on East 24th Street. (Eventually, on New Year's Eve in 1931 I was to find Schueing and my wife, Fay Webb, in the bathroom together in a very compromising situation. After that I never spoke to him again and he quickly faded from the scene. He died later, an alcoholic.)

Sound had just come in and large microphones were RCA's latest creation. But under the hot lights these microphones kept blowing out, even though they were embedded among flowers and other places to keep them out of sight of the camera. I was given a very lovely ballad called "Under a Campus Moon" to memorize and sing to the young mother from New Jersey. Two years later when I asked RCA if I could secure a copy of the film, Eli Oberstein, one of the great recording supervisors who made Tommy Dorsey and several other bands by his dynamic recordings of their music, dug up only two-thirds of the picture, which he found in London, of all places!

It was only possible for me to give an hour or less shooting time to this picture, as at ten o'clock I was to do my first show at the Brooklyn Paramount Theatre. We did four one-hour shows daily with a two-and-a-half hour break between the second and third shows, at which time we usually napped or ate. Thus it was that I was dashing back and forth across Manhattan Bridge from the studio at East 24th Street to my dressing room at the Paramount Theatre and back again to be under the cameras at the 24th Street Studio. After our last show at the Brooklyn Paramount, we hied to the Villa Vallée in New York to perform there until two in the morning, sometimes until three. Naturally, I was relieved when the picture was finally finished and in the can.

A few months later we headed west to RKO Studios in Hollywood to make the ill-fated *Vagabond Lover* with Sally Blaine as the girl and with Marie Dressler, who really was the star of the picture. As we prepared to return to the Brooklyn Paramount at the conclusion of the shooting at the RKO Studios in Hollywood, I was acutely aware that my having fallen in love with Fay Webb in California was going to be complicated on my return to Agnes O'Laughlin, who fully expected me to carry her to the altar on my return.

Meanwhile, I was totally unaware that Ginger Rogers, the young lady I had admired the first day of the shooting of *Campus Sweethearts*, had, by some mysterious happenstance, apparently fallen in love with me. She had terminated her marriage to Jack Pepper and, unknown to me then, was about to open in a George Gershwin show called *Girl Crazy*, a show in which Ethel Merman was to come full-blown into great stardom, and that featured Willie and Eugene Howard, with whom I was to perform later on in two of *George White's Scandals*.

Ed Schueing had introduced me to the Sydney Binghams, whom I found to be a very pleasant couple. Sydney, as head of the New York Subway System, was able to do small favors for NBC from time to time due to the tremendous power that he held in the national life of the city, and his wife, a rather plain woman but a fine executive, purchased all the food for the dozen odd Schrafft Restaurants in New York City.

The Binghams asked me if I would like to attend the opening of *Girl Crazy* at the Alvin Theatre. I knew that Ethel Merman was going to be in it; that it was her debut in the musical legiti-

Ginger Rogers

mate field, although she had appeared with me in 1929 at the New York Paramount Theatre for a week. The great Al Siegel, who was a fine pianist and composer of several hit songs, had demonstrated an outstanding ability for taking unknown girls with singing talent and making them truly great stars. He had been working carefully with Ethel Merman, whom he had discovered at a party. Someone had told him that this young girl, who was a secretary during the daytime, had unusual power and quality of tone. On this particular night of the opening of *Girl Crazy* Siegel had been felled by the flu, but insisted on being brought to the theatre in an ambulance with a temperature of 104° to direct her from the pit as she sang the hit song of the show, "I Got Rhythm." It was indeed a night of triumph for both Al Siegel and Ethel Merman, as she skyrocketed to fame on that evening.

I don't recall whether Ginger Rogers did much singing or whether she did more dancing, but she had an important role in *Girl Crazy*. After the show, which was a hit, the Binghams, Ginger, and I went to her suite at the Warwick Hotel, *the* top hotel for all outstanding personalities in show business. Ginger lived there with her mother, who had prepared a party for thirty or forty persons to celebrate Ginger's debut in this hit musical.

Suddenly—how it ever happened I can't conceive—Ginger and I were alone in a large room where previously the guests had been dancing and drinking.

"Let's get the hell out of here!" she said.

We drove to Central Park Casino, the *in* club of the moment being run by A. C. Bloomingthal, a friend of the mayor, who was later to go to Mexico City to become an impresario in the hotel and nightclub field there. Through the power of the mayor this choice spot for a nightclub somehow had been permitted to be created on city land in Central Park. I knew that Leo Reisman and his Boston band was playing there. I had watched them at the Brunswick Hotel in Boston the fall when Yale played Harvard in my senior year. I was only vaguely aware that he had a pianist who was going to become an outstanding personality in the world of music recording and show business—Eddy Duchin. Eddy, I believe, first conceived and popularized performing at the piano in what many of us called "the Boston style." It was a simple matter of closing the eyes and moving the head back and forth as the pianist played certain passages. Being a fellow orchestra leader, Reisman naturally was most cordial. As Ginger and I danced we smiled to each other as he presented his delightful music.

Toward the last of the evening a rumpus suddenly erupted. Unknown to Ginger and me was the fact that not only Walter Winchell was in the room, but also Earl Carroll, who apparently detested and hated Winchell. As Winchell was about to leave Carroll strode across the floor and took a swing at Winchell's jaw. They were quickly separated and Winchell left; everything returned to normal.

Finally, as the evening came to an end Ginger and I went to my car and as we sat there I was to receive my first invitation to marriage. Don't get me wrong—Ginger did not actually propose; she just made it clear that she would like to be Mrs. Rudy Vallée. I was flattered, of course, but I had the unpleasant task of telling her that I had left my heart in Santa Monica; that I had promised Fay Webb I would marry her.

Years later in 1934, when I was making *George White's Scandals* with Alice Faye at Fox, before it became Twentieth Century-Fox, I was eating at the Beverly Hills' Brown Derby with Richard English, a fine writer. (English had been assigned to "give me the works" for some magazine or newspaper. He apparently found me entirely different from what he had been told I was like, and he became one of my closest and dearest friends; in fact, he was to manage me for several years before his untimely death.) As Dick and I sat there I became aware that Ginger Rogers was a few booths up.

Dick said to me very slyly, "Boy, if a girl looked at me the way she's looking at you and I was with her, I'd certainly be very, very annoyed!"

Ginger's marital history, I believe, included Lew Ayres; when that ended she married a fellow in the marine air force. I remember when my Coast Guard band and I played a dance at Camp Elliot in San Diego in 1943 that she was there to welcome him back, as he had been overseas for some time.

In 1931 Fay Webb and I moved into our apartment at 65 Central Park West, only to find that both Ginger Rogers and

Claudette Colbert were also tenants in the building. Ginger had appeared in a picture called *Young Man of Manhattan*, in which she had uttered the immortal lines, "Cigarette me, big boy! Cigarette me, big boy!" and the young man to whom she had given this ultimatum, she was to marry.

In 1933, when I went to make the picture *George White's Scandals*, we broadcast my "Fleischmann Hour" from the small, ugly commissary or restaurant room at RKO Studios. We had engaged Ginger to do a dramatic sketch with Leslie Howard, but it seemed she had developed a very severe skin infection and it formed a sort of green moss on a small area on the left side of her face. This being radio, it did not in any way affect her portrayal of the dramatic sketch broadcast, but she was terribly embarrassed and I suffered for her as I realized how very embarrassing it was.

Today Ginger continues to be as effervescent and bubbly as ever she was in 1931 when we were both playing in Detroit—she at the Fox Theatre and I at the Michigan, the four- and five-a-day show band policy of those days. One day as I was outside the Michigan with my motion picture camera Ginger and her mother were also taking a walk between shows, and they posed for me, waving very gaily. Yet, we did not get together because I was still married to Fay Webb.

Recently we met in New York at the Americana Hotel, where we both went to watch the artist of the evening. She looked as radiant and as lovely as ever—a very fine person. I'll always be glad that our paths crossed, and that, for a little while at least, Ginger Rogers came into my life.

Pat Dane:

The Girl

It was in a beautiful room—the Cocoanut Grove at the Ambassador Hotel, that in its heyday had seen so much fun, gaiety, and excitement, especially in old Hollywood—where I first saw Pat Dane. The *Follies Bergère* had come to Hollywood to open at what was then the El Capitan Theatre but is now the Paramount Theatre, showing motion pictures. On a weekend in Palm Springs while playing tennis at the Racquet Club, Les Stoeffen, a six-foot-two, blond giant of tennis whom I envied for his beautiful, equally statuesque wife, had told me about the *Follies Bergère* and revealed that he knew several girls in the show. He arranged for me to have a blind date with one of the girls on opening night.

The show was quite enjoyable. When I went backstage for my date I was prepared for the worst, but she was fairly attractive of face, with a slight accent and much continental charm. "Let's go to the Cocoanut Grove, just the two of us," I suggested.

Shortly after we were seated my gaze was riveted to a party of four about forty feet from our table. This was the fall of 1940 and the Grove had begun its decline, which was to become catastrophic. Not even Sammy Davis could save it! It had been my

6

That Everyone

Wanted

good fortune to have two ten-week engagements with my orchestra of eighteen men and several acts of my own choosing in the fall of 1938 and 1939—two very happy engagements, as we were able to more than justify our cost, and Friday and Saturday nights were invariably close to capacity. The Grove is a large room, seating at that time over 1,200 persons. On this night there couldn't have been more than 200 persons, but the young girl in this party of four stood out like a flaming beacon.

This time it was not the girl of my dreams. It was not Fay Webb or Agnes O'Laughlin, but rather a very young face with the most beautiful skin, easily evidenced even from that distance, and a face not unlike that of Gail Storm. Her chief characteristic was youth and saucy impudence, or, as the French say, *insouciance*! She faced us with full red lips over beautiful white teeth and exceedingly lovely black hair, with a slight wave. I made note that one of the two gentlemen with her was bald, and then I turned to entertaining my guest for the evening.

As we were leaving, I spoke to the maitre d'—Reuben, a Russian Cossack who had been at the Grove for many years and was my maitre d' during my two terms in 1938 and 1939. "Find out who the beautiful girl is at the table of four over near the post," I whispered.

When I called the next day Reuben was glum. "I haven't been able to find out the name of the girl or anything about her," he reported.

This was unusual as Reuben was a man of much experience and crafty and wise in the many things a maitre d' is called upon to do. I was at my wit's end—I had to find this girl! I immediately phoned Sybil Brand, a very dear and trusted friend who had tried unsuccessfully on two or three previous occasions to find me the "right" girl.

The Westmore brothers, all five or six of them, so well versed in the art of makeup and care of the hair for the stars in motion pictures, had a shop on Sunset Boulevard, chiefly dedicated to the women of the film industry. It was rumored that the Brands, Sybil and Harry, had invested considerable money in the House of Westmore. I suggested to Sybil that she alert all the girls in the shop to look for this ravishing girl with the beautiful complexion, the unusually clear eyes, the beautiful smile, and with the youthful impudence that exuded from her so obviously. Several weeks passed with no success.

The Music Corporation of America meanwhile had booked me into a very fine supper club, the Victor Hugo in Beverly Hills, where I was to follow Harry James. James' big band, which some thought had been a little too loud for the room, had still done good business. It was while I was in the room listening to Harry James' music that I was introduced to Joan Crawford by Hymie Fink, one of our best photographers for film magazines. As I sat talking to Joan I began to wonder whether or not I should pursue her romantically, as she was free at the time and so was I.

On another evening at this same Victor Hugo I had been the guest of the Harry Brands, who had invited Betty Grable in hopes they might hatch a romance between the two of us. I chided Betty for having axed Jackie Coogan. "Let's have a dinner date in the not too distant future," I suggested. On the night of our date, however, I came down with a severe cold and it never materialized.

My band and I had a good run of six weeks at the Victor

Hugo. I conceived of something new in the format for a floor show. It was simply the reading by some of the best Hollywood radio personalities of some of our Barrymore Sealtest scripts. We put long, low portable footlights on the floor and read the radio scripts just as we would in the radio studio. At that time Hans Conreid was more than willing to perform for me there, and since he did an excellent imitation of John Barrymore we had much

Pat Dane

fun with these beautifully written scripts in addition to several other acts of the typical nightclub genre. Barrymore came in one night and seemed to enjoy Hans Conreid's characterizations of the"Great Profile."

One night I was electrified as I saw Hedy Lamarr coming into the room. She was then married to Gene Markey, for whom I had done a picture at Twentieth Century Fox and for whom I had a great admiration. Hedy sent me a note with a little plastic cow that she had purchased from one of the cigarette girls in the lobby suggesting we all have dinner together sometime in the future.

On another night I was even more electrified as it looked for a moment that the exquisite face of the girl I had seen in the Cocoanut Grove was in the room, but it turned out to be Rita Hayworth with Ed Juddson, her Texas husband whom she was to divorce later.

And then it *really* happened! It was the last night of our engagement at the Victor Hugo when a party of eight came in and walked by the band platform. The hostess of the party was Margarita Wagner, who had come to the Cocoanut Grove in the fall of 1939 with one of our prominent judges and who had invited me to her table. Margarita was quite attractive, and seemed interested, but we became just very good friends. She was beginning to manufacture the fine cosmetics that are now a major part of her life.

At my first opportunity I joined her group, but as I approached them I was stunned to see that one of the gentlemen was the man with the bald head from the Cocoanut Grove. His name was Lafe Ludwig, one of Los Angeles' top physicians—but even more gratifying was the fact that he rather proudly told me we were fraternity brothers in SAE, and as we shook hands he gave me the "grip."

I lost no time in getting to what was on my mind. "Who was the beautiful girl you were with at the Cocoanut Grove?" I asked, and to my delight he gave me her phone number. It was a Saturday night, and I was surprised that she answered my call. I was guesting the next day, Sunday, on the Chase and Sanborn Radio Show with Edgar Bergen, Nelson Eddy, and Dorothy Lamour. "Would you like to go?" I asked her.

"I would be delighted," she said.

I retired that night feeling very exhilarated and happy, with the hope that this might be a very happy experience.

I rang her bell on Spalding Drive in Beverly Hills. The door opened and there on a little table in front of the door was a photograph of Desi Arnaz. She saw me studying the picture, and laughed, saying, "He's great in the hay, too!"

I discovered that the best word I could use for this fabulous young creature was "kitten." Pat Dane had no inhibitions whatever. She was perhaps the most nonintellectual girl I've ever known, but since I've never been at ease with brilliant, smart, and sophisticated females, it was a relief to be with someone who was just a simple child, with no restraints, either verbally, mentally, or physically.

After the broadcast we went somewhere to eat, probably the Beachcombers, and then to my little house back of Ciro's off the Sunset Strip that I had purchased only a few weeks before.

The evening was so delicious, so delightful, so sexually satisfying that she moved in and was my house guest for at least three months. But as the weeks wore on, with no demands of any kind from her for any gift, cosmetics, jewelry of any kind, I found myself becoming disturbed by her inability to maintain a serious conversation on almost any subject.

I had terminated my ten-year broadcast for Standard Brands of the highly successful variety show, the "Fleischmann Hour," which was broadcast on Thursday nights from eight to nine o'clock ten years from the date it started in New York in October 1929 and ended in California in October 1939.

It was now the last of November and I received a call from a man named Herbert Korholz, who explained that he had a broadcast for me and would like to discuss the matter with me in New York City. "I'm going to play the Royal Palms in Miami over Christmas and New Years," I said, "but I'll be happy to see you there to discuss it."

Christmas was approaching. I informed Pat Dane that I was going to Miami and would take her with me. But a week before Christmas at the Beverly Hills Hotel, I saw Matty Fox with another brunette who, like all the others, intrigued me greatly. I learned that her name was Patricia Morrison, and I recalled that she had broadcast with us in New York doing songs from a Cole Porter show.

I was able to secure her phone number and called her. "I would like to meet your father and mother and have a chat with you," I said.

This was a week before Christmas and my departure for Miami. I went to the Morrisons' residence with a few gifts for Patricia and her father and mother. I sat before the fireplace talking with the three of them. Her father's slight Scotch brogue made it evident that Patricia was of Scotch extraction.

As we went to the door I asked very bluntly, "Patricia, will it do me any good to care for you—seriously, I mean?"

"Yes, it would!" she replied.

That night I had been invited to Edgar Bergen's home for a Christmas party. Pat Dane and I attended, but as I picked her up in the afternoon to take her to the Bergens' I frankly told her what had happened. "I've fallen in love with another Patricia," I said.

The poor girl, whose skin was very white anyway, blanched even more. "Who is the girl?" she asked.

"Patricia Morrison," I told her. "I don't think you should go to Miami with me under the circumstances."

I had already given Pat the ticket and her temper flared. "God damn it!" she screamed. "I'm going regardless!"

Naturally, at the Bergen Christmas party in a room filled with so many persons Pat and I were separated. As I passed behind Edgar Bergen and Ken Murray, I overheard Ken asking Edgar who the ravishing creature was picking up some food from the buffet table. I tapped Ken on the shoulder. "Ken," I said, "she's with me. Her name is Pat Dane, and she's all yours!" Ken Murray instantly set about trying to interest this beautiful creature, but with no success.

Our plane left early that evening. I gave Pat the lower berth and I took the upper. I had picked up several postcards, and in my berth, as best I could, I began writing the love notes to Patricia Morrison. Our plane landed in a heavy snowfall in Nashville, Tennessee. While there I sent a night letter back to Patricia Morrison and a special delivery letter professing my deep devotion. I had decided that Pat Dane and I would stay at my favorite

Patricia Morrison, the first girl I ever proposed to the same day I met her

hangout, the old McFadden Deauville. In 1931 it had been *the* hotel, with the French chanteuse Lucienne Boyer, who wore a beautiful purple velvet gown and shared the spotlight with George Olsen and his orchestra. But there at the desk waiting for me was a night letter from Hollywood. My heart sank as I read it. It said simply that upon reflection Patricia Morrison had decided it just wouldn't work after all. Naturally, I did not relate this latest news to Pat Dane. She must have wondered at the sudden return of my ardor and solicitude for her comfort!

She came nightly with me while I performed with my band at the Royal Palms. There on New Year's Eve was Howard Hughes, a man with whom I'd had dinner five years before. (Pat later explained to me her relationship with Hughes.)

Sherman Fairchild was a young inventor, sportsman, millionaire playboy. He had succeeded very well in his various inventive ventures and enjoyed giving parties on the third floor of the Stork Club Building every other week, usually with Eddy Duchin, Sy Coleman, or other great pianists, playing dance music for the guests who were mostly the *in* crowd of that year. Howard Hughes, always looking for beautiful women, had spied a beautiful girl on the floor, just as I had done at the Cocoanut Grove, only he had cut in on her. But before he could find out anything about her, her husband had cut in and she was gone.

"At that time," Pat said, "I was married to a Jewish boy who was a captain in the air corps. My real name is Thelma Burns; my mother is Jewish." I believe they came from the Carolinas.

Hughes was absolutely distraught and pleaded with Sherman Fairchild to give more and more parties in hopes that the girl might show up again. Several weeks later she *was* back, and this time Hughes grabbed her before anyone else could cut in, took her aside, and asked her name.

"Thelma Burns," she said engagingly.

"Your name now is Pat Dane," he said. "Here's $1,000 and a round trip ticket to Beverly Hills."

Now, here he was at Art Childer's Royal Palms, alone. Evidently he had heard that Pat Dane and I were seeing each other and had flown there in hopes of taking her away from me, or at least talking to her.

Even though I had hurt her in my aborted romance with

Patricia Morrison she still wanted nothing to do with Hughes. I suggested that she at least visit his table for a short time, which she did. Thus, along with the Bettejane Greer episode, you have another good reason why I am not likely to grace the boards of any of the Hughes' hotels in Las Vegas.

Pat and I flew back to California together, but not before I had discussed a new show with Korholz—something his father-in-law, a man named Finneran, had conceived and sold to National Dairies—to be called the "Sealtest Show."

I explained an idea that had been germinating in my mind and it seemed to please Korholz. We agreed upon it as the format for the new show. I liked the price they offered me, which was slightly more than I had received for doing the "Fleischmann Hour." The agency handling the show and to whom Finneran had sold the idea for the format was in Philadelphia. McKee and Albright was a small agency, but Roy McKee had married one the Borden girls, and with her help had stolen the "Sealtest Show" away from J. Walter Thompson.

Roy McKee flew to Hollywood from Philadelphia with a very brilliant, pipe-smoking supervisor of radio shows named James McFadden. I invited McKee for dinner in my Harold Way home. He entered the door at twilight—about six o'clock—just as Pat Dane came tripping down the stairs attired in a black velvet gown. I have seen double takes in my day, and at that moment she looked just irresistible; I don't think Roy McKee ever got over the impact of seeing this lovely creature descending the stairway.

As I became absorbed in the staging of the "Sealtest Show," somehow Pat Dane and I drew farther and farther apart. Eventually she was back in her own apartment. Subsequently, in the summer of 1940 when I went to my lodge in Maine, coming back into New York to do the "Sealtest Show," I received a call from Pat. She was staying just below the Essex House at the Hampshire House. In the meantime she had played a small part in one of the Andy Hardy pictures with Mickey Rooney and the legends about her performance in the shooting of the film are both hilarious and unbelievable.

I believe it was Norma Shearer's brother Douglas, who was the genius of sound at MGM Studios, which was the Tiffany of all film studios in those days, who was deeply in love with Pat Dane. She brought him over on a Sunday afternoon to our bar in the lower building. He realized that she didn't care for him, but he still enjoyed being with her—as everyone did. It wasn't because she had an *in* with him that she defied the MGM top brass; it was just that she didn't fear either man or beast or the devil. When someone remonstrated with her for appearing late on the set of the Andy Hardy picture, she, who had a choice of profane language almost exceeding mine, proceeded to tell the director, producer, and everyone else within earshot exactly what she thought of them and the picture, which incidentally was one of the best of the series, and her part in it was especially well done.

But Pat was Pat and she had no yen for a career or anything else in particular. I flatter myself that there was something in me that pleased her, and this must have propelled her to New York, in hopes that I would invite her to the Maine lodge. I did. We spent two or three lovely weekends there and this beautiful kitten almost entrapped me for another long siesta as a semipermanent house guest.

Somehow she came within the purview of Tommy Dorsey— as volatile, unpredictable, wild, and stormy an Irishman as ever took out a union card. For several years he was first trombonist in my "Fleischmann Hour" broadcast—and for $50 yet. But he jumped from my studio to a dozen others, raking in an easy $600 or $700 a week on all the top radio shows.

Sometimes it was necessary for me to bawl someone out (as only I can do when someone deserves it), and Tommy used to sit there looking at me as though I were a tyrant! In 1938 or 1939 on my way home to Maine I dropped in at the Metropolitan Theatre in Boston (where I had performed first in 1931), and went backstage to say hello to Tommy, who was playing there with his band. It was gratifying to have him put his arm around my shoulders and laughingly tell me how he understood the grief of trying to handle and direct musicians, who for the most part are decent human beings but are also sometimes just children, and who but for their great musical talent would not be the sentimental, easygoing idiots that they sometimes are!

Possibly some of you remember the fight between Jon Hall and Tommy Dorsey over Pat Dane at a party Tommy was giving at his home. When Jon Hall paid too much attention to Pat, Tommy knocked him over the railing to plunge one or two stories to the ground, where, in the fall, his nose was gashed quite badly.

Their marriage must have been a stormy one because I knew Pat and the type of handling she required, which I'm sure would not have come from Tommy Dorsey!

One evening near the end of the war, circa 1945, when someone in Tommy's band—actually his vocalist—threw a cocktail party in Hollywood for all in the Dorsey band, someone suggested that we go to my lower building, which had a large bar and much more room and all the liquor anyone would want to drink. It had been raining all afternoon and there was a heavy fog as we drove to my castle in the hills. We found our way down to the lower building. I was tending bar. Pat, Tommy, and several others in the group were sitting at the bar, when suddenly Tommy—who by now was half drunk—began to berate and eventually slap Pat Dane for no reason at all. I had taken great care not to do anything that would arouse Tommy's jealousy, and yet it must have been the fact that she had at one time spent many nights and hours with me in that same playroom that really provoked him. There was nothing any of us could do—she was *his* wife. Eventually she left the room and went out into the rain and the fog, coming back after about half an hour. Tommy was so drunk that he was nearly asleep on the couch, and all was well again.

I have often wondered whatever happened to Pat Dane, née Thelma Burns. Dorsey subsequently divorced her and married another woman, his fourth or fifth wife, who incidentally was not with him the night he choked to death in his sleep. I've often wished that Pat would either call or drop me a note. She is one of my happy romantic memories—a charming, kind, tempestuous, and lovely, lovely kitten!

PART II

THE BIZ!

Radio's

I'm a product of radio—that powerful medium which at one time was a great part of our lives but since has become, like silent movies, a voice lost in the wilderness. There is no more big money for the individual performer in radio, and although radio does considerable business and is heard by millions of motorists, there are few persons who listen to it when they have the opportunity to watch the newer and more powerful medium of television.

My first experience with radio was in the fall of 1922 when I entered Yale University. I was asked to go to an old, deserted loft on the top floor of the A. C. Gilbert building, where I would find a device known as a microphone, into which I would play solos. I went. I'm not certain whether Lee DeForrest, who helped create the vacuum tube that made radio possible, was present at the time, but I was to meet him later. He, too, was a Yale man.

In 1923, when I happened to be in New York playing a dance engagement, I heard that a saxophonist was going to broadcast from downtown NBC studios. I took the subway to the lower side of New York City and watched Herb Finney, a young red-

7

Child

headed saxophonist from Indiana. Finney went to the Savoy in London about 1923, and in 1924 I followed him there. Both of us were employed by the same management—he with a large orchestra, I with a small group of seven Englishmen known as the Savoy Havana Band. Our nightly broadcasts were heard as far as Morocco, where there was much fierce fighting. We were told that the broadcasts were even heard in the trenches! For some reason, though, *I had not yet listened to a radio broadcast myself!*

After graduation from Yale in the fall of 1927, I went to New York to seek my fortune. I had no idea my destiny was to be greatly shaped by a medium with which I'd had only slight contact before. In New York I had a guarantee of only one job a week from the Vincent Lopez office. It was to pay me $14. Since I was living in the SAE house at Columbia University, which cost me $5.00 a week, I couldn't spend more than $1.50 a day for food. But I had all the clothes in the world, as I'd bought them in London while playing at the Savoy, so it was easy for me to exist even though I had only that one engagement.

I finally broke down the Ben Bernie office, which offered me

This is where I made records for Columbia in London from 1924 to 1925.

fifteen engagements if I would include New Year's Eve among them. That's when everyone works—many mediocre players have been paid three or four times their worth just to play New Year's Eve. The first of my dates, however, was in December in Baltimore. Under the guidance of Herman Bernie, eleven other musicians and I took the train from Penn Station. We were already dressed in tuxedos, carrying our instrument cases, of course, in our hands. When we arrived at the station in Baltimore we were greeted by a young man, who turned out to be one of my classmates at Yale, whose sister was making her debut; we were to play for her coming-out party. The party was held in a gymnasium with the tables and the orchestra underneath the running track. The oval in the middle was where the crowd danced.

During the course of the evening in came the Paul Whiteman Rhythm Boys. It was evident that Whiteman was in town playing one of the Loew's Theatres, and evidently they had been engaged to perform at the coming-out party. The Rhythm Boys were Harry Barris, Al Rinker, and Bing Crosby. Barris played the piano, which was a small upright positioned smack against the wall underneath the running track. As the Rhythm Boys performed, Crosby and Rinker faced the crowd of diners, also underneath the running track.

In those days there was no sound amplification. Above the chatter of the diners the Rhythm Boys might just as well have stayed in bed; no one was paying the slightest attention to them. But suddenly a hush fell upon this crowd of Baltimore's elite. One of the Rhythm Boys was singing a song called "Montmartre Rose," and even though he lacked any amplification or means of channeling the sound waves to us, his voice commanded instant silence. Whether he sang one or two choruses I don't recall, but when he finished the crowd applauded wildly and cried for more. As though he were oblivious to their shouts and applause, almost as though he were hard of hearing, he threaded his way back through the tables and passed by our sax section, not more than a foot and a half away from me. I was struck by the lack of expres-

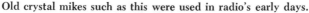

Old crystal mikes such as this were used in radio's early days.

sion on his face, which was a mask of complete indifference. Bing Crosby was a hit and didn't even know it!

Four years later, in the summer of 1931, I received a phone call from song writer Con Conrad. I was performing that summer at the New York Paramount Theatre and doubling at the Hotel Pennsylvania Roof. Conrad's chief claim to fame was that he was one of the composers of a very popular multimillion sheet music and record hit of the twenties, namely, "Margie," and also a catchy tune called the "Continental." I had met Conrad somewhere before. He was a tall, slim man with a moustache; he reminded me of Basil Rathbone. Conrad was a fast talker and evidently the nickname Con resulted from the fact that he was not above using devious means. He asked if I would have dinner with him as he wanted me to meet a young Italian boy. I told him I would meet him at Schrafft's between one of my shows, sometime around six o'clock.

He introduced me to Russ Columbo—a person who was anything but a young boy! I had pictured a Sal Mineo or perhaps a young Vic Damone. This Italian boy was a man of approximately thirty. He was six feet tall, well groomed, and wore Johnson and Murphy shoes (which were sported only by men of the world who could afford them), with a little gold pin underneath his tie to hold the points of the collar together—something affected mostly by the sophisticated young men of Wall Street who set the pace of fashion in those days. As we began to eat I suddenly realized I had seen him somewhere before. "Weren't you in the MGM picture *Dynamite* with Charles Bickford and Kay Johnson?" I asked.

He smiled, and said, "Yes."

After Columbo excused himself to make a phone call Conrad confided to me that when they had come East by train they had brought with them in their compartment a portable phonograph, which worked by cranking it, and all the Crosby records they could find. During the entire three-and-a-half day trip they played these records over and over again so that Columbo could get every trick and nuance of the Crosby delivery. I remembered a bit of gossip that I had heard somewhere—how Gus Arnheim, who was playing at the Cocoanut Grove in 1929, had been featuring Crosby as a singer, and on the nights when Crosby decided to belt the grape, which he did quite often, and was not able to make it to the microphone, Columbo, who was one of the string section (he played the violin), would sing for him.

On Columbo's return to our table Conrad informed me that he was trying to sell Columbo to Earl Carroll and to have Carroll put him in the current *Vanities*, running at a theater in New York City. The *Vanities* was not quite up to the standard of the *Ziegfeld Follies* or even as important as *George White's Scandals*, but the *Vanities* was still a show well worth seeing. For Columbo to be a part of this current *Vanities* would be a splendid opportunity to sell him to a radio network. Conrad asked if I would be willing to put Columbo on about 12:30, before we closed our evening at the Pennsylvania Roof, so Earl Carroll could hear him sing. I agreed. Conrad had no orchestrations but I knew that my boys could fake almost any song that Columbo wanted to sing, in any key.

Conrad and Columbo came earlier, and about 12:15 in came the impresario, Earl Carroll himself, whom I knew exceedingly well. He was with an entourage of at least six of his show girls, presumably to mask the fact that he was going with Beryl Wallace. Several months before, when I was living at 10 East 60th over the Villa Vallée, this lovely girl Beryl Wallace called one night expressing the desire to come to my room. I declined, knowing that Earl Carroll was deeply interested in her. An hour later, after giving the matter further thought, I called her back and asked her to come over. She declined then. Before dawn it was a succession of calls, refusals, calls, refusals, and in the end we never did get together. She and Carroll were later to die in an airplane as it took off from Philadelphia airport and struck some wires. Everyone on board perished.

About 12:40 I announced to our well-filled Roof audience that they were going to hear a young singer from California who was auditioning for Earl Carroll and I would appreciate their attention. Columbo sang in dance tempo so those who wished to might dance. He was halfway through the first song when it was obvious to anyone who had heard a Crosby record that he was doing an out-and-out imitation of Bing Crosby. As I heard him sing "Ah, But I Surrender Dear-ear-ear" with the familiar Crosby half-trill on the word "dear," I fully expected shouts from the crowd of "imitator!" "phony!" But at three minutes to one they were clamoring for more, and I believe we played ten or fifteen minutes overtime that night before they were satisfied.

Columbo didn't make the *Vanities* but he did make a record of a song called "I'm Just a Pris'ner of Love," which launched him to fame and fortune, an NBC contract, and an engagement at the Waldorf Astoria.

Bing had already arrived in New York, being summoned there by Bill Paley, the president of CBS, who had heard several Crosby records and had instructed CBS executives to bring Crosby East and put him on five times a week, broadcasting at the strategic hour of 5:30 to 6:00 in the evening, when the housewife was most likely to hear him. But Bing was really hitting the bottle at this time, and night after night there were lame excuses for his nonappearance before the microphone. In a panic they sent for Dixie Lee, his beautiful wife, in hopes she might straighten him out.

It now became a battle of Crosby and Columbo, not that I was forgotten entirely, as someone had already written a song called "Crosby, Columbo, and Vallée." Some NBC publicist took advantage of the fact that Columbo was tall, dark, and handsome. Bing was about my height, and although passably attractive, did not have the come-hither Latin appearance of Columbo. Someone conceived the idea of a woman, dressed in black with a veil over her face, to appear nightly in the Waldorf Astoria Empire Room to listen to his performance. There was speculation that the woman was Carole Lombard, and she may well have been. This woman of mystery made all the columns, and Columbo was well on his way to success, which could have eclipsed that of Crosby, whose fame, in spite of his drinking, was already very great due to his records and his fine performance when he was before the microphone. Just how the rivalry might have ended is anyone's guess.

Had Columbo not returned to the Coast, tragedy might never have happened. There are many versions, but I believe the true one is simply this: Columbo and a friend were in an antique shop, examining an old ball pistol (a pistol that fires a round metal ball). Apparently no one was aware that it was charged with powder, and his friend pulled the trigger. The ball ricocheted into Columbo's temple, killing him.

After the Baltimore coming-out party, where Crosby was such a hit, there were a series of other engagements in and around New York City. About the third week in December I bumped into a young good-looking fellow named Bert Lown, who had been doing society work with small orchestras for coming-out parties and social affairs in Westchester society. We discussed my taking a steady job.

"I would," I said, "if I could lead the band."

"That's possible," Lown informed me.

Then I learned that I was to lead a small orchestra at the Heigh Ho Club at 35 East 53rd Street—just below the Stork Club—on the night of January 8, 1928.

My last engagement for the Bernie office was at the Commodore Hotel on the night of January 7—the occasion: the Jewish Theatrical Guild dinner to raise money for the Guild. It was a testimonial dinner in honor of William Morris, Sr., the founder of the great agency. There was no dancing, as the tables filled all of the carpeted floor. I was one of ten musicians from the Ben Bernie office; there were ten from the Paul Whiteman office, and we were needed as much as another nose, as we played for only two of the acts. There were about thirty star acts that evening—all performing gratis, of course.

On the east side of the long room in which the banquet was held a temporary stage had been erected, and back in the southwest corner was the dais, where all of the celebrities, admirals, generals, rabbis, priests, etc. were gathered with William Morris, Sr., the guest of honor.

It was my first chance to see George Jessel in action. I marveled at the smooth way he handled his chores of introductions and his smooth flow of phrase as he reminisced. Mayor Jimmy Walker arrived late, as he always did. The ceremony at the dais was finally concluded and everyone turned their chairs to the east side of the room to watch a list of entertainment that would have cost a fortune had the acts been paid. The show began with Lou Holtz as one of three masters of ceremony. Vincent Lopez played his "Nola," and departed. There were the Keller Sisters and Lynch; but when I saw the great Van and Schenk, whom I'd seen at the Palace only a few months before, my cup runneth over! It was truly a great collection of personalities—I sat there with my mouth open, admiring these acts, realizing I was seeing a show that would have cost me several hundred dollars if I had paid to see it.

Monday afternoon, January 8, I asked seven musicians to meet me at a small room in the Roseland building where Bert Lown had his offices. Lown had heard an agent talking about the prospective Heigh Ho Club engagement. The reviews of the club's opening on New Year's Eve had been very bad, especially in the *New Yorker*, where a woman columnist who called herself *Lipstick* (Peter Arno's wife) wrote that the floor was rough and the band looked very Jewish. Lown had described me to the owner of the club as being aristocratic-looking, a college man, and perhaps just what they wanted. The choice of musicians was left to me, so I brought two of the boys from New Haven— one who played a fabulous piano and later wrote the tune "Sweet Lorraine"; another, Joe Miller, who played tenor sax. The other five were all fine musicians having played for Lown in engagements at society dances in Westchester.

While I was working with other dance orchestras for a short rehearsal, particularly those in New Haven, I had observed that invariably the leader had us play only choruses of various tunes that everyone knew; but very stupidly he would always have the band play all the tunes *in the same key*, sometimes for hours, and sometimes for the entire evening, because he and the boys who had been hastily assembled had no way of knowing how or when to change key, where to make the new chord change, or what notes to play. I had resolved that if I ever led a band I would never play two choruses of two songs in the same key, but always would mount upward—F, G, A-flat, B-flat, and so on. We spent an hour at the rehearsal doing nothing but changing keys, my pianist giving us the correct notes to play and showing us exactly where to make the change.

One of the boys, Jules DeVorzon, was a short, pop-eyed Jewish boy from the Bronx. He boasted a gold front tooth and a very beautiful wife, and today is selling real estate in Palm Springs. His daughter was once Miss Palm Springs. DeVorzon, with his trained voice, was to do the singing. I was merely to lead, play saxophone, and choose the music we were to play.

I first met Don Dickerman that evening of January 8. He was deceptively tall, very well built, extremely strong, and an authority on all things pertaining to pirates. He also possessed a great knowledge of underwater life and the sea, having been with the explorer Beebe on the famous Galapagos expedition in the South Pacific. In fact, the interior walls of his Heigh Ho Club had beautiful murals in which Dickerman had depicted in silver and gold leaf and other colors some of the fish and other creatures he had seen under water with Beebe on this expedition.

Dickerman owned three small clubs in Greenwich Village— the Blue Horse, the Country Fair, and the Pirate's Den. It cost very little to enjoy oneself there, but he had convinced George Putnam, the publisher and husband of Amelia Earhart, that they should create a really swank, very select club on 53rd Street for the Park Avenue gentile elite. The result was the Heigh Ho Club. George Ott was selected as the maitre d'. He spoke six languages, and was short, bowlegged, and very quick of movement. He also had no scruples about doing anything to anyone at any time! Why Dickerman chose him I don't know, except that as a maitre d' he was an extremely capable man and knew his business inside out.

On the night of our debut there couldn't have been more than fifteen persons present. It was a beautiful room with excellent food—no liquor, no gambling, just good food and our little dance band. The dance floor was very small. We wore tuxedo pants with satin Russian blouses buttoned at the neck, long sleeves, and a sash around the waist. Back of our band was a dark cobalt blue background with a beautiful live white cockatoo directly behind my drummer. Every time the drummer raised his sticks, the cockatoo's crest would go up—which was really something to see!

We played three or four numbers for our first set, not playing the orchestration from top to bottom, only the choruses. We lacked the brass section to play the arrangement as it should have been played. I observed Dickerman sitting in a chair with his feet straight out—and a scowl on his face. DeVorzon had sung two of the numbers during our first set. As we ended that first set I went over to Dickerman. "How do you like our music?" I asked him.

"I don't like the singer!" He growled.

I saw the job floating right out the window and went back to

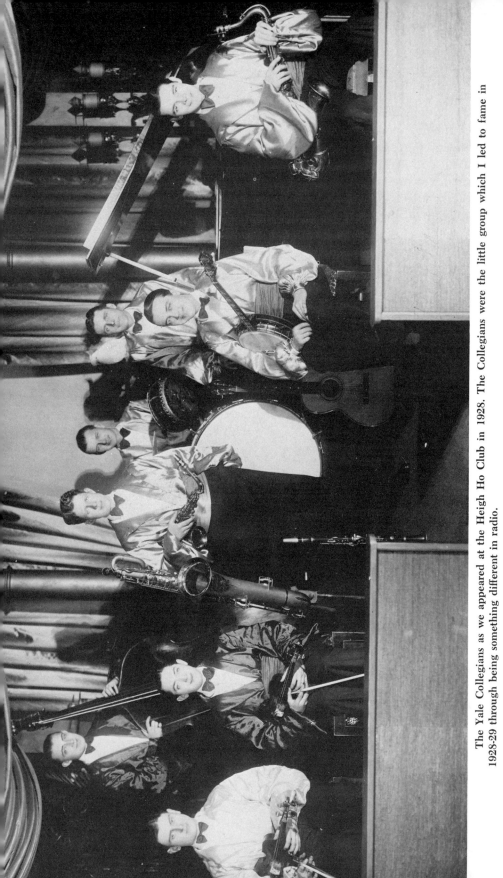

The Yale Collegians as we appeared at the Heigh Ho Club in 1928. The Collegians were the little group which I led to fame in 1928-29 through being something different in radio.

the band platform and spoke to our pianist. "Cliff. Do you remember the song 'Rain' that we played at the Yale spring dances in New Haven?"

Fortunately he replied, "Yes."

It was a song that had been written by a man who staged musicals for amateur civic groups throughout the country. These shows were put together by an impresario named Ned Wayburn, and one of his producer-directors had written this song for one of the shows in a small town in Pennsylvania. Our Yale Collegians band had gone on tour in the summer of 1927, and one of our boys had come across this tune. I sang the lead; on the second chorus a sudden storm was created by sound effects behind the stage and the flickering of lights. We put on slickers; then the lights came back on, indicating that the sun was out again, and we took off the slickers and finished the song. I had taught "Rain" to a band when we were playing the spring dance at Yale. Cliff Burwell, a New Haven musician, had played piano at these spring dances.

Now, for our second dance at the Heigh Ho Club, I played a chorus of "Rain"—on two clarinets in the low register. I then sang a chorus, followed by a chorus on my baritone saxophone, and I sang still another chorus and finished.

Again I approached Dickerman, who was now smiling, as he said, "You do the singing."

That little statement—that little command—changed the whole course of my life!

We continued to play at the Heigh Ho Club eight hours a night from seven until three in the morning—Saturdays, Sunday, and holidays, and a tea dance on Saturday, for the magnificent sum of $90 a week. Near the end of February an event that was to take us to the heights was about to happen. Lown informed us that he had talked a small radio station into broadcasting us from the Heigh Ho Club. This was station WABC, the Atlantic Broadcasting System, with offices in Steinway Hall in New York. Later, WABC was to become the flagship station of the Columbia Broadcasting System for William Paley.

On the afternoon of our first broadcast a very pleasant gentleman by the name of Sampson came to give us some instructions. He wore a tuxedo and very heavy, shell-rimmed glasses. He was a

Yale man. He informed us that *they could not afford an an-nouncer and I would have to do the announcing!* I fancy he expected that I would fall through the floor or faint. But I had observed the way Billy Phelps at Yale could make things very interesting; I had acquired some of his techniques and looked forward to my new role of radio announcer.

As you stepped out of your cab to come into the Heigh Ho Club (Heigh Ho being an old English greeting), our German doorman—short, wearing a long impressive officer's coat with epaulets on the shoulders—would say, "Heigh Ho." So I decided to say, "Heigh Ho, everybody, this is Rudy Vallée announcing and directing. . . !" I made this announcement over the music of a Yale football song, which was to become our theme song on every broadcast from the club. I tried to make the songs interesting by a little bit of gossip about the writers or the writing, or the song itself. I made up groups of songs or similar types of songs—maybe five songs from the Ziegfeld *Showboat*, which had just opened, or five songs that all had a quality of the Orient.

The next afternoon after the first broadcast I came into the club and there were twelve or thirteen letters lying on the desk. I opened them and they all said the same thing: "You are *different! Different!! Different!!!*" I showed the letters to one of the boys in the band who had worked for Lopez and asked him if he thought that Lopez ever received letters like that.

He was astounded. "No," he said. "I'm sure he didn't!"

At first we were broadcasting only three times a week. Suddenly WABC asked me if I would broadcast every night. I said we'd be glad to. About five weeks later I received a call from WOR—one of the radio stations with excellent pick-up reception in New York City—asking me if they could broadcast us. Since we were there eight hours a night, that was no problem; we had all the time in the world. Later, WMCA at the McAlpin Hotel also asked us if they could broadcast us.

"Hop aboard!" I said.

To avoid duplication of songs on each program that followed the other, I would go downstairs into the cellar next to the storage refrigeration boxes, tear up old menus, and type up a list of songs for each broadcast, taking great care not to duplicate. As we had a selection of about one hundred tunes, this was not too difficult to accomplish each evening.

To my surprise Dickerman was rather displeased about the broadcasts. He felt that they took us away from the patrons who were dancing while we broadcast. I explained the situation to him: "In the next few minutes after the broadcast, I will be singing these same songs through my megaphone for the patrons of the club only, and since they are there for the evening, they really don't miss a thing." Actually when he was worried about patrons, I could have said, "What patrons?" There were nights in February, March, and April when we didn't have three or more persons to play to all evening, because the club was strictly formal, strictly gentile, and so far the Park Avenue elite had not materialized. In late April, however, our broadcasts were beginning to have their effect, and Ott was letting in people who were not formally dressed and some of whom might have been Jewish. As long as Dickerman didn't come over from his three clubs in the Village we were safe, and it was a pleasure to have someone to whom we could play and whom we could see dancing.

It was clear to me why our first radio listeners were intrigued with our broadcasts from the Heigh Ho Club; they told me why in their letters. When I announced my name, they immediately pictured a George Raft, a Rudolph Valentino, with patent leather hair and almond eyes—a more or less oriental facial appearance —but I talked quite nasally and sounded something like the Coolidge twang; yet, I philosophized in the manner of a college professor, which was the result of the hours spent at Yale in the classroom of William Lyon Phelps, who could take the most mundane subject and make it glow with warm and interesting facts and fancies. Most of the letters were frankly curious as to what sort of man I might be. I theorized that when we did show ourselves in the theatre or on a tour, there would be long lines at the box office!

I'll never forget one night when a woman, a rather homely one, came to the bandstand. I was standing in the middle of the platform, while the rest of the boys were seated on either side of me. She looked at me, and asked, "Which one is Rudy Vallée?" I pointed to Joe Miller, who, although short, had a well-shaped head, with dark, straight hair and a cute, turned-up nose. She went to him and he immediately pointed to me, and said, "That's Rudy Vallée." Whereupon she came back to me and practically held her nose as she waved disdainfully and walked back to her table!

Dickerman, by nature, was indeed a real snob. When I showed him a wire from the Fox Theatre in Detroit offering me $1,500 a week to become an emcee for their stage shows (the vogue in those days was for the orchestra and the acts to work on stage), he was incredulous! He just couldn't believe I would actually take such a job—that I wanted to appear before and play for these common people in a theater! We were fortunate at having a few celebrities come to the Heigh Ho Club. Babe Ruth came in one night, shook hands, and was most cordial. And we did get quite a few of the very elite from time to time.

The Heigh Ho Club was to close during the summer. In the spring of my graduating year at Yale I had been offered two engagements—one the very swank Milton Point Casino at Rye, New York, and the other the Sands Point Casino at Port Washington, New York. A kind lady had sung my praises to the man who was chairman-director of both clubs. I was again able, through her help, to secure for Bert Lown the Milton Point Casino engagement, which now was sought by many New York society bands. The very stuffed-shirt group who owned the casino had decreed that I could not mingle with the guests. I was not allowed to sit at tables or make a phone call at the club. But this did not annoy me, as I knew it would change very shortly.

All that summer we broadcast over WMCA for an insignificant local sponsor who sold Herbert's Blue White Diamond. *The eight of us* received the sum of $110 for each hour broadcast. But the broadcasts were so successful that, when the announcer stated if anyone wanted a picture of Rudy Vallée, he or she might have one by writing for it, the sponsor received over 50,000 letters—from one announcement on this small, one-lung station!

Then came the fall and our return to the Heigh Ho Club, with no increase in money, and the same long grind of eight hours a night and tea dances on Saturday. Lown began to realize he had made a mistake in selling us to Dickerman the second year for the very small salary we were all receiving. Lown and Ott began to scheme of a way to get us out of the club and into another spot where they would pay us three or four times as much money.

While we were playing the Heigh Ho Club in the fall of 1928, from time to time Lown would assign me, without the band, to a short appearance at a hotel in Brooklyn or in the Bronx, or in some part of New York—it might be a coming-out affair or something else—but for all these arduous appearances I received not one penny! My absence from the club was noted by Mrs. Dickerman, Don's mother, who in Don's absence was running the club. When she upbraided me for leaving, I explained that Lown was my boss—if he gave me an order to go somewhere, I had no choice. Actually, I was usually out of the club for no more than two hours, which meant I was in the club for six hours doing many, many songs—enough to satisfy any rabid patron who might wish me to sing all evening.

In November 1928 Dickerman, with one of his eight wives, went to Cuba to discuss the possibility of creating a King Arthur's Castle nightclub for some Cuban promoters. The night that he returned from Havana and came to the club, we were packed. He sat on the right side of the room and I could see that something was wrong—he was scowling again. I went over to his table. "How was your trip?" I asked in a pleasant tone.

"I had a lousy trip," he grumbled, "mainly due to a lot of things I've heard about you."

Unknown to me, Lown and George Ott had sent wires saying that some of the men escorts were very upset about the fact that their girls were asking for my autograph and were fawning over me—anything they could wire him that would indicate I was doing a bad job.

Dickerman looked at me sternly. "I'll see you downstairs at three in the morning," he said. At the meeting downstairs, with the cashier working on his books, Dickerman said, "Of all the dirty double-crossing skunks I've ever met, you're the worst! Take your band and get the hell out of here!" He turned to the cashier. "See that they don't take anything! I don't want them any longer!"

What an irony. We had been packing the club almost every

night recently and I had never taken one night off, and here we were, without any notice, out on our ass. But it took me only a few days to land a spot that had been suffering very badly. It was called Versailles—not the Versailles of East 50th Street, but a room that today is the famous Copacabana at 10 East 60th Street. The Versailles of 1928 was owned by Scalawag, a rascal who cost me a fortune. He had pretended that he had never heard of me, but this elegant scoundrel airily said that he would give us a try.

"Put in a radio wire and watch what happens," I said.

The place had been deserted every night. Walter Gross, who was playing there with Eddie Davis and his small, fine orchestra, told me that many nights they didn't even have one person the entire evening. In three weeks' time we were packing them in. Eventually (to flatter me) the place came to be called the Villa Vallée.

The time had come for me to prove the power of our radio broadcasts. Bill McCaffrey, a Keith booker, was persuaded to give us a chance to show our stuff in one of the key Keith Vaude-ville theatres for $400 for Friday, Saturday, and Sunday. Two shows a day. I saturated the air with announcements during the weeks before we opened at the Keith 81st Street Theatre, with the result that on the opening day the hordes of our radio fans pushed the manager out into the lobby. You couldn't get near the theater. Inside they screamed and threw things into the air when we played certain songs. It was one of the most fantastic, dynamic, exciting events that had ever happened in the world of Broadway; and *Zits Weekly* (which rivaled *Variety* at that time) said, "A bombshell bursts on Broadway!"

On opening night the big booker of all the Keith theaters took me upstairs into an old dusty office and asked if I would play all the Keith theatres including the Palace. Goddamn it—if I only had had a smart manager, I would never have settled for $1,500, as he was prepared to offer us $10,000 a week! Too late I realized I needed a manager. The National Broadcasting Company had a small agency called the Artists Service Bureau, managing mostly concert artists; the only "pop" artist they signed was Vincent Lopez. A few days after our Keith debut I signed with them for the usual 10 percent, because I knew that NBC was tops in radio and we needed that lifeline of the broadcast—to go forward and to keep ourselves alive.

Thus it was one year later on the night (Sunday evening) of the next Jewish Theatrical Guild dinner in 1929, that I was invited to be one of the acts for the dinner at which I had been a member of the orchestra the year before. I arrived at the Commodore and went back of the big room, where there were booths for persons to hide and drink. In one of the booths was Mayor Walker with Grover Whelan, the city greeter; they were having a drink. Since Prohibition was still in effect, this little hiding place was perfect.

Walker sent for me. "Rudy," he said, "may I have the honor of introducing you tonight?"

"I would be thrilled, your Honor," I answered.

When Walker would get a little tight sometimes, he'd phone me at the Heigh Ho Club or send a wire asking me to play his favorite songs at one or two o'clock in the morning.

Walker introduced me, and as I stepped onto the stage, the audience rose to its feet, applauding and cheering. I looked down and there were twelve of the boys with whom I had worked the year before. That was the power of radio: In one year's time it took a little band of eight pieces led by a young punk from Maine and made them the toast of the East—eventually, through coast-to-coast broadcasting, to become the most important contributors to radio programming!

The Real

George

Talk about eccentrics! What quirk in a man's nature could impel him to wear a dark blue suit, a white shirt, and a black bow tie morning, noon, and night? Saturdays, Sundays, and holidays? In the box office, backstage, on the street, at banquets, everywhere? Well, such a man was George White, producer of *George White's Scandals*, who, to my knowledge, never dressed otherwise. One could only assume that he slept in similar attire. This strange, diminutive individual was reputed to be worth between $3 and $4 million in 1929.

George White was to affect my life very definitely beginning in June 1931. Our first formal meeting was typical and I should have sensed the headaches to come. I was first summoned to his august presence in May 1929 during my third or fourth week at the New York Paramount. A telephone call had informed me that White wished to see me in his offices at the Apollo Theater stage entrance on 43rd Street, a few hundred yards from the Paramount. It was quite logical that White would want to see me, as just a few months before I had turned down an offer to appear in Florenz Ziegfeld's production of *Whoopee* at the New Amster-

8

White's

Scandals

dam Theater. Between shows at the Paramount I heeded the summons and at the proper moment was ushered into the great man's presence. Actually, I was not ushered into his office. In the first place, it was in the back portion of the Apollo Theater, where White had previously presented his other *Scandals* and was a shabby, two-by-four room with a tiny spot to sit outside. I could see him at his desk and he could see me.

He kept me waiting for at least forty minutes and as I finally got up to go back to the Paramount (one block away) for my next show, he suddenly called me in: "Hey you! Come in here!" He went back to his work but finally looked up. "What do you want?" he asked.

"I believe you sent for me," I replied.

Then he said belligerently (as if he didn't know), "Who are you?"

Of course, I replied, "Rudy Vallée."

He said, "I didn't send for you."

Right then and there if I'd had any brains, I'd have told him to go to hell as I was tempted to do so many times during his dying days at a hospital in Santa Monica. I got up and started to leave.

"Have you ever thought of going into the *Scandals*?" he yelled at me.

I replied, "No, but I would like to," and that ended the dialogue.

In my junior year at Yale I had witnessed his *1926 Scandals*, a smash, naturally enough, with the talents of Harry Richman, Frances Williams, and Ann Pennington, plus songs written by DeSylva, Brown, and Henderson, who gave him "Lucky Day," "Birth of the Blues," and "Black Bottom." At this show I had been the guest of a wealthy Yale boy who was enamored of one of the McCarthy Sisters appearing in the show. I had left with the feeling that I had seen a very fine production.

In the spring of 1931 I realized that, although we were hitting $40,000 average weekly grosses at the Brooklyn Paramount Theatre (monotonously, as a matter of fact), I had pretty well run my course in this medium. Although the Paramount hierarchy seemed to be satisfied with my work, in a few more short months they would realize, as I did, that it was time for a change. We could expect to be dropped unceremoniously from the roster of the Brooklyn production. Therefore, when tentative feelers were sent out by the men of the music-publishing industry that, if I wished, I could be in the next *George White's Scandals* production, I very frankly said that I would be happy to entertain such an offer.

The great George White—blue suit, white shirt, black bow tie, and all—was persuaded to catch one of our Brooklyn Paramount stage shows. That particular week I was doing an impression of Chevalier that registered so strongly with the audience, I was forced to appear for three and four encores. When I finished we had dinner at my favorite hangout, Manny Wolfe's. In spite of Prohibition it was wide open—no knocking at the entrance, no peeking through the little trap doors, no phony passwords. During this dinner we discussed the terms, the date of rehearsal, the opening, and, in effect, practically set the contract.

A few nights later in a small office in the DeSylva, Brown, and Henderson building, Lew Brown and Ray Henderson presented (with Lew Brown singing and demonstrating as only he could) the songs they had written for the eleventh edition of *George*

White's Scandals. Two of these songs have made show business history—"Life Is Just A Bowl of Cherries," and "My Song," but not "The Thrill Is Gone" and "This Is the Missus." The attitude of everyone present was patronizing, as though I were a fledgling who knew little or nothing of show business. To them I was a rank amateur, a dilettante who needed much nurturing and training. Naturally, I was extremely annoyed. But I bore their patronizing. I wanted a shot at another medium in the field of entertainment. After Brown and Henderson had auditioned the numbers we all left the small room together.

"There's one thing I want to ask you, George," I began.

"Yeah? What is it?" he demanded.

"Can you work my impression of Maurice Chevalier into the show?"

He snorted. "Vallée, you've got to remember one thing—this is the *Scandals*, not a goddamn five-a-day grind at some lousy theater."

"But I killed them at the Paramount with it—three encores. After all, those were *people* in the audience!"

"Do me a favor—just remember you're on Broadway now. This is the big time."

"All right, all right," I grumbled. "But—if there *is* a place for the Chevalier bit, will you promise me *I* can do it?"

"Yeah, yeah, sure. If we can fit it in, you'll do it."

Two weeks later I secured my release from Paramount Publix. I then married Fay Webb and, during our short honeymoon in Atlantic City, was summoned to my mother's bedside by plane, as she was near death. A nightmare of *Scandals* rehearsals followed, lasting from ten in the morning until eight, nine, and sometimes ten o'clock at night. I would sit in the dark expanse of the Apollo Theater for days on end without being asked to say "boo," or to sing a chorus or to do anything for the four weeks of the performer's time that the Actors Equity gave the producer at no cost whatsoever to him. The males in the show all received instructions from White to memorize the lyrics and melody of every song that any other man did. In the event of a performer's illness, any one of the other men could step into the breach at a second's notice. My part in the show was something I could have learned (as I did) in a matter of a few hours. I have always memorized melody and lyrics (I read music) exceedingly rapidly. This was a bit upsetting to Henderson and Brown, who had been accustomed to teaching the average performer his songs by rote. Since I appeared in none of the outstanding sketches, my few entrances and exits and my limited contribution to the show was something that could easily have been accomplished in two days of instruction and rehearsal. All the same, I was forced to sit and sit—interminably.

Our opening was to be held in Atlantic City in August 1931. The last-night dress rehearsal in New York took place in the Apollo Theater before leaving for the out-of-town tryout. The final scene took place in a lavish set in which the entire cast was supposedly in a German nightclub. Each of the principals was called upon to do a small bit as a reprise of something he or she had done previously in the show.

The comedian of the eleventh edition of *George White's Scandals* was Willie Howard, who in my opinion was one of the greatest natural comics the world will ever know. To Willie Howard were given some of the funniest and cleverest sketches anyone could ever hope to have in a musical revue. Even Ray Bolger, who probably had hoped, as I had, for a part in some of the comedy sketches, was confined to his own spot in the show and to his dancing. While Bolger did have one small part in one sketch with Howard, the skits and blackouts were almost exclusively written for and dedicated to Willie Howard's great talent with an assist from his brother Gene. But in this German cabaret finale, after doing a series of impressions of Jessel, Jolson, and Cantor, Willie Howard walked offstage, came back with a straw hat, and performed as that great French personality Maurice Chevalier. While Howard's impression was a *caricature* of Chevalier, and well done, too, it was not a true *impression* of him. I, on the other hand, had studied especially prepared Paramount films of Chevalier doing some of the songs from the picture *Paramount on Parade*. I had played his records morning, noon, and night, and had studied the motion picture until I knew every nuance, every movement, every gesture, every grimace—everything that went into giving his performance the appeal it had for his audience. I couldn't believe my eyes. Recalling my conversation with George White, I looked at Brown and Henderson. Both of them averted their glances; they knew I was being given a royal double cross. I was naive enough to believe that one or both of these men would go to White and remind him of his promise to me—that if a Chevalier impression was to be done on the show, it was to be mine.

Neither White nor perhaps anyone else in the entire company was aware of the importance to me of this, my first appearance in a musical revue. I was primarily a radio personality, and I knew that the critics of the press were lying in wait, ready to tear me to pieces if I did not acquit myself with something outstandingly different. Of course, they expected me to sing a few songs; that was what I was supposed to do. But I realized that unless I did something quite different from what everyone would accept as a matter of course, this show could be the kiss of death for me.

Opening night in Atlantic City came, and the German night-club finale found Willie Howard again doing his caricature of Chevalier. When the individual who represented me, who had little or nothing to do with my securing the part in this show (but who nevertheless was securing a 10 percent commission for the National Broadcasting Company), visited us in Atlantic City at the first matinee on Wednesday afternoon, he realized as keenly as I did that something had to be done. An appeal to Willie Howard fell on deaf ears.

"The impression is great for me!" Howard pointed out to White.

Then he began to do some thinking—or maybe his brother pointed out that on their return to New York Willie and he might wish to guest on the "Fleischmann Radio Hour," but that I might refuse to book them. At any rate, Willie changed his mind. A few days later he reversed himself.

We had previously appealed to White, who had ignored the fact that he had promised me I would do it. "Dammit, Rudy— Willie Howard is too important to me and the show," White had said, with the implication that I was not in the least to be reckoned with. "I can't ask him to drop the Chevalier bit. That's all there is to it!"

It was fortunate for me that in the end I was given the opportunity to do this bit of mimicry. It turned out to be the only thing that brought me any real praise, not only in New York City but on the road. With no undue false modesty, it was one of the production's highlights and achieved such results as "stopping the show" for sometimes as long as forty to fifty seconds, which (if you've ever timed it with your watch) is a long time. There were some persons in the audience who actually believed that Chevalier was there on the stage. One night Chevalier sat in the audience with my father and when I finished, he said to my dad, "*He* does *me* better than I do *myself!*"

Our *Scandals* then went to Newark for another two-week try-out, where Ethel Merman joined our cast. Our little epic had opened in New York on September 14, 1931, and it had run until February, when it went on the road. Probably George White always felt that I brought his New York run to a close, but even I

In the fall of 1931 a caricature of each member of the *Scandals* cast was put up in the lobby of the Apollo Theater.

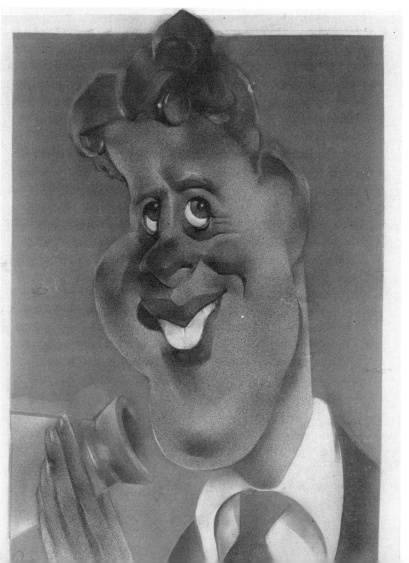

could ascertain from *Variety's* weekly list of grosses that it was time for us to get out on the road and make some real money. We were in the trough of depression and White was just stupidly hidebound enough by the tradition of musical revues to believe that I could not be left out of the production for two weeks without the necessity of closing it.

"George, you've got to give me two weeks off," I pleaded. "I hate to say this but I'm about to crack up."

"What the hell's the matter with you?" he barked at me.

"Oh, I don't know—the grind, the rat race, and, of course, there's Fay. She's been on the Coast for over three months."

"I hate to give you the show-must-go-on routine, but do you realize I'll have to close it if you leave? Put all those kids out of work?"

"You don't have to close the show. If it's okay with the Pennsylvania and my radio sponsor for me to take a couple of weeks off, why can't you see it the same way? How about a replacement —how about Morton Downey?"

"Nah!"

"All right—how about Bing Crosby?" I said. "He'd be great."

"Now come on, Rudy! He wouldn't mean a damn thing to my show. Look, I don't want to argue with you—take your two weeks. I'll close the show and we'll reopen in Boston when you get back."

I was well aware that Crosby was very hot on records at the time. He'd probably have been so popular in the *Scandals* that White wouldn't have cared if I *ever* returned. But White would have none of it. White wasn't the only one who missed the boat on Crosby! I once worked up an impression of Crosby (whistling and all) that was so believable it fooled one of the members of his original trio. He happened to hear me do it (while his back was turned to the stage) at the Pennsylvania Grill one night. Later on he asked me, "Where'd Bing go!" This imitation received tremendous applause at the New York Paramount, but Borros Morros, who was the dictator of shows at the Paramount Theatres at the time, asked me to drop it. "Bing's all washed up!" he said with great finality. "You and I should make what Crosby will earn in the next ten years," I answered. That was in 1931. Now, some forty years later, Crosby is Old Fort Knox himself!

And so the *Scandals* closed. I went to California, flying in an old trimotored Ford plane, chatting with Will Rogers, who got on at Amarillo, Texas. Although I wired Fay Webb at every place along the way where telegrams could be sent, mine was the agony of watching Will Rogers greeted by his family while I stood alone at the airport and waited one hour for the arrival of my wife.

I rejoined the show in Boston, where we played a fortnight, grossing $50,000 each week. Then we embarked on a tour of major cities and occasional one-night stands throughout the country. White, whose original interest in me had been my radio reputation, realized that if he could secure an occasional armory or large auditorium (sometimes with extra wooden seats to take care of the thousands who turned out to see a radio personality in person), he would achieve financial grosses unknown to touring musical revues. We finally reached Chicago, where the sponsors of my program informed me that if we went farther I would have to resign from the radio show. Although I carried eight key men with me, the difficulty of finding additional good musicians in towns such as Canton, Ohio and often even in larger cities was seriously affecting the quality of our broadcasts. I informed White that I could not go farther than Chicago. Evidently he had in mind to tour the production to California, maybe staying out for as long as three-quarters of the year, milking every town and hamlet that could possibly play the *Scandals*. I had no choice in the matter. My radio show was at stake. The eleventh edition of the *Scandals*, therefore, folded in Chicago in the spring of 1932.

Those were the bleak days. While Roosevelt was trying to get elected, I was campaigning my way back to New York. Willie and Eugene Howard, Ray Bolger, I, and others from the defunct eleventh *Scandals* played the Paramount Publix Theaters—and that wasn't a bad talent package, now that I think of it. Then we were back in the land of the rat race for a few weeks and on to a tour of one-nighters from which I returned to New York each Thursday for the "Fleischmann" show.

On these tours I realized I needed a girl singer badly and my thoughts turned to Alice Faye. I had come to know her and to like her immensely during the *Scandals* run. She was a cute blonde lovely in the chorus, very friendly, with a smile warm enough to melt the heart of an Eskimo. In the Atlantic City *Scandals* tryout in 1931 one of the semiprincipals, a girl with a big

With Alice Faye in the film, *George White's Scandals*, 1934

song that stopped the show opening night, developed laryngitis. I
suggested Alice as a replacement but George White turned her
down. Oddly enough, I had never really heard her sing profes-
sionally. The only times I had seen her perform were in those
impromptu numbers she would do for kicks at little parties the
Scandals company enjoyed from time to time after rehearsals.
Her unique way of handling a song stuck with me, however—I
knew she had great authority and physical appeal. So she joined
me on the grand tour in Harrisburg, Pennsylvania, and the first
night this ex-chorine was the smash I thought she would be. Next
stop: A featured personality role on my Thursday broadcasts.
Alice also performed with my company at the Hollywood Restaurant in 1933 and was an unqualified smash, night after night.

It wasn't long after she came on the "Fleischmann" show that
the papers were served to me asking that my separation agreement

with Fay Webb be set aside on the grounds of duress and fraud. Alice was as fiercely loyal as a mother rhinoceros at bay with brood. One of my favorite memories of Alice is of a time in Island Pond, Vermont (my birthplace) back in 1933. I forget just what the cause was, but an altercation concerning me was taking place in a small restaurant at two o'clock in the morning. Alice was outside but wanted to get inside to join the argument. It required a strong Canadian lumberjack to hold her back from the fray. Picture it—there was this huge, six-foot Canuck with a tassled toque and a Jerry Colonna moustache holding my diminutive vocalist a few feet in the air as she kicked away at his shins to escape his grasp. The more he laughed at her sttruggles, the madder she got. Fortunately, reason returned to the dissidents and the scene was serene again.

At this juncture White called me at the Essex House to offer me the lead in a filming of the *Scandals* to be made at Fox, which had not yet become Twentieth Century-Fox. I felt I must do something to atone for *The Vagabond Lover*, so I indicated my willingness, even though Fay Webb's attorneys were waiting to pounce.

"Just name any figure you want, Rudy," White said at the outset. "I want you to make some money. After all, Fox Studios has all the loot in the world." Then gentle Georgie reversed his tactics. "They've got me buying the talent now," he whined. "Honest to God, all I can offer you is $2,500 a week for four weeks' work. Ten grand."

I made a few mental calculations. "For God's sake, George," I said. "It will cost me nearly that to move my broadcasts out there! Plus the fact I'll have to give up the Hollywood Restaurant job and theater dates. After all, I can't underwrite the picture!" The disastrous premiere of *The Vagabond Lover* crept back into my mind. When all is said and done, a man has to try to make restitution for certain dastardly crimes! "Okay, George. You've got me; I'll do the picture."

Sometime before I had tried to sell White on using Alice Faye in this production he had let me persuade him to catch her performance with me at Loew's Theater in the Bronx, but he had been noncommittal. After he had gone to the Coast to prepare the picture, he suddenly wired me that he had secured a special song for her in the picture. Just coincidentally, the song title sums up my estimation of George White: "Oh, You Nasty Man!" At the time I had formed an agency to handle talent, and as Alice was one of our artists, we signed a satisfactory picture contract for her and we all entrained for Hollywood. Suddenly Lillian Harvey resigned as star of the picture. Alice's rushes doing "Oh, You Nasty Man" had already been viewed by the Fox brass and were adjudged sensational. Zanuck and the Fox brass said to White, "We want this girl for the lead!" White, for the first time in his life, was sunk. "But I don't own her!" he replied. They asked, "Who does?" White could have died, but replied, "Vallée!" So they came to me on bended knees.

I sent for Charlie Feldman, a young attorney whose girl friend Raquel Torres chummed with my wife Fay Webb. At lunch at Fox, with the figure of $500 in my mind, I asked Feldman what I should ask for.

"Five hundred dollars a week," was his answer.

Later, Feldman founded one of the most powerful talent agencies in Hollywood representing Cary Grant, Ingrid Bergman —you name them. So I always felt I may have given Charlie Feldman his start as an agent.

Alice got the lead and became a reigning star for years. Later, she decided to forego a full-time screen career to be the wife of Phil Harris.

George was a cutie and never hesitated to use anyone to further his aims. During the filming he arranged to have me stranded for a very long time atop a high pillar on the set from which the ladder had been removed. It got huge headlines and a barrel of publicity, which helped the picture's grosses. As White received a percentage, my ridiculous plight made money for him. As for me, the picture cost me about $75,000 in legal fees, transportation, etc. Wouldn't you think this would have cured me of this small-time Svengali White? Some of us never learn!

So this blue-suited postman rang for the third time. White asked me to play a part in the twelfth edition of *George White's Scandals* in 1936, but after looking over the songs and the general outline of the show, I felt that, to put it as charitably as possible, it was not going to be a very outstanding production. Even though Willie and Eugene Howard were again to be in it, the little intuitive voice that had guided me pretty well up to this date said, "Stay out of it." Cliff "Ukelele Ike" Edwards was assigned the part I refused and, when I caught the show in Newark, I was greeted by shouts of "Bow wow" from Bert Lahr, Willie Howard, and Cliff Edwards when I visited their dressing rooms. These animal-like cries were uttered to indicate to me that the show was a "dog." As I watched the show unfold, I realized only too well that it was a veritable bestiary—not only a dog but a turkey.

Among White's many decisions that have led me to question his judgment was a sordid happenstance in the 1931 *Scandals*. My mother had died two weeks before the rehearsals. When we arrived at Atlantic City the composers Brown and Henderson were still trying to put over a song that they felt was one of their best. It bore the title "If I Thought I Could Live Without You, I'd Die." Ethel Barrymore Colt sang her rendition of it—to a baby in a cradle; it didn't work. White tried several other renditions of the number by other members of the cast. One of the most ridiculous was Willie Howard's rendition. At that time he was at least sixty years of age, out on stage with a black, shiny wig. He sang it to a woman of graying hair, obviously supposed to be his mother. Before the second-week matinee began, I was informed by the stage manager that Mr. White had sent an order for me to sing the song in place of Willie Howard.

I dispatched the stage manager to point out to White that the matinee audience (made up mostly of women) would resent my apparent attempt to capitalize on the death of my mother by singing a song to a woman who was supposed to represent her. I pointed out that it would not only be embarrassing to me, but it would cause resentment by the public. Most certainly they would feel that this was playing a bit too obviously on their sympathetic potential. The stage manager returned to inform me curtly that White had said, "Do the song!" Always, like a good soldier, I obey orders even when I know they are stupid or wrong. When I was halfway through the song I could feel the general air of shock, astonishment, resentment, and indignation from many sections of the audience. Any performer can sense those things in a moment. No sooner had I come off the stage after singing the song than White had rushed backstage to apologize, saying he hadn't realized, he didn't think. This, believe it or not, *after* I had taken particular pains to explain to him what would obviously happen were I to do it.

After watching, with a certain amount of visceral pain, the opening night of this 1936 turkey in Jersey, I moved to Pittsburgh with my band and company of entertainers to play the Stanley Theater.

The butler in the residence of a Yale classmate, where I was staying, brought the phone to my bed one morning at one o'clock. "Rudy?" a metallic voice said. "This is George."

I had just dropped off to sleep and nothing registered very well. "George?" I mumbled. "George—."

"George White, goddammit! The show's in trouble. Bad trouble. We're in Boston and business stinks!"

I could have reminded him that I had said I didn't think he had a good show when I turned it down and about the lousy things he had done to me in the first *Scandals* and on the picture, but good-time Rudy never did rub it in when he should have. "I, ah, I'm sorry to hear that, George," was about all I could muster. I was still half asleep.

"Rudy, you gotta save the show," George pleaded. "It's a good show and all we need is a big commercial name to type it. Will you do it?"

"Now come on, George. First of all, I don't think it's such a hot show and besides, I'm involved with a hell of a lot of theater bookings. I just can't make it. I'd like to help you and all that, but you know how it is." I wanted to get back to sleep; I was bushed.

He hung up. But George White never gave up, never took no for an answer. First thing I knew he flew to Pittsburgh. White drove to my classmate's residence on the outskirts of Pittsburgh that night, awakened me, and knelt by my bed, as he pleaded with me "to step into the show to save it. It's not for me so much," he went on. "Think of all those kids who'll be thrown out of work. Would you want *that* on your conscience?"

This got to me. Maybe I felt guilty, having had such an easy time all during the depression. I don't know. Maybe White was the greatest salesman since the apple peddler in the Garden of Eden. Or perhaps I am one of the great all-time pushovers, a patsy par excellence.

So I managed to cancel the rest of my tour, learned the songs, the routines, and agreed to join the show in Washington in a few days. I made one proviso with White: I wanted to do an impression of Fred Allen in the show. (Ever since I had first seen Allen

at a little theater in Connecticut in 1926 I had admired his material and delivery. I had tried out this Allen impression at the
Brooklyn Paramount and the Hollywood Restaurant with great
success.) White agreed to this demand. "By the way, George," I
said, remembering the Maurice Chevalier hassle, "do you mind
putting it in writing?" With this understanding signed, sealed,
and delivered, I joined the company for the opening night in
Washington. But just a few minutes before curtain time I was
told not to do the Allen impression. As I write this sentence so
many years later I still burn a little at White's perfidy. But the
crowning act was yet to come.

Again I obeyed orders, but by now I was so disgusted I failed
to show up in the finale, causing much comment in the press. All
the same, I did do the impression beginning the second night in
Washington and we moved on to New York. After the down-beat
opening-night reviews and with a few more performances under
our belt, it became obvious that neither my presence, the presence
of even the fabulous Bing Crosby, nor that of anyone else for that
matter could save this doomed production.

Then my attorney phoned me with some very singular news.
"White wants you out of the show," he said in a voice full of
disbelief.

"Out of the show?" I asked incredulously. "Has he finally
gone completely out of his mind? But why on earth—."

"He's evidently trying to cut the payroll to keep the show
running," said the attorney.

"This is just great—after I gave up those theater bookings.
They would have paid me three times what I'm getting from
White. I just can't win. Suppose the show maintains its gross
without me, or by some fluke does better business. *That* sure as
hell won't help my career any!" I seethed in silence for a moment.

"Rudy—are you still there?"

"Yes. I'm trying to cool down enough to think. I'll tell you
what—you tell White I'll take a cut if he will ask me—privately."

Came the evening of the fracas. It was March 17 and I went
to the theater from the annual dinner of the Friendly Sons of St.
Patrick. With no notice White again sent me a message not to do
the Allen impression. As I saw him scurrying about backstage in
his blue suit with a green carnation in his lapel, I thought "How
can I be so goddamned stupid as to have gotten involved with

this character again?" After the performance I started for my dressing room only to be stopped by White's arrogant two-fingered whistle, which was always his signal for us to come running. The rest of the principals clustered around him as he asked several of them if they would take a cut. As I started to go to my dressing room he yelled at me to come back.

"Will you take a cut, Rudy?" he asked me in front of everyone.

I was furious that he had not deigned to ask me privately. I tried to remain calm. "You've made the profits," I said. "Why not take the losses?"

Then to my amazement, he said, "I lost enough money with you on the tour of 1932."

Recalling the gymnasiums and auditoriums in which we worked, with no dressing rooms, the large audiences, and the fabulous grosses for those days, as well as the critics' reviews, which had stated that the audiences had turned out mainly to see the radio personality—I felt this was too much. I was no longer calm. "You little prick!" I said. "You know very well that's a goddamn lie!" I was in tails and I had my hands in my pockets.

White glanced at some of the chorus girls watching the scene from outside their dressing rooms. In the manner of a prize fighter he approached me, with a smile on his face. I thought he was only clowning. Without any warning I felt a stinging blow on the bridge of my nose and realized too late that he had struck me. Before I could get my hands out of my pockets, the stagehands had separated us and the fracas was over. I had just had an operation several months before on my nose, which I had broken falling out of a hammock in the Navy in World War I. White's blow had landed right on this sensitive proboscis, but fortunately he had done no real damage.

I was barred from the theater pending a hearing before the American Arbitration Society. The case was to be tried before three men: one, my representative; one, White's representative; and a third, the medical writer for *Time* magazine.

Bert Lahr, who was in the show, was asked by White to testify against me. Lahr was very embarrassed and contributed nothing to the case for either side.

Then they put on Peggy Mosely, a slim brunette who had worked in my first *Scandals* back in 1931 and in this second

Scandals. She was my girl friend in a number that I sang as we were returning from a late party. In front of her door I would pretend that I had left my gloves in her apartment and together we would stand near the footlights as I would sing "I Forgot My Gloves." She would nestle against me with my arms around her. Sometimes when I was near to cracking up from overwork, I'd begin to giggle. She could feel my giggling and she would begin

With Peggy Mosely in George White's *Scandals* (1936). I'm singing "I Forgot My Gloves." This is the girl who said she had never heard words like those I shot at White backstage when he socked me in the nose.

giggling too, and one night I broke up completely. White rushed on stage as they lowered the curtain, with old man Valloooooo and Peggy in convulsions of laughter.

This same girl was now testifying that she had never heard such language in her life! The White representative had stated that I had called White "a little prick." When the medical man from *Time* suddenly queried, "And how many years did you say you had been in show business?" I knew that we were "in"!

His vote made it two to one. After due deliberation they ordered White to reinstate me in the show. White had threatened that if he was ordered to do so he would close the show. Rather than see the members of the cast suffer, I did not return. Cliff Edwards went back into my part, the same Cliff Edwards who, when I asked him if he would mind my stepping into the show, had said that it was perfectly agreeable with him. (I later learned that he often lurked in the wings cursing and reviling me as I portrayed the role he had left; he should have realized the only reason I stepped into the show was to try to save it and keep everyone working. His resentment further manifested itself as he testified against me at the arbitration proceedings.) Edwards returned to the part, but his triumph was short-lived. The show folded one week later, as it should have done months earlier, leaving me sadder but wiser.

When George White, the little hoofer from Toronto, Canada, sent for me to humiliate me in his office in 1931, he was worth $4 million. When he was on the prison farm where he was sent for one year for hit-and-run driving (as he was driving away from the race track at Del Mar, he had run down a young pair of newly-weds as they came out of a church to cross the road; White had driven away, leaving the pair *writhing in death*), he was so destitute that a Marine private overseas, hearing that he lacked the money for dental work, sent the money to him!

Even though White did profit handsomely from the Fox *Scandals* picture, which cost me over $70,000 to appear in it for him, he spent the last years of his life alone, broke, and unloved. Eventually he died of cancer.

I have just one final thought: Was he buried wearing his blue suit, white shirt, and black bow tie?

The Tony

I had come to know Tony Martin slightly through an incident in New York in the middle thirties. At the time I was interested in Judy Stewart, a beautiful brunette who occasionally performed as a dancer. Judy seemed to like me but never really cared deeply for me; so some of the things she did came not as a surprise to me.

In the thirties there was a successful and elegant supper club, the Versailles, way over on the East Side on 50th Street. I had taken Judy there on the night of Tony Martin's opening, and it was obvious to me that Tony was interested in her.

The following week I went to my lodge in Maine but decided to return to New York Tuesday night instead of Wednesday, as I usually did. Two of my friends from Rye, New York, the Watermans, suggested we go to the Versailles for a late dinner. And who do you think was seated along the wall, all by herself—waiting for Tony to finish his two shows? You guessed it—Judy Stewart! I found myself a little hurt, yet delighted at Tony's and Judy's discomfiture. The Watermans left and I went over to join the two culprits.

9

Martin Caper

"After all," I told Tony, "I'm not married to the girl."

That clandestine affair put an end to the interest I had in Judy; from then on it was never quite the same.

By the fall of 1939 I had moved to Hollywood. I invited Alice Faye to go with me to the fabulous Trocadero—the gayest spot along the Sunset Strip. It was the happiest scene of night life in Hollywood in the halcyon days of the late thirties. As I danced with Alice I noticed a great interest on the part of Tony Martin. I believe he was there stag and I was not surprised when, a few months later, he and Alice became man and wife. But it was not a happy marriage and eventually was terminated.

In 1942 a man as young as Tony Martin was fair game for the draft board. He somehow wangled the rank of chief petty officer (the man who really gets things done in the navy, just as the top sergeant really runs the army). Considering the fact that Tony Martin never had any military experience, as I had had in World War I, he should have realized that he was a fortunate young man to receive a rank that sometimes takes fifteen, twenty, or twenty-four years for a real old salt to achieve.

At a Warner Brothers Studio Club party (February, 1938) held at the Biltmore Hotel in Los Angeles. Left to right, Jack L. Warner; Gladys Gladd, wife of Mark Hellinger, columnist; Jack L. Warner, Sr.; myself and Judy Stewart.

Tony was never one to hide his light under a bushel. As a matter of fact, there were critics who often said that when he performed he always seemed to be looking at himself in a mirror. In another era what Tony did to achieve the rank of chief specialist might not be particularly frowned upon, or be dishonorable. In the Civil War, for example, there were individuals in Washington who paid other men to take their places in the ranks; throughout history commissions have been bought or won through contacts. But it was different now. Tony's commission was linked to an automobile gift to a lieutenant commander stationed at the naval base in San Francisco; he owned a very successful plumbing business in Los Angeles where I had purchased supplies when I first moved to Hollywood. It ended in Tony's dismissal from the Navy.

It seemed to me that when he appeared on the floor of a

nightclub either during the war or after that, the father and mother of some boy who had lost his life as a seaman in the navy would not only refrain from applauding his singing, but also might even boo him while he was performing. I did not reckon with the short memories of most human beings, and there were those who didn't even know that the affair had taken place. Today when I ask someone if he remembers the Tony Martin incident in San Francisco, I am greeted with an uncomprehending stare.

Tony was smart enough to enlist immediately in a branch of the air force that carried supplies to fighting men all over the world. He first went to New Haven to my old alma mater for training and then flew many loads of supplies over the Himalayas. From what I am told, he did a bang-up job until the end of the war.

There was one aspect of this sordid mess for which Tony will

Tony Martin (*center*) at his induction into the Navy on January 2, 1942. LCR. M. N. Aroff (*left*) was tried before a general court-martial on July 27, 1942 on charges of accepting an automobile from the singer "as a fee, compensation and reward for facilitating the enlistment" of Martin as a chief specialist in the Navy. (World Wide Photos)

always be faulted by those it affected. Thereafter, when any person who was in show business sought and asked for a commission in any branch of the service, he immediately put upon the spot any high-ranking officer who signed the papers giving him the commission. Invariably he would be asked: "What did you get for okaying the commission!"

I didn't mind having to go in as an enlisted man; yet, it was a fact that I had become a worldwide figure earning in excess of $200,000 a year. Any surgeon or doctor who was in the $75,000 or $100,000 a year bracket usually received at least a captaincy but more often the rank of major or lieutenant colonel. John Philip Sousa led a navy band in World War I. He was immediately made a lieutenant commander and finished as a *commander* in the navy. Conversely, he was not only a band leader but had written some of the most memorable music for marching bands.

Pianist Eliot Daniel was a near victim of the Tony Martin incident. Daniel was a Harvard man who graduated with Eddy Duchin. Eliot had been the piano mainstay of my broadcasts ever since he joined me at the Hollywood Restaurant in New York in 1934. It has always been my privilege to have the finest pianists in the musical world—men like Walter Gross, Walter Scharf, Frank Leithner, and Carmen Cavallaro. But Eliot Daniel was the most well-rounded pianist I've ever known. Whether it was dance music, show music, picture scores, operatic, or symphonic, no one could excel him. His ability to memorize quickly and to be able to follow a singer or performer who took great liberties, as I did with a song, made Eliot truly outstanding and worthy of every dollar I paid him.

As soon as I took over the Coast Guard band I began augmenting it until we finally had a fine band-orchestra of forty-five men, made up of the finest musicians in the entire country. I had asked Eliot to join us, but he told me his draft number was almost up and he was going to Boston to get a lieutenancy in the navy. Thus, on our first date at a Coast Guard station at Lompoc I was forced to use another pianist, who, though excellent, lacked the command of the piano as exemplified by Daniel. Suddenly Eliot was on the phone calling me from Boston to tell me they could not give him the commission because of what had happened in San Francisco, and that he was coming back to join my

Coast Guard band. He was not a moment too soon. In fact, we kept the medical department at Long Beach open until ten o'clock that night, because on the following morning Eliot would have been in the army.

It was about three or four months following the horror and infamy of Pearl Harbor. America was frantically trying to make up for its total unpreparedness. Airplane factories were working around the clock. On the California coast we were greatly apprehensive that at any moment the Japanese might attack. There may have been one or two destroyers and perhaps a battleship stationed at San Diego, but I doubt it.

Lewis Stone, the judge in the MGM pictures of the Mickey Rooney–Andy Hardy series, had always had a secret yen to be in uniform with the rank of a colonel. He created what was called the *California Evacuation Corps* made up of those of us in the motion picture industry who had *a station wagon.* We were totally unauthorized and bought our own uniforms. Lewis Stone talked Warner Brothers into letting us drill two nights a week at the old Warner studios on Sunset Boulevard. The California Evacuation Corps was not lacking in stars. Robert Young, Caesar Romero, practically every top male personality who had a station wagon, met to drill on Tuesday and Thursday nights. Later, we went to the Warner Brothers Ranch for what is known as a *bivouac!* Our three-day encampment included Cliff Arquette, whom you know as Charlie Weaver; Buster Keaton; and a well-rounded group of men, some of whom had had military experience. Victor Borge, whom I had placed on the Bing Crosby show, had asked me if he could join our Evacuation Corps. It was amusing to see Lewis Stone seated on a cot outside his tent with his overseas cap, sporting the rank of colonel, as the rest of us went about our various tasks of preparing our meals, drilling, or what have you. Before the bivouac we had a meeting where I pleaded with the boys to study the maps and to mark the shortest routes to the hospitals. In the event the Japs did come in our task was to remove persons from burning buildings, those who had been bombed or hurt, and get them to the nearest hospital.

One of our group, convinced that there must be a fifth column of Japanese in Los Angeles, believed they should be removed and taken to a prison camp somewhere in the Middle

West. He felt the only man to help us do this was Wendell Will-kie, who was on a speaking tour that had led him to Los Angeles. The next morning at eight o'clock Willkie graciously greeted us in his suite at the Biltmore Hotel and listened to our story and fears concerning the nisei and the native-born Japanese. In the event of an attack it was felt they would suddenly be able to assist the attackers and cause possible damage and loss of life. On Willkie's return to Washington he set in force the necessary legis-lation to accomplish a most dastardly and cruel action resulting in 100,000 Japanese being incarcerated behind barbed wire in prison camps through the Middle West. I later tried to atone for my part in this despicable act when a young Japanese-American couple, Johnny and Fumi Ito, moved into our house. Fumi served as housekeeper and my secretary while we helped put Johnny through college. I am godfather to their two adorable children. Johnny had served in our armed forces, but poor Fumi with her father and mother had been one of those I had caused to be transported to the Middle West to be cooped up like criminals.

I have said that Victor Borge became a member of our Cali-fornia Evacuation Corps. He had approached me on learning that I was drilling two nights a week at the Warner Brothers studios. He told me the draft was getting very close to him. I expressed amazement at this; he had two or three children and I couldn't understand why the board would be taking a married man, especially one who was not even a citizen of the United States. Borge asked me if I thought that joining our Evacuation Corps could be of any help in avoiding the draft. I replied that it might, but that his fate was in the hands of his draft board. I later advised him the same when he asked if performing with my Coast Guard band would keep him out of the draft. I, too, was getting close to being called up. It was incredible to me, as I was forty-one years of age. My radio program was responsible for the employment of at least thirty-five persons and it seemed that would help. Such was my ego—I didn't realize how easily I could be replaced. Joan Davis took over the show with scarcely a ripple on the entertainment scene.

I hied myself down to the navy offices near Chinatown. I recited the fact that I'd had a year of Reserve Officer Training Corps at the University of Maine, served as lieutenant commander naval aide on the staff of the governor of Maine for four years, and also had a college degree. I was curtly told that the only rank I could achieve would be that of a seaman 3rd class. Nothing daunted, my attorney and I went to Santa Ana to talk to General Couzens, who had become the darling of the Hollywood film crowd. He had made it possible for several film personalities to receive a commission in the air corps. But our visit was fruitless. We were told that the chance of even making the rank of sergeant was doubtful.

I had engaged the services of an attractive and capable secretary whose name was Mona. I related to her my unsuccessful attempts to get a commission in the navy or the air corps. Then, almost too casually, she told me that Max Sturges, a former musician and lawyer for the Musicians' Union, had put together an eighteen-piece Coast Guard band and was looking for someone to lead it. To Mona he had expressed the desire to ask me to do it.

A meeting of Coast Guard brass was arranged at the beautiful home of Owen Churchill in Los Angeles. Churchill was a true aristocratic Angelino. Among the guests was Captain Towle, who was in charge of the Coast Guard base at Long Beach. Sturges was present, along with Commander Thomas—as enthusiastic as Towle about the formation of our band. I had given the meeting serious thought and had decided upon my course of action, in view of Tony Martin's unfortunate incident. After a most delicious dinner there was a strained moment of silence. I then proceeded to break the ice.

"I am keenly aware of what is in your minds and I'm going to be very frank and honest about the situation as to what rank I should have as the bandmaster of the Coast Guard band of the Eleventh Naval District. I don't want any of you to be embarrassed as you undoubtedly would be if you gave me a commission in gold braid. I am quite willing to enlist as a chief petty officer and to remain in that status until Captain Towle feels that I should receive a commission."

With a feeling of relief we all raised our glasses in a toast to my appointment as a bandmaster. There followed two of the happiest years of my life as I directed one of the finest aggregations ever organized to produce fine instrumental music. I frankly was almost grateful to Tony Martin for the fact that I was not a commissioned officer, as being an enlisted man gave me much more freedom in certain respects than I would have had were I wearing gold braid.

When a few months later the band had been augmented to forty-seven men, my cup runneth over. The majority of the men, particularly the brass section, were artists whom I could not have afforded to have in civil life. When I gave a downbeat to our fifteen-piece brass section I felt an exultation that not even Arthur Fiedler could experience when he directs his Boston Pops Orchestra.

Now that I had Eliot Daniel as first piano, Robert Maxwell (a $1,000-a-week artist before he joined us), and a percussion section second to none, I proceeded to lay out a two-hour concert-show that was easily worth $5 a seat. We played the bases of all the other services and on a war bond tour to the East, we performed in theatres, college auditoriums, and stadiums, where we received a standing ovation when we played our final selection. Finally, as we approached an evening in the Hollywood Bowl at which we were to fete the secretary of the navy, I realized that for me to direct the massed bands of all the services as an enlisted man was like a surgeon doing an operation in his pajamas. Captain Towle agreed that the time had come for me to be promoted and on that evening I wore a white mess jacket, tuxedo pants, and the shoulder bars of a lieutenant senior grade.

With the Eleventh Naval District 45-piece band/orchestra stationed at Wilmington. At the time of this photograph I had been promoted to lieutenant and the band consisted of top musicians of the country, including Robert Maxwell on the harp.

Photograph taken shortly before opening of The Pirate's Den. *Left to right in back row:* Bob Hope, Tony Martin, Ken Murray and others. *Front:* Myself with Jimmy Fiddler.

As for Tony Martin, who had been working valiantly in the branch of the Air Force that flew needed supplies "over the hump" to the men in Burma, he had indeed redeemed himself.

Today, Tony Martin has had a rebirth of his career which might well have been inspired by the example of Robert Goulet and his wife, Carol Lawrence, teaming up together. The Martins, now Tony and Cyd Charisse, have been winning accolades and huzzahs not only in Las Vegas but at the Waldorf Astoria, where the reviews have been as warm and favorable as Tony and his lovely wife could wish. As of this writing Tony is slated to do the *Life of Harry Richman* and no one will do it better.

In 1961 when we were shaking down our production of *How to Succeed* in Philadelphia, Tony was doing his single act at a huge nightclub in Cherry Hill, New Jersey. He and his entourage of three young men were staying at the Warwick Hotel, where most of our cast were also staying. One afternoon as Mrs. Vallée, with one of our poodles, entered the elevator in the Warwick, Tony and his three henchmen followed her into the car. Mrs. Vallée heard Tony mutter to one of his boys, "Find out what floor she gets off at."

Ellie has a delightful and mischievous sense of humor, which came to the surface as she said, "Why, Tony! Don't you recognize me? I'm Mrs. Rudy Vallée!"

The Day

Milton Berle

This is the saga of Milton Berlinger, alias Milton Berle, alias Uncle Miltie, whom someone dubbed the "King of Television," a title he richly deserved. He is one of the most talented persons in this difficult world of show business, and yet one of its most contradictory characters.

My mind is hazy as to when I first met him. But in the very early thirties I became aware of his august presence. Several other personalities, spurred by envy, no doubt, informed me that Berle was a comedian about whom three outstanding observations might be made: (1) He was not above stealing anyone's material if it was worth using. (But that is a trait common to all of us in the entertainment world.) (2) He always arranged for his mother to sit in the audience, where through many shows she would not only start the applause but also as a good Pied Piper would try to bring the laughter out of an otherwise dull audience. (3) He never knew when to finish and get off the stage.

I couldn't believe anyone would be so stupid as to overstay his leave. But as I watched him perform at some affair—I don't believe it was in a theater, but a gathering such as a cocktail

10

Ran Off

the Stage

party, with several personalities being called upon to perform—
he went on and on and on even when it was clear to anyone but a
deaf egomaniac that the audience was bored to tears.

Yet, paradoxically, but for Milton Berle I might never have
realized that it was also possible for one lone person to hold an
audience completely spellbound for an hour or more. Today,
with only piano accompaniment, I do a two-hour routine of songs
and humor and usually receive a standing ovation when I finish.
Sammy Davis, Jr. does it, but he needs a large orchestra with
tremendous brass and strong timpani rolling to finish most of his
musical numbers. Belafonte, Danny Kaye, and several others ap-
proximate Davis in his approach to a one-man show, but Chevalier was the first, I believe, to do a ninety-minute, one-man
show with just a piano.

Berle, the many-sided individual wearing three hats, is a
formidable person. He is at once a producer, a director, and an
entertainer, with emphasis (in my opinion) on the director. I
believe his ability as a director exceeds his ability as a comedian,
although I know he will not enjoy my observation. As a self-

styled "King of Television," he was the first, by his own efforts alone, to dominate the TV air waves with a great and superbly produced variety show. Although his Texaco show started just about the same time that Ed Sullivan began his conquest of the new medium with his "Toast of the Town," Sullivan at first relied upon his aides to help him eventually have the top-rated variety show that sent Berle to the showers. As a result of my own experience, though, I could only greatly admire the smooth way Berle put together his "Texaco Star Hour" on television.

Although Berle was not a musician or an orchestra director, he really in effect was his own arranger and orchestra director. It was Milton who decided upon the Texaco theme song and who probably created the quartet that sang the catchy Texaco tune. He probably wrote most of the theme song, too. The musical

Milton Berle

bridges were pure Berle, as I watched him create them and dictate them to an arranger to be put on paper for the orchestra to play. The guests were entirely his selection, and he chose their material. He edited it and assigned to his writers the job of incorporating any ideas that he felt would strengthen the performer's part of the telecast. Ironically, perhaps, it was Berle himself who was the weakest part of his own program. His return to television, after a vacation from it, was an unmitigated disaster largely because he relied less upon his guest performers.

In December 1973 Berle was to appear with Jerry Lewis at the very popular Deauville Star Theatre in Miami Beach. John Huddy, entertainment editor of the *Miami Herald*, told what happened.

"Here's what happened to provoke Lewis' wrath," said Huddy. "He and Milton Berle were to do an act together in the Star Theatre, integrating their routines, blending their famous Burlesque style comedy. Lewis was more than willing to do just that—but Berle, who had a reputation for telling others how to do their act, did not cooperate. In the end the two comedians decided to perform back-to-back. Separate shows. Lewis, whose act needed updating anyway, then made a blunder: He allowed Uncle Miltie to go on first."

Speaking for myself, I can't believe that Lewis could have been this naive. Surely he must have long ago become aware that Berle had an almost criminal, callous disregard for anyone else on the bill with him. Huddy called it a "blunder." I would call it sheer suicide. According to Huddy Berle stayed on for nearly an hour and a half. That, ladies and gentlemen, is ninety minutes— almost a full-length motion picture.

Said Huddy: "By the time Lewis appeared the audience had had enough comedy, certainly enough slapstick. The harder Lewis worked the more openly the crowd yawned. Many people walked out. The next day the bad news spread like grass fire: The great Jerry Lewis is bombing on the beach."

It was, of course, Lewis' own fault. He should never, but never, have permitted Berle to precede him.

Perhaps I should explain my contention that I have always considered Milton Berle a very contradictory person. At the March of Dimes' January 1973 dinner for Frank Sinatra as man of the century, Berle was chosen (even though the dais also seated Jack Benny) as the "funny man" to rib Sinatra. Berle has never been more a delight or more brilliant than he was that evening in 1973. Few know that he is also a gifted song writer and stylist. Much of his material, however, is written by a former clothing salesman, Stan Davis, who is without a peer in writing for certain persons—notably Berle.

Years ago in the late thirties Berle wrote a column that appeared in *Weekly Variety*—I believe he wrote it for the fun of it. It was called "The Berling Point" and was a breezy reflection of the times. As I began to realize the need for some humorous material for me in my increasing personal appearances without my orchestra, it emboldened me to speak to Berle. "Milton," I said, "would you consider letting me use some of your material for an occasional appearance?"

"Of course," Berle said. He gave me the material, and when I asked what I owed him, he refused any recompense. "Forget it!" he said magnanimously.

Then in December 1973, at the opening of the $3 million renovated Oakland Paramount Theatre in Oakland, California, I watched and listened to a Berle who was unbelievably, catastrophically, amateurishly, and incredibly wretched! It was a black-tie affair, with speeches from everyone. There were celebrities from Hollywood and all the elite of the Bay area, including former Chief Justice Warren, who, with his wife, sat at our right. Champagne was freely served in the lobby and various beautifully decorated rooms throughout the theater. John Scott Trotter directed a large orchestra from the pit and played a long medley saluting the stars who in yesteryears might have played on the stage or the screen of this theater. It was a very pretentious and prestigious show: Robert Merrill from New York, a group who performed an incredible Hindu dance, a large choir on stage, the Salvation Army Band to play "The Star-spangled Banner," the promise of some new, top black artists, some old-timers like Donald O'Connor, and, for humor—Milton Berle.

I was told later that when Berle arrived with his entourage of four persons, he was suffering from a bleeding ulcer. That, and only that, could account for the amateurish performance that one of the most brilliant raconteurs offered that evening. It wasn't only that it was rambling, wandering, straggling, and totally out of keeping with the event of the evening—it was downright offensive and nauseating! He opened with one of the most harmless but bewildering chestnuts, as he stated, "Boy! Am I unlucky! If they sawed a woman in half, I'd get the part that eats!"

I have never worried about youthful members in the audience. The chances are they know all the sexual matter in advance and if they don't mere words are not going to corrupt or hurt them. As a matter of fact, it was the youthful element in the audience that seemed to enjoy Berle's sallies into sexual and totally irrelevant nonsense. Only a small group of these youngsters applauded the worst portion of his performance, which was the reading from a paper of a poem set to music—a poem on the Watergate mess. It could not have been conceived by Stan Davis, and Berle's reading of it was more than pathetic. He closed the first half of the show, but not before he had visibly discomfited Chief Justice Warren, who muttered something during one of Berle's most nauseating jokes.

Unless you have watched Berle work in a nightclub you cannot imagine just how sadistic this man can be. His work as a single is usually satisfying enough. But when he works with a woman, usually one physically well endowed, Berle becomes a lecherous, offensive, Jerry Lewis type. He seems to take a great deal of pleasure in manhandling the unfortunate girl, who has agreed to work with him probably because she needs the money and the exposure that being in his act will give her. The important thing about all of this is that he doesn't have to do it. Apparently this is a mental block in Berle. He doesn't realize that in pleasing a few men and women in his audience he is losing the respect of the majority who do not wish to see such a lascivious display.

That Milton Berle is a very gifted and talented performer in many directions is acknowledged by nearly everyone in show business. But like Jerry Lewis, who is equally gifted, Berle knows he has exceptional talent, and *there is nothing worse than a gifted person being acutely aware that he possesses this gift!* This contempt for his peers is most evident in Berle when discussing what you are going to do on his show. I don't think he is aware that as you talk he makes it evident that he is not listening to you but is off somewhere miles away. Having already decided in his mind what you can and cannot do, he half listens but is watching something else going on in the room and you are keenly aware that he is just barely tolerating you.

Few persons who are thus gifted can keep their feet on the ground, and their contempt expresses itself in various ways. On his telethons Jerry Lewis shows it best by the way he swaggers around twirling the microphone and grimacing, using the same facial contortions Berle often uses, not unlike the expressions of a spastic child (with the tongue protruding and an idiotic and almost frightening mask of a real moron). If Berle and Lewis only knew how this angers some of the more genteel members of their audiences, they just would not do these arrogant things.

Berle's greatest betrayal of not only his ego but at once his insecurity is his reaction to applause. I have watched him too many times not to realize that applause is to Berle what catnip is to a cat. Applause causes him to experience a euphoria that is something to behold. First, his face lights up, and there is a mixture of joy and incredulity, as though he is not quite sure that what he is hearing is real. Then he relaxes and drinks it in. After savoring it for a few seconds he feels impelled to do something, whether it be vocal or just some movement. He moves about, sometimes like a whirling dervish—pirouetting, then mincing in the stereotyped gay manner, maybe running to the wings; in fact, anything can happen if the applause is very great and long.

Eventually he says something inaudible as he moves his mouth in one of his famous moues, and not being particularly creative or alert to say something different to this rapturous audience, he retreats to the commonplace, "Thank you, ladies and genemen." Yes, that's the way he has been saying it for many years and today, unless he is carefully watching himself, he reverts to his old "genemen."

Berle also inaugurated one of the most annoying and audience-insulting customs to plague our American nightclub and show stages. It was probably in his first hosting chores that Berle, after introducing a performer, found himself on the stage as the performer terminated his or her act. Suddenly, he was confronted by something for which he was totally unprepared. The act was over, but now, he, Berle, the host, who had just introduced this person by name, felt that this moment called for something either in word or action from him. I suppose he thought it was really a stroke of genius when he found himself saying, "John Dokes, ladies and genemen! John Dokes!" Berle is also responsible for the arm wave. This is the gesture by which the host urges the audience to greater applause, cries, whistles, or other responses.

Berle's failure to terminate his part of the show after a reasonable stay is the most disturbing of all his intrusions. It is hard on entertainers who have been patiently waiting for their turn to perform. The audience may be tired out and restless by then.

In 1933 I was asked to accept the presidency of AFA—The American Federation of Actors, a union of the lower strata of entertainers, who made no pretense to the culture and high quality of the legitimate and motion picture personalities. I accepted, but bowed out when I realized that I was being used to fill the pockets of corrupt men with the dues of the poor souls who had once been the top names of a defunct and passé phase of show business called vaudeville. Harry Richman and Sophie Tucker took over, and AFA became The American Guild of Variety Artists. While I still headed AFA, though, we had a benefit on November 10, 1935, at the Majestic Theatre in New York City, at which Milton Berle appeared.

In the first three years of my radio and theater fame I did over one hundred benefits each year—most of them on Sunday nights. They were held in New York City at all the top legitimate theaters that did not have shows on Sunday night. A group of from thirty to fifty top personalities would meet at the first theater while other personalities were already performing at two or three other theaters. We passed each other, swapping theaters and waiting in the dark of back stages before going on. This could be an exhausting and trying experience. Instead of the usual hit-or-miss presentation of the personalities who were knocking themselves out to help what might be a completely phony charity, I decided we would secure the time of each act, and assign each performer to be at the designated theater at a certain time, to be presented for a duration not more than ten minutes beyond the time so stated.

We decided that Milton Berle would close the first half, just before intermission. We would have been much smarter if we had given him the last spot on the entire show. All went well until I presented Berle. He was going over very well, but we had given him twelve minutes, and when he had been on for fifteen, it

The clocks here remind me of Uncle Milty because once he gets on stage, even a thousand of them wouldn't help him remember his time to leave!
(Photo from opening night, The Texas Millionaires' Garden of the Gods Club—1952)

was clear that his reputation for not getting off was not going to be challenged this evening. After he had been out for twenty minutes, we rang down the curtain. Down it came, but nothing daunted, our hero calmly lifted it, stepped out, and continued his act, which lasted through the entire fifteen minutes of intermission.

Today Berle is a much more mature person. Possibly his mother's death had some effect on his brash personality. He loved her very much and she was a fine person who lived for his success. The stories of her presence in the audience are all too true. (My wife similarly is one of my best bellringers when it comes to laughing it up when sometimes the audience is not laughing in the right places.) I remember Berle's first wife, Joyce Matthews, one of the loveliest girls I've ever known. Joyce really brought out the best in Berle, even though their marriage ended. Since moving to California and becoming one of the Beverly Hills film colony, he has done some fine things. His work in the Joseph Levine film *The Oscar* was most believable; he has done some excellent television, dramatic, and comedy work. In Florida, in 1971, his portrayal of the little guy in *Last of the Red Hot Lovers* gave me more pleasure of laughter than anything I've known in a long time.

But I'll never forget one afternoon in 1936 when a little retort from old man Vallée caused the great Berle to run off the stage and into the street in sheer panic. The stage of Loew's State Theatre in New York City little dreamt that the enactment of David and Goliath was to occur that fateful Tuesday afternoon.

It was my week at Loew's State, a theater that played shows four and five times a day to audiences of two to three thousand persons. I had a band of eighteen men and four acts I had personally chosen for my tour of theaters that year. It had become the custom at Loew's State for the act or performer who was to follow the current act to come out on the stage Tuesday afternoon, the second show, and take a bow. It was as simple as that. Berle was to follow us, and his bow was scheduled for the second show, Tuesday afternoon.

As we finished one of our numbers I looked around. There was Berle in the wings. My heart sank as I surveyed his appearance. He was wearing a camel's-hair coat that looked as though

Loew's State marquee, circa 1935. This is where the Berle encounter took place.

he had been sleeping in it for weeks. On his head was a brown felt hat, with a sweat band that was badly discolored. I, on the other hand, was a fashion plate incarnate—white flannel trousers, double-breasted dark-blue jacket, white shirt, with a four-in-hand tie, and black and white shoes.

After two more numbers from the company I stepped to the microphone and gave Berle an eloquent and well-deserved introduction.

He strode in, cigar in hand, hat and coat still on. I moved back into the shadows, out of range of the spotlight, indicating that the stage was his. He began by informing the audience that he was to be there next week and promised a good show. Then, to my astonishment, he seemed to run down for lack of something to say. I should have remembered his inane words when an act had finished and he couldn't think of something to fit the situation.

Suddenly Berle whipped off his hat, held it out to the audience, and then, turning to me, smirked: "This hat belonged to Rudy Vallée, *but I had it cleaned!*"

It was apparent that the audience didn't like this remark coming from one man about another man who had just graciously introduced him. There were a few nervous giggles.

I didn't change my expression, and Berle turned back to the audience and continued to ramble on. But again he came to a stop, and again he ran out of something to say. This time he turned back to me, and, as he surveyed my attire, said, "Hmmmmm! Very nice!"

I have never pretended to be a quick-witted person. I usually think of the perfect retort days after the incident. But here for some reason, without hesitation, it popped out of me: "Sorry I can't say the same about you!"

The audience had been waiting for this moment. They responded with a roar that built into a hurricane of laughter, jeers, derision, and boos that sent Berle running off the stage and outside, where I fervently hoped he wouldn't be run over by a taxi!

Voyage of

For years I had the feeling that one day I would return to London. More than a decade had passed since I had worked at the Savoy. The opportunity came sooner and much more pleasantly than I had expected. Our advertising agency apparently had convinced our sponsor that it would be a timely and brilliant idea for me to do two "Fleischmann" broadcasts from London during the coronation in the summer of 1937, using all European talent and English musicians.

This decision was telephoned to me while I was playing in Miami Beach in the spring of 1937, and on my return we discussed all phases of this plan. It was decided that I would miss one Thursday broadcast by sailing on a Monday. That would put us in the docks at Southampton, England the day after the Thursday broadcast, which unfortunately we would not be able to hear at sea. It was agreed that Edgar Bergen would take over the show I missed and fill in for us as master of ceremonies and top comedian. Thus, we would have approximately six days in England to put our show together. The London J. Walter

11

Misadventures

Thompson office had already interviewed and pretty well set most of the personalities, including the lord mayor of London, and an old American friend of mine who had become a British citizen, Sid Phillips, a brilliant arranger and director. Phillips was engaged with twenty-five of London's best musicians to handle the musical chores for me, although I was to direct the band as always.

Thus, on a beautiful Tuesday afternoon we backed out of the French pier on the luxurious *Ile de France* and turned the nose of our ship toward Europe. While the *Ile de France* had been dwarfed in size by the *Normandie*, it was still a luxurious boat with cuisine to tempt the appetite of Duncan Hines himself, the choicest of fine wines and all you wished of them gratis at dinner or luncheon. Except for the fact that before sailing I picked up some sort of an infection that gave me a high fever, the trip was a wonderful experience. I felt better the third day out and discovered that among our passengers was George M. Cohan. He kept pretty much to himself and when I sent word to his stateroom to ask him if he would become a part of the ship's concert, which I had been asked to emcee the last Friday night on board, he declined even to take a bow.

I had become acutely aware of the fact that George M. Cohan, towards the end of his days, for all his great talent and fine artistry as a performer, had become an embittered man. His wrath was particularly directed at the new electronics of sound on film, the microphone, and the speaker of radio. Cohan had been born, so to speak, in a theatrical trunk, and had come up to his glowing success the hard way by playing all the "tank" towns in his vaudeville days. He had known much privation, actual suffering, and hard work. Somehow he could not accept the fact that, in one short year of broadcasting from an obscure nightclub on the East Side, a boy from Maine could achieve a fame even greater, as far as recognition by numbers of people is concerned, than he had won over a period of twenty years.

I recalled a night when after five long shows at the New York Paramount Theatre, at a time when my weekly salary was at its highest, I received a wire from George M. Cohan asking me to appear at the annual Friars Frolic at the New Amsterdam Theater. I walked two blocks to the New Amsterdam between shows on that Sunday afternoon to inform Mr. Cohan that I would be backstage after my last show at the New York Paramount awaiting my introduction, and that I would do a couple of songs with my own pianist from the Paramount, thereby not requiring any rehearsal with the orchestra that afternoon.

At approximately 10:45 that evening I found myself backstage at the Friars Frolic with several other performers, and I introduced myself to the great producer Sam Harris (formerly Cohan's partner), who checked me on his list. I then peeked out from the wings to watch Chevalier and Primo Carnera both do an imitation of Chevalier. I watched the other acts that were the last half of the evening show, when suddenly I noticed that the curtains were being lowered, and that the band was playing "The Star Spangled Banner," signifying that the evening was over. To my amazement I was the only person left alone backstage.

My vanity was not affected deeply by this slight. If it was intentional, then I knew that Cohan felt I was an adversary worthy to be challenged. If it was because he thought me unimportant—too unimportant to be introduced even though he had asked me to perform—it would leave me puzzled as to *why he had asked me to perform in the first place!* Some of the Friars were mortified beyond words, however, and descended upon me at the Pennsylvania Grill the following night, exhorting me to take a high post as their dean, a position second only to that of Cohan's. They wanted to give me a testimonial banquet at the Astor Hotel, and the man who had sponsored me suggested I resign. I laughed it off and told them lightly that it was not terribly important to me, that it was forgotten, that I could accept none of these things they felt would be the proper recompense for this slight.

The daily sight of Cohan hunched up at the stern of the ship watching the wake of the *Ile de France* also reminded me of the night that he was toastmaster at the Friars' testimonial dinner to Maurice Chevalier at the Astor Grand Ballroom, with the most impressive array of religious and show business personalities I have ever seen under one roof. As Chevalier was about to leave America to return to France, this was his farewell appearance in the United States, and our dais that night was truly a who's who of New York City, which is to say the United States. Four motion picture cameras covered the event from the balcony, and in the sea of faces that filled the ballroom floor were more diamonds, ermines, and minks than I have ever seen gathered under one tent.

There occurred that evening the most spontaneous and explosive, laugh-provoking incident I have ever witnessed at an affair of this nature. Jesse Lasky, a pioneer picture producer who had originally brought Chevalier to the United States, was reminiscing about it, and evidently being a little tired, he lost his train of thought. Absent-mindedly, he said, "Where am I?" Like a jack-in-the-box, George Jessel popped up and close on Lasky's words said, "You're Jesse Lasky, this is the Hotel Astor, and the banquet for Maurice."

I was on the dais where I could observe Cohan very closely, being about three chairs from him, and it seemed to me that he had had a cocktail or two, as he was exceedingly flushed when it came time for him to introduce the guest of honor. It was quite evident, to me at least, that Cohan felt a distinct hostility toward this personality, who quickly and dramatically had captured the United States in three pictures in the short space of one year. I can remember Cohan's words so well as he fondled the gavel in a manner that distinctly indicated he felt an inner urge to rap Chevalier over the head with it. Out of the corner of the famous Cohan mouth came this introduction: "We *admire* you, Mr. Chevalier, we *like* you, Mr. Chevalier, we love you, Mr. Chevalier, and it now gives me extreme pleasure to introduce that star of stage, screen, and that . . . er . . . what do you call it . . . radio. . . ."

The ship's concert proceeded nicely without Cohan. It afforded me an opportunity to get to know the incomparable Hildegarde better, as she was on board, and she really killed 'em. There was also a small, dwarflike, deformed German named Joseph Schmidt, who in my opinion was as close to being the reincarnation of Caruso in a German body as could be imagined. I had heard a record from a German motion picture, *My Song Goes 'Round the World*—a song that Schmidt sang with such beauty and power that I purchased a dozen records and set about making the English translation of "Frag' Nicht." I did this song in both German and English on my broadcast. Schmidt was returning to Germany and, unknowingly, to his death in a concentration camp. He was a shy, pleasant individual, who at first refused to do anything during the concert, but later, after the proper encouragement, did several numbers.

My good friend Jimmy Campbell, the music publisher, arranged for us to be speeded through the British customs with all of the cameras, electrical equipment, and gadgets that I carry with me for comfort, pleasure, and utility. Within two hours from the time we docked I was ensconced in a suite at the Savoy Hotel, where twelve years before I had labored as a lowly saxophonist, and had been fired for the first time in my saxophone career, because I had insisted on returning to college, ignoring the fact that the Savoy management had extended my labor permit at great cost and trouble.

It was our first night on the town, and my pianist and I, after a delightful roast beef dinner at Simpson's on the Strand, found ourselves at Ciro's, which even then was the playground for British royalty and the elite of London. Ciro's orchestra was Ambrose (who owned it) and his music, one of my favorite British recording artists, and one of the most prolific and imaginative of British orchestral recording artists. It was not until we arrived at Ciro's that I discovered our own American artist Helen Morgan was appearing there nightly. There was no line of chorus girls or assisting artists. She was the show. Shortly before midnight Ambrose announced this personality whose immortal rendition of "My Bill" and "Can't Stop Loving That Man" from *Showboat* had endeared her to American audiences. But when this sensitive singer, whom I had watched completely captivate her audience at Tommy Guinan's Playground in New York in the Fall of 1927 and in the Ziegfeld production of *Showboat* in 1931, appeared on the floor of Ciro's, I realized with a sinking heart that she was in no condition to perform that evening, and I wished devoutly that I had not been present to witness the tragedy that occurred. She was in the middle of the song when she became sick, threw up, and fell to the floor. It was a heart-rending thing to see, embarrassing for everyone present, particularly for those of us who admired her and wanted her to be at her best. Her performance was cut short, and Ambrose assisted her to her dressing room.

I felt that there was only one thing to do, and I asked Ambrose if he would let me step into the breach to see if I could do something to save the situation. He explained to me patiently that Ciro's never presented anyone from the audience. However, I insisted, and reluctantly he introduced me. I tried to erase the unfortunate impression that had just been created by a fellow American. It could have been that the audience appreciated what I was trying to do, or perhaps they really did enjoy the numbers that I offered. Anyway, they kept me there for forty-five minutes, and I wound up with a ten-minute slice of musical Americana, a Rodgers and Hart composition that is one of my favorite offerings—"All Points West." It is a dramatic monologue with songs of a train announcer *who has never been on a train himself,* and who envies the lucky persons who board the trains whose departures he announces. Near the end of the composition the poor train announcer is shot in the melee as police are taking a criminal to Sing Sing. Although the railroad stations I announced were unfamiliar to this British audience, the theme is a universal one, and when I finished the composition, the audience was standing and roaring its approval and appreciation. After I returned to my seat Ambrose asked me if I would perform at Ciro's for a week during my stay. I had already agreed to play two vaudeville theaters, sandwiching in the appearances between our broadcasts, and I realized that I would be taking on more than I should really attempt, but I agreed to play Ciro's the last seven days of our stay in London.

The heart of London was sealed off with barricades that made it necessary for us to drive several miles on the outskirts of London in order to reach the Savoy Hotel, which was only a quarter of a mile from Ciro's itself. With the coronation only ten days away, the entire population of London was dedicated to this glorious event, and every phase of the city's industry and activity was centered upon it.

Had I realized the tempo of conditions that prevailed during the coronation I would not have accepted the cabled offer that we received when we were three days out from London to play the Finsbury Park Theater and the Holburn Empire Theater, nor would I have accepted the invitation of Jack Hylton, the famous

Seventeen years later (1954) I was in London with Jane Russell, Jean Crain, Scott Brady, and Alan Young making a United Artists picture. The best British motion picture that year was *Beau Brummel*. Attending its showing at the Film Festival, we even got to meet the Queen.

bandmaster, to be his guest at a soccer game the coming Saturday, and that evening to witness his triumphant production of *The Red, White and Blue* at the celebrated Palladium Theater. In the first place the population of London was much too busy rehearsing for the coronation itself to go to a vaudeville theater during these hectic days, and my experience at the Palladium was to be one I shall never forget.

Saturday morning Hylton's chauffeur arrived at the Savoy to take me to Jack's apartment, where after a light lunch we left for the soccer game, which was played before an audience of over 120,000 people. I left the game early to return to the Savoy for a nap, and at 8:30 was seated in a box to watch one of the finest musical productions I have ever witnessed in a theater. At intermission Jack asked me to come to his dressing room, where he asked if I would take a bow. Naturally, I told him that I was prepared to contribute something to the evening's entertainment, and he asked me what I was going to do. Recalling the great success of "All Points West" at Ciro's, I told him that I would like to do that number. At that moment Jack was being dressed for his next appearance on the stage, and he suggested quietly that I do something else. Remembering my triumph at Ciro's, I reiterated my intention of doing the Rodgers and Hart composition.

Hylton said nothing more, and I wonder to this day why he didn't give me his reasons for asking me *not to do it!* He could have simply explained that two-thirds of his audience, particularly the balcony and the back portion of the floor, consisted of visiting firemen from the Lancashire district of the British Isles (a segment of British life comparable to our Ozark or Tennessee hillbillies) who had come to see the soccer game. With considerable boredom they had endured Jack's production of *Red, White and Blue* and were impatiently waiting for their idol, a lean, saturnine individual named George Formby, who, unknown to me, was to be presented after me. So sure was I that I would prove Hylton's distrust of my choice of number groundless that I rushed in where angels fear to tread. Of course, I had my pianist Eliot Daniel with me, and I informed him that we would do "All Points West" when the time came for my introduction.

I pride myself on having a sense of showmanship, a sense of

timing, and a feeling for the appropriate thing to do. But if I had had any intelligence at all I would have realized several things when Jack did introduce me. The hour was late (it was approximately 11:10) and I should have known that the audience had been seated (except for the intermission) since 8:30. I should have made a quick salutation to Jack and exited gracefully. As I stood in the wings awaiting Hylton's introduction I observed a lanky character with a small ukelele in his hand and vaguely wondered who the hell he might be. Once out in the spotlight I acknowledged the audience's perfunctory applause and paid a tribute to Hylton for his splendid recordings, and the fine show he had brought to America several years before. Usually such a tribute would have brought down the house. The tepid quality of the reaction should have told me something was wrong. But there is no fool like an unseeing and obstinate one. "Now," I said to myself, "this is my opportunity to prove to Jack Hylton that I know better than he what his audience would like." I described the composition I was about to do, and started "All Points West."

I was about two and one-half minutes into it when to my horror there began in the back of the theater the sound most dreaded by all performers. It was *the sound of organized, systematic clapping!* That portion of the audience in the front half of the theater, for the most part in formal attire, turned and tried as best they could to quiet or stop this organized demonstration of hostility. Knowing that I had approximately five more minutes of the composition to do, I debated whether I should turn tail and leave the stage, or whether I should continue. In between these two conflicting emotions I subconsciously wished that the floor would open up and swallow me. By some miracle the clapping ceased! I finished the composition and received a nominal amount of applause, though nothing comparable to the reaction I had received at Ciro's the night before.

It was an unnerving experience that I will never forget, and I still wonder why Hylton did not simply explain that the large Lancashire portion of his audience was waiting impatiently for their idol George Formby, and would tolerate no one or anything else at that hour of the evening. Obviously, had he informed me of this situation I would never have attempted anything beyond a one-minute chorus of a song, if even that. I have a feeling that the memory of this fiasco remains in British theatrical circles today, and it is probably the reason why I have never received an invitation to play the Palladium.

Our first broadcast fared much better. It boasted an outstanding cast of European performers, with the lord mayor of London, Will Fife, Richard Tauber—the German tenor, and several other outstanding continental favorites, with only three musical compositions in which I worked with Sid Phillips and the orchestra. It was rather a fantastic thing to contemplate that our broadcast, which emanated at one o'clock on Friday morning, was reaching New York by cable-radio at eight o'clock on the day before, and even more ironically frightening, it was reaching the California coast at five o'clock in the afternoon.

By the evening of the broadcast I was already on the fourth day of my doubling between the Finsbury Park Theater and the Holburn Empire. The matinees at both theaters (I was doing two shows a day at each house) were sparsely attended since, as I have said, most of the British people were preparing for the coronation itself. The evenings found the audiences larger, and quite cordial to the little routine I had whipped up for this appearance. I played the saxophone and related how I had played at the Savoy Hotel with the all-English Havana band some twelve years before. Frankly, I was much relieved when the vaudeville appearances were over, and I looked forward to my opening night at Ciro's.

But my hopes of a triumph at Ciro's were to be short-lived. I sat downstairs in the cellar of Ciro's awaiting my introduction when I observed that, after the band had finished its last dance set, someone had announced the show was about to go on but something was wrong with the public address system. A feeling of fear clutched my heart as I heard the speaker's voice on for a second, then off for several seconds. My introduction was delayed some ten or twelve minutes while evidently futile attempts were made to repair the amplifying system. Even though I was reassured by some glib individual that the system had indeed been fixed, an intuitive hunch told me that I was going to be in trouble.

Ciro's was a long room, with a capacity of about 400 people. It was packed, with an expectant and receptive audience. My voice and vocal chords are not powerful, and I depend completely upon a public address system to give me much-needed resonance and assistance. Without the proper amplifying system I might just as well have stayed in bed. My first number was received well enough; the second item began to really bring them into camp, and then it happened. In the middle of my third number the system went dead, came on for a few seconds, and then went completely and finally dead. Again, I wished that the floor would open and that I might disappear through it, but realized I was obligated to go on as best I could. I would have been wiser to have simply walked off than to try to fill the spacious room, when more than two-thirds of the impact of what I was doing was completely lost. It could have been such a glorious triumph, as it was a friendly audience and one that I knew wished me well, but the fact that this establishment failed to have a technician capable of keeping the vital bond between the performer and an audience in perfect condition completely ruined what might have been a happy, exciting moment in my career. If I had been a girl I would probably have gone home and cried myself to sleep. As it was it was one of life's darkest moments for me, and in spite of the fact that the succeeding evenings were as happily successful as I could have desired, I could not erase the bitter taste of the agonizing moments of that first night.

But the supreme catastrophe had come on our second and last broadcast from the British Isles, and this misfortune was in no way attributable to any fault of mine. We had assembled an even more brilliant cast for this program to the British Isles and the United States, and what with J. B. Priestley; the London Scottish Pipers; the Weston Brothers, two extremely talented boys from Cambridge; Florence Desmond, the gifted British mimic; the Royal Horse Guards Band; French actor Fernand Gravet; another appearance of Will Fife; and American musical comedy star June Knight, we felt we had a diversified and outstanding broadcast to beam back to the United States.

The program itself went off without a hitch, and we all retired to June Knight's apartment in a swanky hotel. Just as we were about to toast and congratulate ourselves upon a fine program, we were informed that *three minutes before our program went on the air* the zeppelin *Hindenburg* had crashed and burned at Lakehurst, New Jersey. I knew, of course, that for at least an hour following this tragic disaster no American radio audience would be paying any attention to our program, good, bad, or indifferent, and that in our smug, placid ignorance we might just as well have been broadcasting to the North Pole. But I also had the common sense to appreciate the fact that life is like that, and that we at least had done our best, and what was done was done.

After a reunion with some of the musicians with whom I had played at the Savoy Hotel, and a final evening in my honor at the Savoy itself in the room where I had once performed so many long, dreary hours on my saxophone for tea dances and the dinner and supper enjoyment of the elite of London, we sailed from Southampton on the German liner *Bremen*. It was necessary that we take this Nazi luxury liner in order to be back in time to do our Thursday broadcast. As we backed out of Southampton, with all the fleets of the world lined up for the coronation, I took pictures of the Nazi officers of the ship as they crowded to the starboard side of the ship, intently studying the ships of the various nations that were to be engaged in mortal combat with the Third Reich only a few years hence—ships they and their comrades would destroy in their futile dream of conquering the world. The officers didn't like it as I trained my camera upon them, but I secured highly prized shots of men who were conspiring at that moment in their dreams of destruction.

My Jewish attorney, who hated the Nazis with an implacable hatred for what they had done to his people, had confided to me that as much as we disliked sailing on a German boat, we would find that the cuisine was without a parallel in all the ships of the world. I can only say that he was more than justified in his gastronomic estimation of the North German Lloyd's *Europa* and its sister ship, the *Bremen*. But a morbid ceremony took place each evening after the dining room was closed for eating, with the gathering of all the ship's crew that could be spared from their tasks in the spacious salon above the dining room, where in abject worship they foregathered around a bronze bust of Hitler to sing Nazi war songs.

We were happy to disembark on the morning of the Thursday of our broadcast, happy to be back from a trip that from my standpoint at least had been a series of misadventures, brightened only by the excitement of the coronation itself. Even that took place in a downpour.

The Assassination

As the big Eastern Airlines' DC 2 left the runway at Miami airport, I settled back in my seat to read the *Miami Herald* of Wednesday afternoon, February 8, 1939. There, staring at me from the front page in a box (an actual frame of heavy lines to focus attention upon it) was an item from the Walter Winchell column as lethal and damning as the bite of a cobra! At first I just couldn't believe what he had charged in that little square in the middle of the front page, but there it was in all of its impact intended to terminate my career as an entertainer in show business completely and shamefully!

I could hear the statement as it would be delivered by Winchell on his Sunday night radio broadcast to the millions who not only listened to him, but who believed implicitly in whatever came from his rapacious mind: "Rudy Vallée, whose temper is getting testier every day . . . slugged . . . a bus boy . . . who got in his way . . . backstage at The Royal Palms nightclub . . . in Miami, Florida."

The full impact of Winchell's charge hit me on my first reading of it, but as I reread it again and again, the realization of

12

That Phffft!

what it could do to me left me almost completely spent and in a state of collapse. You must weigh the words "slugged" and "bus boy" with great appreciation of their meaning to know how deadly and damaging they could be to my image as a decent human being.

Millions of parents had appreciated my efforts to bring them something pleasing and entertaining over the air waves and on the stage; by their applause and attendance at my personal appearances and by their letters they had expressed their enjoyment of my radio programs and had made my name a household word. Now, by this brutal act, I had completely forfeited any further right to their respect and interest. For such a man to become so arrogant as to slug a mere boy who was slaving in a nightclub for a few dollars a week there could be only one penalty, and that would be to cease to tune him in when he broadcast and to write to his sponsor to explain why, and to boo him off the stage whenever he dared to show himself in a public place again.

I doubt if Winchell fully realized that this attempt at assassination could so quickly and completely obliterate me from any further activity in any field of endeavor. Naturally, my first thought was simply to wonder how he had dared to print this murderous charge without first giving me the chance to answer it. It just didn't make sense, as he was too intelligent a newsman not to know that, if the charge were to be proven as fact, it could only mean the end of Rudy Vallée as a popular star in show business. Unlike so many performers I had never fed him any items of gossip to be used in his column, but I couldn't believe that my failure to do this would have earned his dislike of me.

I first came to Winchell in 1933 when I and my band were performing at the Hollywood Restaurant at 48th Street and Broadway. My two successful seasons in this room were most happy ones for me, as we played to packed houses every night and our audiences were made up of the cream of New York's society as well as the bourgeois. In the floor show were eight, tall, beautiful show girls, and Winchell and other newsmen usually dropped in possibly to date some of these lovely ones. When I put Alice Faye into the floor show, Winchell wrote most favorably of her part in it.

The more I reflected on his using the story without first phoning me the more I was convinced that the source of the story must have been unimpeachable for him to have had it put on the front page instead of burying it in his column. But I realized that right now the truth about the incident must appear in his column as quickly as I could get it to him. In those days the planes going between Miami and New York stopped at several places along the way. As this plane prepared to land at Jacksonville I began to write the true account of what happened at the Royal Palms, which I then wired to Winchell from Jacksonville. Fortunately, it was possible to send a fast wire at the airport, and what I said was simply this: DEAR WALTER, PLEASE CORRECT YOUR STORY CONCERNING ME AND THE BUS BOY AT THE ROYAL PALMS. IT HAPPENED IN THE KITCHEN, NOT BACKSTAGE. I GOT IN HIS WAY AND HE HIT ME. SINCERELY, RUDY VALLEE.

My reason for the flight to New York City was to perform on radio, presenting my Thursday night "Fleischmann Hour" from the NBC studios. I left my musicians in Miami, using NBC "house men" to do the broadcast, and then returned to Miami by

Walter Winchell

train after the broadcast to continue my four weeks at the Royal Palms. I had tried unsuccessfully to reach Winchell while in New York, and as I settled down in my compartment on the train I opened the *Daily Mirror* to read the Winchell column, hoping to see my wire just as I had written it. But there, in typical Winchellese, was an astounding call to the newsmen of Miami, Florida: "Attention all newsmen of Miami and Miami Beach, Florida! Go over to the Royal Palms and find out who is right—Rudy Vallée or Walter Winchell."

It now had become a matter of integrity! Who was lying? Who was telling the truth? My heart sank as I realized that this thing was being blown into a full-fledged scandal that could really bury me once and for all. I hardly slept at all, and the next day at noon the train pulled into Savannah, Georgia. The train had hardly come to a stop when the stationmaster burst into my compartment to tell me that my attorney was on the phone in his office. We both tore back while the train was held until I finished my phone call.

My attorney, Judge Hyman Bushel, spoke quickly yet calmly, knowing that he was the bearer of very bad news. "There is a warrant out for your arrest and you are going to be served with a criminal action suit and another civil action suit. I am going to suggest that you get off the train at Hollywood, Florida very early in the morning where our old friend Benny Gaines will meet you and drive you to the police station in Miami for fingerprinting and release on bail. You will probably avoid all the photographers and the press by getting there so early."

I thanked Hymie and sped back to the train. As I alighted about six o'clock the next morning, the day was beautiful with birds singing in the sunshine, but there was nothing but gloom in my heart as I shook hands with Benny Gaines. Bushel, who had been a magistrate in New York, had wisely suggested that we get to the court in Miami before the press could be there, to be fingerprinted and possibly set free on bail. I received a call while at the station from a former district attorney named Fred Pine whom I had met some time ago. Pine very simply stated that he wished to represent me and without fee. I explained to him exactly what had happened.

In order to get backstage at the Royal Palms without going

through the audience, it was necessary to go into the kitchen and exit from the kitchen through a door that left you outside, and then to walk back of the building to the stage door of the stage itself. On this Sunday night I entered the kitchen, wearing a powder-blue, shawl-collar, tuxedo jacket. I suddenly felt a sharp blow between my shoulder blades. Instinctively I turned and struck out at what had hit me. It was a food tray with dishes and several glasses on it held in the hands of an overweight but tall youth with rosy cheeks and one front tooth missing. Somehow he had not seen me in front of him as he entered through another door into the kitchen. I realize that to raise one's voice even when the provocation is very great is a cardinal sin in our land of the free. But on this occasion, I felt no qualms about bawling him out. I did not, however, lay one finger on him, although when I hit the tray, it may have hit him in the upper part of his left arm. When I took off my jacket and saw the grease stains where the tray had hit me, I really let him have a few choice expletives! Of course, he blubbered, but I could dally no longer as the show was about to begin, and I left him standing there with real tears running down his round face.

As I related all this to my attorney and we discussed the matter we both arrived at what must have happened after the encounter in the kitchen. I recalled how on successive evenings as I went through the kitchen I could hear mutterings from one of the two chefs to the effect: "Wait untila Winchella hears about a dis!" (He was Italian, I believe, but the message got through to me although I didn't really give it any serious thought.)

Pine pointed out to me that we must have witnesses as to what actually took place on that fateful Sunday evening. I didn't believe that there were any waiters in the kitchen, but we knew that the kid would have several waiters swear that I slugged him and so it was necessary for us to hire our own witnesses to testify with equal vehemence that I did *not* strike the boy.

The trial was set for Monday morning, February 14, in the courthouse in Miami. As I walked through the halls of the courthouse, I almost bumped into one of the most beautiful redheads I have ever seen. She was a court stenographer, though not for our trial, but as we met I could see that she was most charming and completely free to accept my invitation to dinner at the club that evening to—I hoped—celebrate the winning of my case.

The case took very little time, and strangely enough neither side called any waiters to testify. The boy did show a small, blue bruise about the size of a dime on the muscle of his left arm. The judge, however, dismissed the charges and I left the courtroom with a light heart and feeling that justice had been properly served.

I had received a call from an old friend of my radio days, Stanley Hubbard, who owns the biggest and most powerful radio and TV station in St. Paul, Minnesota. It was his custom to winter in Miami and to enjoy his beautiful yacht, which was anchored not far from the Royal Palms. Hubbard had been very confident that I would emerge from the courtroom victorious and had suggested that we celebrate after my last show at the Royal Palms by cruising up and down the canals and waterways that abound in and around Miami. Thus it was that I lay back on the soft cushions of the yacht with the redhead cuddled in my arms, sipping champagne and luxuriating in the cool of the evening as we floated up and down the waters of old Miami's shores.

Actually, and I can now confess this with complete candor, the trial was a farce!

Fred Pine was a truly great lawyer who had enjoyed the friendship of the members of his profession, and the Sunday night preceding the trial he had invited me to dinner with him at a fine eating place. He had arranged for us to be able to listen to Winchell's broadcast as we ate. We felt sure that Winchell would have something to say about the bus boy incident, and sure enough, it came near the end of his broadcast. Only Winchell could utter such a fantastic statement as poured forth from the radio speaker that evening. Only this former hoofer-turned-columnist whose column became a must for all of us in and out of show business, and whose contributions to the lexicon of journalism in words such as

> renovated, middle-aisleing it, terminated-ended, phffft!, giggly water (liquor), chicagorilla, debutramp, revusical, hard times square, blessed event (to have a baby), phewd (a smelly feud), moom picture, Joosh (Jewish), radiodor (bad radio program), park rowgue (a bad newsman), pash (passion), shafts (legs), infanticipating (expecting a baby)

made his column the model for all his many imitators, could do an unexpected total about-face as he did that evening. After all the agony he had caused me to endure, after his great discourtesy of failing to ask me for my version of the incident, Winchell had the audacity to cry: "It is to be hoped that the participants in this much exaggerated affair will kiss and make up!" Hmmmmm?

From the time of his near assassination of me in 1939 until his death Winchell was to be plagued by family misfortunes—loss of reader interest in his column, dental torture, and finally a long and losing bout with cancer. His daughter Walda went through four messy marriages; to break up one of them with a hippie character, Winchell had her committed! His son committed suicide. As he neared the end Winchell was a lonely, embittered man who must have realized all the hurt he had given so many others by revealing embarrassing and petty things about them. If anyone had dared to reveal his escapades with other women under the nose of his wife, or the one girl of his life whom he kept in a room at the St. Moritz, which was his home for so many years, he would have had their heads.

It ended well for me, but I still wonder—why did he want so badly to see me killed off at the height of my career?

The Sealtest

I didn't realize when Herbert Korholz asked if I would be interested in a new radio program that it would turn out the way it did. Soon I was involved in a show that was destined to start with a bang, flounder, and then return to life and high eminence through the efforts of Ed Gardner (Archie of "Duffy's Tavern") and John Barrymore (the Great Profile).

Korholz was an amazing individual who had started with absolutely nothing, except a prison record, and had turned that nothing into billions of dollars, eventually controlling many large and important corporations. He was a trim, well-dressed man, with eagle eyes and aquiline features. When he spoke there was an enigmatic quality in his voice, enhanced by a trace of native German—a blend of toughness and masked intentions. On the evening I met him at the Royal Palms in Florida his sharp features were wreathed in an unaccustomed warmth, except that there was something about his mouth that suggested cruelty. However, as I unfolded my idea for a show he seemed to react favorably, and I lost all the suspicion that was in the back of my mind.

13

Double Cross

The new broadcast was again to be with NBC, again to be on Thursday nights, but only a half-hour in length, unlike the "Fleischmann Hour." I thought I had conceived a very unique, informative, and exciting format, *if* the writers could be found to develop it. The idea was simple. It was to be a *rehearsal* of the show, and the rehearsal itself would go on the air as a finished product:

As the persons who came to attend the rehearsal ascended by the elevator (with appropriate sound effects), some of the females would ask the operator who was appearing on the "Sealtest Show." This operator would give the stars idiotic names and explain that you were not to applaud at the end of any musical number, dialogue, or interview. Once inside the studio you became aware that the Vallée entourage consisted of two studio cops, Jimmy Gleason and Ed Brophy, who were always arguing, with Gleason saying, "Talk American, talk American!" Fritz Feld, the diminutive comedian who was in our picture *The Palm Beach Story*, was to be my excitable French librarian; Vince Barnett would be a very gay and effeminate clarinet player. I was to have two secretaries: one beautiful, educated, cultured, and refined; the other a gum-chewing nitwit, always screwing the language up badly. Willie Fong was to be my Chinese valet, always calling me from home. As he was telling me that he was ironing, the telephone would ring. When I would ask what happened, instead of telling me that he had left the iron on the pants and they had been burned, he would reply, "Wrong number!" Gabby Hays would be my ranch foreman. When I would inquire about the ranch, he would say there was meat scattered all over the place. When I would ask if he had watered the cattle, he would say, "I thought you asked me to slaughter the cattle!" We also would show the listening audience the way an orchestra is rehearsed by putting mutes on the instruments, taking them off, stopping to rearrange a passage or change the notes, etc. The basic idea was to show them some of the things, humorous and

Left: With me doing a radio program in 1935 is Baby Rose Marie, the tiny singing sensation of the early 30s. *Right:* Rose Marie (1951) rehearsing with Phil Silvers and preparing to make her Broadway debut in the musical comedy *Top Banana.* She is now one of the regulars on the popular "Hollywood Squares" quiz show.

otherwise, that happen when putting together a half-hour broadcast. In the hands of good writers I felt this could be done, and
done well. Korholz was most enthusiastic about the idea.

A month later—February 1940—I was out on the Coast with
Finneran and Korholz, meeting with the man I'd chosen to direct
our show, Vic Knight. (Knight had successfully handled two or
three years of Eddie Cantor's radio broadcasts.) Suddenly Korholz informed me that he and Knight had met a young fellow
named Paul Henning, who had given them an idea they felt
would be sensational. Henning, a young boy of country ante-
cedents, had just come in from the Ozarks, where he went fishing
every chance he got. Years later Henning would create not only
the "Beverly Hillbillies," but "Petticoat Junction" and "Green
Acres." Today he counts his millions and clips his coupons in his
San Fernando Valley home.

Henning said he had written forty historical scripts that
would be perfect for Rudy Vallée. Apparently they overlooked
the fact that they had bought Rudy Vallée because he *was* Rudy
Vallée and did things that Rudy Vallée was expected to do. In
portraying the part of Christopher Columbus, for example, he
would be playing a role that probably could be done by any actor
worth his salt at one-twentieth the fee Vallée was to receive for
doing the "Sealtest Show."

Henning's format for getting into the dream in which I became the character was very simple. My retainer, valet, and
houseboy was to be Slapsy Maxie Rosenbloom, and on the first
show I supposedly had just finished reading a book about Columbus, and then, sparring with the former prizefight champion,
I would be knocked out. Enter dream music and the next eighteen minutes or more I'd be Christopher Columbus, and Mary
Bolland would play Queen Isabella. On the second program I
was to be Captain John Smith with Martha Raye as Pocahontas;
again, either I fell from a ladder that Slapsy didn't hold properly,
or again he somehow caused me to be knocked out. Each show
would have a short, light song or two written especially for the
show to be sung by the four fine vocal voices of the Kings' Men,
who were a gift from Paul Whiteman. On paper the ideas looked
quite good, even though I was to mirror a totally alien personality every week.

My friends at NBC, especially John Swallow, the head of the

NBC complex on the West Coast, all felt I should put up a fight for the rehearsal idea. Finneran, whom I knew only slightly, was a promoter who'd gone to all the dairies throughout the country persuading them to pool their monies and form the National Dairies to popularize the word "Sealtest," the Sealtest label of laboratory protection, meaning that the milk and the ice creams and all the dairy products were made the proper way.

Finneran, I felt, was a ruthless man who would not be dissuaded from anything in which he believed firmly. However, I was able to persuade Korholz to let us have *two* test broadcasts before live audiences—one night my rehearsal idea and the other night the Paul Henning historical sequence. I had both recorded, and the NBC crowd were unanimously in favor of the rehearsal idea; but Finneran and Korholz made it clear that they were in the driver's seat and it would be the Henning historical series.

Two weeks from the March 20 broadcast date my house guest, Alfred McCosker, a newspaper man who had risen to the commanding power of the Mutual Broadcasting System, discussed my dilemma with me.

"If you refuse to do the historical series," he advised, "Korholz and Finneran will see to it that the columnists accuse you of being too big for your own good."

"But I'm liable to be killed off in the process of finding out whether this idea is good or bad," I replied.

McCosker agreed, but suggested: "Play along, Rudy, and see what happens." And I, who am supposed to be a difficult S.O.B., agreed to give it a try!

The historical ideas were beautifully presented. I have them all on discs and scripts. Henning is a gifted writer, not only in humor but in plot and development. But for some reason the public didn't go for it. We dropped from a March opening of *seventeen Crossley* to a June rating of *four!*

The double cross! It had not been enough that Korholz had double-crossed me after accepting my idea in Miami; but now was to come the real cutthroat, Machiavellian attempt to destroy me. Finneran and Korholz suggested to the sponsor: "Let's dump Vallée, and go to MGM and try to get Mickey Rooney or somebody from the MGM lot with a variety show, or something like it."

I will always be grateful that Roy McKee, Edward Albright,

and Jim McFadden were men of integrity, honor, and decency. They pointed out that I had reluctantly agreed to do the historical sequences and that I had done them to the best of my ability. They called for a small housecleaning of everyone but Henning and yours truly! Vic Knight had already quit; Slapsy was dropped. We then moved to New York so I might go to my lodge in Maine while doing the broadcast Thursday nights in NBC Studios. As we reached New York I was given a list of six radio producer-directors to take the Vic Knight post of direction and production. At least three of them I recognized as being men of wide radio experience and ability. However, there was one name that caught my eye, and without any hesitation I decided that Ed Gardner would be my choice as the man to pull this show out of the fire and send it upward in ratings.

During my "Fleischmann" years I had played the Canadian Exposition in Toronto twice, for two weeks each time. We had done our broadcasts from the grounds of the exhibition and on the first appearance in Toronto for the exhibition was broadcast Dr. DaFoe, who had just delivered the Dionne quintuplets, with my father and DaFoe and me chatting about it. On the second appearance at the exposition in 1936, our regular producer had become ill; in his place was a tall, emaciated, excitable, heavy-drinking (not on the job), very volatile, Teutonic character named Ed Gardner. Gardner was to become Archie of "Duffy's Tavern"; he talked then exactly as he did on the "Duffy's Tavern" show (which he created).

The Canadian musician's union penalized me, making me pay for the equivalent of one Canadian man for every one musician I brought from the United States. We tried to keep our dress rehearsal under the hour so I would not be penalized an extra $1,500 if it ran two or three minutes over the hour. For the past ten weeks we had been using a comedy team, Howard and Shelton, a sort of Abbott and Costello. The scripts were very humorous, and their act ran seven to eight minutes. *Gardner had promised that we would not use Howard and Shelton for the dress rehearsal*, as it might run us overtime. To my surprise, the morning of the dress rehearsal they were in the front row. I informed them we were *not* going to use them in the dress rehearsal.

Gardner had completely forgotten his promise of the night before, and argued, "How am I going to judge the feel of their act in the show if they don't perform?" I reminded him that we had used them for fifteen weeks; that we knew exactly how they talked; that I brought them on and off with "London Bridge Is Falling Down" as a musical signature; and that after our dress rehearsal or before it, with a stop watch in the room, we could time their act with no problem at all. Gardner's Teutonic stubbornness made itself very evident—he threw his script down. "We're going to use them in the dress rehearsal," he said emphatically. So when we came to the point where I introduced them and played "London Bridge," up they dutifully came from the audience, but just as arbitrarily I went into my next band number. The twenty musicians instantly drowned out the two men, who, after a minute of futile dialogue, abandoned the microphone! Gardner instructed Miss Hermanson, his J. Walter Thompson secretary who traveled with us, to take down all changes in script, to call John Reber in New York, and to tell him that Mr. Vallée was not obeying his contract. We finished the dress rehearsal well under the hour, with the reappearance of Miss Hermanson, who stated that Mr. Reber had insisted Mr. Vallée obey the contract!

On our return to New York we occasionally presented excerpts from the Broadway shows. Performers who had Thursday matinees could not be at our regular afternoon rehearsals but came after they finished their matinees. Invariably, John Reber, who was of Pennsylvania Dutch extraction and had a farm in Reading, Pennsylvania, and who masterminded all the radio programs for J. Walter Thompson, would be seated in the front row to watch our afternoon dress rehearsals. On our return from Canada the first Thursday, I read the introduction to a twelve-minute excerpt from one of the Broadway plays; when no afternoon performers appeared, I put on the goddamnedest act, slamming the script to the floor, and breaking my baton, with Reber holding his sides in convulsions of laughter. Ed Gardner in the control room probably wished he were somewhere else.

Gardner's failure to keep his promise regarding Howard and Shelton's appearance in the Canadian dress rehearsal rankled me for a while but as I looked over the list of men to take over our ill-fated Sealtest series, I put his past treachery out of my mind and asked him to meet me at the Essex House. He was flat on his rear end. He hadn't worked in several weeks. I spoke bluntly but very plainly. "Ed, this show is in trouble. It is your show top to bottom. You pick the idea, the personalities to fit the idea. *You pick everything* but the songs I sing." That was a great sacrifice of authority for me to surrender everything but the choice of my songs, but I had complete faith in this man.

Subsequently we moved little by little away from the old man in armor, the historical clanking, and the overmelodramatic scripts that Paul Henning had written for us. Henning was still with us for his original salary of $250 a week; McKee and Albright had decided to pay Gardner $500 a week for production and direction. Our first or second or maybe it was the third show in New York was the "Hatfields and the McCoys," with Walter O'Keefe, Dinah Shore, Joan Edwards, and me. It was still somewhat historical but had more comedy and was more believable. Dinah Shore had just made her first hit record, "Don't Go Near the Water." She gave us much help in listener interest. Gradually Gardner weaned us away from the Henning idea, and on the fourth show there suddenly appeared a man whose truly great genius in the art of comedy and the writing of it was later to be so evident in *Guys and Dolls* and *How to Succeed in Business Without Really Trying*—Abe Burrows! Abe was to ride herd on the writers, of whom there were now four or five, as Gardner knew where to find them, knew their abilities, but above all knew how to guide and channel their gifts. (I'll never forget when I visited Abe in his apartment in New York in 1961, as he was still at work on Act I of *How to Succeed*. He told me that every time he wrote he always felt Ed Gardner behind him, guiding him; that Ed had great taste!)

But then the inevitable had to happen. Ed decided on the life and times of Diamond Jim Brady—in the Gay Nineties. It was well cast, and I had very frankly given little thought to the songs on the show, realizing that they would have to be songs of that era, like "Bicycle Built for Two," "East Side West Side," "Herald Square," and songs popular at the time Diamond Jim Brady was at his peak. However, I had promised one of my closest friends, Al Porgie, who was in the music business, that I would do a song of his called "Looking at Yesterday." I felt it would fit quite comfortably in with the other older songs. We gave my pianist Eliot Daniel the job of clearing the songs to be used in the show. All music had to be cleared with NBC, which was necessary by radio network edict. When I asked if he had cleared the songs, he replied, "Yes, *all but 'Looking at Yesterday,'* " which Gardner had stated would not be used on the show. Recall now my complete abdication of all authority, *except* that I would choose my songs, something I had stated to Ed Gardner when he needed the job very badly.

I offered to change the lyrics to fit our story and also informed Gardner I would sing only one-half of the chorus, which was just enough to give my friend Porgie the ASCAP credit he needed for the rendition of his song on a top radio program. But this was going to be the second time that Gardner showed a strange streak of irrationality, something that plagued him all his life. Our Tuesday night script test was as usual in the studio, with a live audience but only a piano for the music. I noticed several figures in the sponsor's booth. I knew it was not the Philadelphia agency execs, but probably Finneran and Korholz. I did the short version of the song and noticed great agitation in the sponsor's booth. But the dress rehearsal was over; so I retired to the cubbyhole dressing room NBC had provided for the personalities on the shows, and was adjusting my tie when there was a knock on the door.

"Yes?" I asked. It was a millionaire socialite named Artie Deutsch learning the business as a $100 a week "go-fer."

"They want to see you out front," he replied.

"What about?" I asked.

With a smirk of half-triumph and malice he replied, "That song!"

My Irish-French surged up in me. "Tell them I won't be on the show Thursday night!"

Roy McKee later phoned me from Philadelphia at the Essex House at one o'clock. He stated that Gardner would be fired, but I stopped him. "I don't want anything to happen to Gardner." I then simply said that, "I can't work with associates who don't believe in me and don't have faith in whatever I might do on my own show."

McKee pleaded with me, honestly and earnestly, "Rudy, we wanted you from the start; when they wanted to dump you, we wouldn't let them do it. We'll do anything for you. I'll catch the 1:30 out of Philadelphia if you want me to, but please don't let us down."

McKee was a fine person; I realized I owed him and his agency much loyalty. "All right," I agreed, "I'll continue."

Perhaps it might have been better had I quit then and there, as for several weeks I did the show like a walking zombie. Whereas I had done the warm-up with a few bits of humor and maybe a song before the show, I now did nothing. I read my lines in a monotone and did nothing but what the lines dictated me to do and say. Gardner, of course, was literally dying inside as he realized not only what he had done to me, but to himself and to the show. But—how long can you stay angry? Four or five shows later I realized I must put my anger aside and really do my best.

After the last show in New York Gardner sounded me out on what would really make it the top-rated show for many weeks. He suggested that on our return to California *we should put on John Barrymore!* Perhaps he expected me to rave and rant and scream, "What! Put that old drunk has-been on our show?" But I said very simply, "Ed, there may be nights we'll wonder if he'll be there, *but it will be worth it!*"

Such titans of creative writing as Burrows; Norman Panama and his buddy Mel Frank; Jess Oppenheimer, who created "I Love Lucy"; Keith Fowler, whose father was to write "Good Night, Sweet Prince," the story of John Barrymore; Frank Galen; Charlie Isaacs; and a few others—these men were to give us scripts in which I played straight to John. But more importantly, bringing Lionel Barrymore, Orson Welles, Billie Burke, and so many other personalities—particularly Charles Laughton— would make our shows the most listened to on the air. When we reached the impossible rating of twenty-five Crossley, we toasted ourselves with champagne! Those were show nights I'll never forget. I'll always be grateful to Gardner for suggesting Barrymore, and if his spirit can hear me, I can only say, "You more than justified my belief in you, Ed!"

After many happy programs John Barrymore began to deteriorate. First he used a cane; then he read seated. His ankles were so swollen that I wondered how he could endure it. There came the afternoon when I arrived and was told that John had tried to make it, but was in the hospital. I have seen three great stars in their last moments of coma and death. All reacted the same way.

John Barrymore, who became a regular performer on our Sealtest radio program

First, Willie Howard, a comedian who will never be excelled; William S. Hart, the great western star; and finally Barrymore. I went over to the hospital that afternoon to find Barrymore in his last hour of coma. Like Willie Howard and Hart, here was a dying man with fingers opening and closing, mouth making movements with no sound, eyes opening and closing. I did not stay for that final moment, as I have never wanted to see death. (I did not go to the funeral of my father or sister, regardless of the feeling of the hometown folks.)

I wish I had known Barrymore better, but I just couldn't take him to the Beachcombers after the show as I did many of our associates. I knew that for him to be in the presence of so much liquor was to invite serious trouble. He was always accompanied by a young German boy who carried a bottle of sauterne, which he ladled out sparingly.

John never once did anything verbally or otherwise on the show to cause us to worry or be frightened. Once he did get a laugh that is still re-echoing. It was the fall of 1940, election year, and our writers had come up with a script and a show that I vow I'll somehow see in album form, as it was one of our best and funniest. It was called "The Vagabond Lover Versus the Great Profile." John, on a campaign tour, was being interviewed by young Leroy of the "Great Gildersleeve Show." The kid asked him to what he attributed his fine constitution. John replied, "I get eight hours of sleep a night, eat three square meals a day, and drink five glasses of—." At this moment John stumbled over the line, recovered, and read it, "—drink five glasses of Sealtest milk a day." Then he gave the punch line, as he said quickly, "No wonder I tripped over that one!" The studio audience exploded and almost blew the roof off.

When John finally did his readings from a chair, he began doodling on his script pages. Few persons know that John Barrymore was an artist before he became an actor; he could draw pencil sketches, usually of himself in profile in a few seconds. He left them on the floor, but I rescued many of them and gave them away. Today they are collector's items.

The shows on which he and Orson Welles traded insults between each other or when the two Barrymore brothers slugged it out verbally with Welles are true classics.

I regret I didn't get to know a man who resembled John very much and who was always in the front row at our Tuesday night rehearsals. This man, John Decker, was a fine artist, and it remained for Ed Gardner, as a peace offering, perhaps, to ask Decker to make a painting of me in the Rembrandt style. My painting, along with the four that hang in Chasen's entrance hall, are worth a great deal today, but I would never part with mine.

As much as I do not believe in the supernatural, I must confess that as I listened to the last show Barrymore did with us, it was as if he really seemed to be aware of impending death, and that he knew this was to be his last show. One of the lines from *Romeo and Juliet* he read almost prophetically, as he cried, "Hark! What light through yonder window breaks? It is the east, and Juliet is the sun!"

Victor Borge:

The

Victor Borge is without question one of the most brilliant creative comedic minds performing today; unfortunately, he is also, perhaps, the world's greatest ingrate. Furthermore, he is reluctant to part with any of his money, especially that which he owes to others; even Scrooge might envy him! As I look at a clipping stating that the government had filled a tax lien of $338,000 against Victor Borge for failure to pay income taxes dating back to 1958, I'm sure the government also has its opinion of him.

I have never really expected monetary rewards for helping someone achieve stardom. In the case of Victor Borge, not only was I not rewarded financially, but at no time in his entire career has he ever admitted that when he was brought to me *he had been rejected at every audition* in every part of the country, and that every agency, radio network, and executive in Hollywood had been completely unimpressed when he performed for them. He never mentions the fact that I made it possible for him to be presented on the one show that was tailor-made for his great talent.

14

Ungratefulcholy

Dane

I have pondered this lack of gratitude and have come to the logical conclusion that no personality who has become a star wants to be reminded of his humble beginnings, when he was unwanted, unrecognized, and when his name meant nothing at all. This reluctance was particularly evident in Victor Borge one night when he was performing in the Empire Room of the Waldorf Astoria. I sat there with friends to watch him go through his routine. About halfway through the performance he sort of half slyly looked at me out of the corners of his eyes, and said in an almost inaudible aside: "This is the man who put me on radio."

I first became aware of this trait in Victor Borge when I thumbed through a precursor of *TV and Radio Guide,* a little California magazine that cost, I think, six or seven cents, and that came out only on Saturday. In an interview, Evelyn Bigsby (who today is secretary of a large group of those of us who have been in radio for over twenty years, namely, the Radio Pioneers) asked Victor Borge how he came to appear on the Bing Crosby show. As I read his incredible reply I realized that in addition to his reluctance to pay the commissions he owed my agency for booking him on the Crosby show, he also was even more reluctant to spell out the story of the desperate condition in which I found him in December 1941. Miss Bigsby quotes him as saying, "I was walking down the street and I bumped into Rudy Vallée, who said to me, 'Why don't you go on radio?' "

I've kept every article, clipping, letter, or anything that pertains to Victor Borge. As I reread the March 23, 1957 issue of the *Saturday Evening Post*, containing one of a series of articles by Dean Jennings, I realized that not only did Borge have a very poor memory, but he was also inventive in fabricating many points of his relationship with me and my agency. In fact, I acquainted Jennings with many purported facts in the *Saturday Evening Post* story which were completely at odds with what actually happened or was said. I received a reply from Jennings, which appears on the opposite page.

In early 1941 I created a nightclub in Hollywood to help Don Dickerman. Previously I had invested $100,000 in a little nightclub of his in Greenwich Village, where he already had three in 1929, only to lose it all. He came out to Hollywood in 1940, apparently broke. "Errol Flynn is making a picture about pirates over at Warner Brothers," Don said. "We should have a Pirate's Den here in Hollywood like the one I've had in Greenwich Village for the past thirty years." I thought about it and decided that instead of being the lone sponsor and angel of this club, I would get fourteen other important celebrities to contribute and appear at the club. We had a star-studded list: Fred MacMurray, Ken Murray, Jimmy Fiddler, Bing Crosby, Tony Martin—you name them, we had them. Each star gave $1,000. The Pirate's Den was on La Brea near Beverly, and our opening night was covered by *Time* magazine, Columbia newsreels, and *Life* magazine. Everyone who was anyone was there that night. Unfortunately, it became a lone crusade on my part to keep the club going. Since I was a bachelor and we had excellent food at the club, I ate there frequently.

It was on a Monday night in November 1941 when I received a call from Harry Maizlish, the head of Warner Brothers' radio station KFWB. I had appeared at a few Jewish charities for Harry and I assumed that this was a call for another one. But he told me that he had been ordered by Major Albert Warner of Warner Brothers to get Borge on Hollywood radio. Maizlish was

DEAN JENNINGS

P.O. Box 335
Tiburon, Calif.
April 16. 1957

Dear Rudy Vallee:

I have your long letter on the Victor Borge business and I must say I am not only overwhelmed by
your documentation, but by your restraint. Under
the circumstances I think you have been more than
gracious in your viewpoint.

Needless to say, it must be apparent to you that
I am, or was only the instrument in relating the
events involving you and Victor. It so happens
that of all the detail in this autobiography, the
sequences involving you were the only ones on
which Victor spent considerable time . He rewrote
and rewrote, and obviously knew exactly what he
wanted to say. He also made some changes in the
galleys long after I had finished the series, and
I had no control over that at all.

Your letter makes a very good case for your side
of the controversy, and I was happy to read it.
I have never had the pleasure of meeting you, and
of course there is nothing personal in what was
written, from my standpoint, at least . I do
recall that you were most pleasant when I called
you a couple of years ago in connection with a
book I was doing on Barbara Hutton- which book,
alas, has turned out to be too incendiary to print.
I am now doing George Raft's autobiography for
the Saturday Evening Post, and we will probably
have a sequence in which you had some sort of
a tiff- I hesitate to call it a feud - with George.
If you care to say anything about it now, I'll be
happy to have the information.

Incidentally, having had some friction with Borge
myself since the story came out, I second the
motion on the last line of your letter.

Sincerely,

Left to right: Victor Borge, myself, Dad, and Dr. Reuben Chier

very emphatic about the importance of my meeting Victor Borge. "He's a pianist-comedian," he went on, "who has been making small films in Denmark, writing, directing, and producing them." He explained that he had taken Borge to MCA (Music Corporation of America), William Morris, and all the radio stations, but had been rejected by every one of them. "As a last resort, Rudy, you've presented a great many personalities on radio on your 'Fleischmann Hour.' Give the fellow an audition," he pleaded.

"I'm eating at the Pirate's Den tonight," I told him. "Bring him there and I'll audition him."

As we were introduced at the Den, Borge insisted that I look at his scrapbook. "I'm not interested in the scrapbook," I said. "I want to see you perform personally, in the flesh."

I invited Maizlish and Borge to have dinner with me. Before Borge could stop me, I was on the floor introducing him. In the *Post* article he said there *was a lot of noise* while he was performing. But it was a Monday night, *the room was not crowded*, and there was really very little or no noise.

It takes a great deal to make me laugh, but when he did "Phonetic Punctuation" I nearly rolled off my chair. I think it was then and is now his greatest piece of material—although he makes very light of it. He calls it "practically nothing" in the *Post* article. He also said in the article that he performed for only two or three minutes and that I stopped him. However, he was on for at least thirty minutes (if not closer to forty). I had no intention of stopping him in any way, shape, or form. Frankly, I was delighted with his performance and so was the small audience.

Borge evidently knew I had a half-hour radio show for National Dairies, the "Sealtest Show," because he was most emphatic about his desire to appear on my show. I tried then in vain to convince him that there was only one show in which he should appear and only one show that could use him for a long, long time. In fact, as we were about to leave the club, I made one prediction—that he would be on the Bing Crosby show for Kraft for one year. By his own count he was on it *fifty-six weeks!*

I never told Borge completely and fully just why he should not appear on the "Sealtest Show," but the reasons were very simple and painfully clear:

In the first place, the program was originally handled by the J. Walter Thompson Agency and emanated from New York, but a small Philadelphia agency, McKee and Albright, had managed to take the program away from them, and it was they who decided in 1940 that I should be the host of the show from California.

Pirate's Den publicity shot with (*left to right*) Bing Crosby, Don Dickerman, and myself

Second, the J. Walter Thompson office in Hollywood was run by a mean, arrogant, pugnacious, hard-drinking Irishman named Danny Danker (whose widow married Louis B. Mayer after Danny died). Third, Danny Danker was a Harvard man, which did not endear me to him or vice versa. Additionally, he was deeply in love with Alice Faye, who would rather listen to my broadcasts in his car than do something else with Danker. Fourth, if I had presented Borge on my "Sealtest Show," which I wanted very much to do, it would have been another radio first for me. Danker might then have refused, just for spite, to ever use Borge on the "Kraft Music Hall." Still, it was plain that Borge and even Maizlish didn't understand why I would not present him on my broadcast. Actually, it would have been rather difficult to fit him into our show, because each week Barrymore and I enjoyed a short twenty-seven minute plot in which we portrayed characters with a story line. If we added Borge to our show, giving him ten or twelve minutes—enough of his routine to put him over—it would mean that that show would become a shambles as far as the story line went. My principal motive, however, was that I just didn't want *to see him lose the chance of getting on the "Kraft Music Hall" by appearing on our show first.*

I suggested that Borge come over to the NBC Radio Studio the next night, Tuesday, where we presented our script before an audience (with only a piano instead of the orchestra) to test the comedy parts of the script. Obviously, I would put him on to warm up the audience before we did our show. Usually we did a few jokes—from either Barrymore or me. I called the two men who were running the "Kraft Music Hall" broadcast, both of whom were good friends of mine, particularly Cal Kuhl. The other individual was Carroll Carroll, who wrote most of what Bing Crosby uttered on the show and gave him the peculiar flavor of talk that suited Bing so well. I insisted that both men come to catch Victor Borge's warm-up.

As planned, I presented Borge on our Tuesday test show before we ran through our script. He literally tore the audience apart. He must have done at least thirty minutes and the audience was just plain laughed out. Both Carroll and Kuhl approached me after the preview. "Danny Danker will call you tomorrow morning," Carroll said. "Cal and I will report to him." In the *Post* article Borge had said that as he left our studio he

NATIONAL BROADCASTING COMPANY, INC.

A SERVICE OF RADIO CORPORATION OF AMERICA

3000 West Alameda Ave., Burbank, California

THORNWALL 5-7000

March 25, 1957

Mr. Rudy Vallee
7430 Pyramid Place
Hollywood 46, California

Dear Rudy;

      The events leading up to the booking of Victor Borge
on the Kraft Music Hall, as I remember them, are as follows:

      Cal Kuhl, who was then directing Kraft Music Hall,
told me that he had received a call from you asking him to
attend the preview of your Sealtest Show to see a new
comedian. Cal asked me if I would go instead of him as he
didn't want to. I said I had a date and he'd better go.
We discussed this for about half an hour and finally com-
promised. We'd both go.

      As a result of this visit at which we saw Victor do
his punctuation routine, he was booked on the Kraft Music
Hall to do the same routine. It is my recollection that we
put him into the show on the following Thursday. It is also
my recollection that he was so successful that we lost one
of Bing's songs, a commercial and were cut off the air without any finish to the program.

              Regards,

              Carroll Carroll

CC/pbk

bumped into two fellows *who were indulging in a bit of espionage.* Espionage, shit! He obviously meant Carroll and Kuhl, who
were there *at my invitation!*

Our producer Dick Mack then came rushing out of the Control Room, angry as hell. "Why won't you put Borge on the next
Thursday program?" he demanded.

Things are too hectic after a run-through of a script for me
and it was difficult to go into great detail as to why we could not
use Borge. Mack must have immediately phoned the Sealtest
people in Philadelphia or sent a night letter to them describing
the sensation that Borge had been on our test show, asking them
to give me a bad time as to why we wouldn't use him the following Thursday. This is the wire that came from James McFadden
of the agency, who later came to stay with our show. (Notice
that it was sent five days before Pearl Harbor.)

WESTERN UNION (45)

1220

CLASS OF SERVICE		SYMBOLS
This is a full-rate Telegram or Cablegram unless its deferred character is indicated by a suitable symbol above or preceding the address.		DL=Day Letter
		NL=Night Letter
		LC=Deferred Cable
		NLT=Cable Night Letter
		Ship Radiogram

R. B. WHITE PRESIDENT   NEWCOMB CARLTON CHAIRMAN OF THE BOARD   J. C. WILLEVER FIRST VICE-PRESIDENT

The filing time shown in the date line on telegrams and day letters is STANDARD TIME at point of origin. Time of receipt is STANDARD TIME at point of destination

1941 DEC 2 AM 9 48

SN99 121 SER=PHILADELPHIA PENN 2 1206P
RUDY VALLEE=
            7430 PYRAMID PL

AFTER LEARNING FROM YOU ON PHONE YESTERDAY THAT YOU HAD
DEFINITELY DECIDED TO SELL NEW COMEDIAN TO KRAFT I HAD TO
BACKTRACK WITH ROY AND CLIENT. HAD ALREADY DONE SELLING JOB
TO GET HIM IN OUR DECEMBER EIGHTEENTH SHOW BASED ON GLOWING
REPORTS FROM DICK MACK. EVERYONE DISAPPOINTED THAT A
SENSATIONAL RUDY VALLEE DISCOVERY CANT BE PRESENTED ON
RUDY VALLEE PROGRAM. IF HE CLICKS BIG ON KRAFT WONT WE ALL
BE MIGHTY EMBARRASSED TRYING TO EXPLAIN WHY " RUDY VALLEE
PRESENTS" DIDN'T GIVE SEALTEST FIRST OPPORTUNITY ESPECIALLY
SINCE THEYVE PLAYED BALL WITH YOUR AGENCY ON PENDLETON,
DURANTE, LICH, ETC. FELT YOU SHOULD KNOW REACTIONS HERE.
AM GOING TO GIVE YOU JOB OF EXPLAINING IF HE TURNS OUT TO BE
A WOW. REGARDS=
            J A MCFADDEN.

    WOW.

On the afternoon of December 2 they phoned me from Philadelphia, and, after I explained to them my reasons for not wanting to take the chance of killing off Borge's prospects of going on the "Kraft Music Hall," they understood and were mollified, even though they didn't like it. They agreed to give Kraft the chance of presenting him first. The call from Philadelphia was not the only call I received concerning Borge. Danny Danker phoned me in his usual tone of bellicose belligerency in a voice that was anything but Harvard quality. He made no attempt to mask his hostility, and, with all the contempt he could muster, he said: "I'll give you $150 for Victor Borge." I simply said, "Go Screw!" and he replied in kind and hung up. But an hour later he was on the phone again, this time a little less truculent. When I outlined my idea of a graduating scale going up every thirteen weeks, he agreed.

I toyed with the idea of asking Bing for the privilege of presenting Borge on the Kraft program, as I felt deeply that I was giving Bing a priceless personality, one who would do a great deal for his show. And since not only had the radio stations but the talent agencies and the Music Corporation of America and William Morris, according to the testimony of Maizlish himself, had been consistent in refusing to see the comedic genius of Borge (all of them had turned him down), I felt that my recognition of his ability *should have been appreciated and made known!* But in the end I decided against demanding this of Bing.

I asked Borge to go to our agency offices and sign a contract of management with Rudy Vallée Presents. He did. I, of course, assumed that my associate Ted Lesser would sign him for seven years, which was the legal maximum number of years in California. This is a wire from Borge regarding our not signing the contract until he had a chance to make some changes.

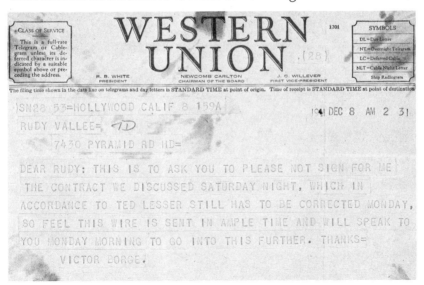

After that I took Borge to Grace Hayes' Lodge, which was the only place in Hollywood at the time paying any money for acts, as Ciro's and the Mocambo did not have entertainment. Grace had never paid anyone over $250 a week, but she agreed to pay Borge $450. But he decided he didn't want to work there. I then asked him to appear at a very important banquet at the Beverly Hills Hotel where all the leading legitimate actors and actresses of the West would be, a sort of Lamb's Club group in the West, where we could perform and, I felt, do himself some good.

Next, I took him to dinner at the residence of Harry Brand, Darryl Zanuck's right-hand associate, in the hopes of securing a screen test or at least a part in some Twentieth Century-Fox picture. While I was upstairs in the powder room, Mrs. Borge apparently told Mrs. Brand that *she and the children had not eaten for a day and half*; that the dinner that night was a saving grace for her and Victor. I didn't know at the time that Borge was pumping gas at a service station in Beverly Hills, and I didn't know that they had not eaten until the Brands told me about it much later.

In the *Post*, Borge said: "No one was interested in my accent and the studios seemed to be well supplied with piano players." Later on that page he added, "I was so pinched for funds I couldn't even afford thirty-five cents for the regular tourist's trip through the National Broadcasting Studios." Yet, on another page he insisted that he "never borrowed money from him nor did I ever owe him money in any form" ("him" meaning Rudy Vallée).

Although I was not aware that he was working in a service station when I came to his rescue, I instinctively knew he was low on funds. I'm not sure whether he had a car, but that night I picked up Borge and his wife to take them to the Brands and returned them to the place where they were living. I had in my pocket $100 in bills. As we walked to the car while Borge's wife talked to my lady of the evening, I quietly said: "Do you need money, Victor?"

"Yes," he replied. "I've only $14 in my pocket."

I gave him the $100. There was no doubt in my mind but that he would repay me or I would secure it from our commissions on the broadcasts, which would start shortly. Later, when he told me he wished to buy a car but didn't have enough cash to pay for one, our office loaned him the money. One of my boys, Ralph French, was very mechanically minded and searched around until he found a good used car.

My talent agency, Rudy Vallée Presents, continued to serve Borge. We more than justified our 10 percent commission, which, according to a memo from Ted Lesser, was apparently difficult to secure:

Rudy Vallée Presents, Inc.

OFFICE CORRESPONDENCE

TO   Mr. Vallee

FROM   Mr. Lesser

DATE   Jan. 9, 1942

The Victor Borge situation relative to pictures is as follows: I had a call from Fred Datig, head of casting at MGM, but it was of no real consequence.

Steve Trilling, at Major Warner's request, is looking out for parts for Victor.   Ihad a chat with Steve about this the other day.

The important thing is the interest that Le Baron has in Victor. I do not have to tell you that when Bill is interested we know that that interest is sincere.   Bill hopes to give Borge the comedy lead in the next Sonia Heine picture.   I took Victor to Le Baron's office and Bill called Mack Gordon and Harry Warren in.   Bill was tremendously impressed and he hopes thatthe script when it comes through, will be sufficiently along the lines of Victor's personality, so he can be used in this very important set-up.

I think it appropriate to tell you that we have not received any commission from Borge - I have dunned him several times without trying to be a nuisance, but he gives me all kinds of excuses.

I have handled enough actors in my time to know who are going to be good pay those who are not - and Borge I can definitely say is the kind who will not.   I have notified J. Walter Thompson to send us his checks and I hope that this will remedy the situation.   In the meantime, Borge owes us exactly $252 - (this is after the deduction for the P. Springs engagement).   I am merely telling you this to keep you abreast of the situation.

I would not mention this to Borge if I were you because I have dunned him myself and I will take care of it.   Certainly if we get the LeBaron picture as I hope to do, I expect to ask in the neighborhood of $10,000 and we will be in a position to collect all of our back commission.

During the war Borge had approached me about joining the California Evacuation Corps. He was worried about being drafted. "I don't think it would do much good as far as your draft status goes, Victor," I said. "I don't think you'll ever be drafted since you're married and have two children." But he joined anyway. Later still, when he learned that my Coast Guard band and I were making War Bond appearances in various parts of California and at other military installations, he pleaded: "Take me with you, Rudy, so I can tell my draft board I am in some way assisting the War effort." What is interesting is that in the *Post* article *he had me coercing him* and forcing him to make these appearances.

It was about nine months after he began working on the Crosby show that I took him with us to the army air base at Victorville, California. We were sitting around the beautiful Yucca-Loma pool before the show. Borge suddenly stated, "I don't like Ted Lesser." He pronounced it as though it were spelled with an "o."

"Why don't you like Ted Lesser?" I asked. He had no reason. "Victor, the Music Corporation of America has been needling you about joining them, haven't they?"

"Yes, they have," he frankly admitted.

I knew this must be the case, as Jules Stein, the mighty president of this great talent agency, had called me four or five weeks before and had asked to buy Victor Borge's contract. I had replied, "You didn't want him then, and you can't have him now." They then began the technique used by a great many agencies to woo clients away from a rival agency. It's very simple. Simply say, "Vallée's too busy in the Coast Guard to take care of you and Ted Lesser has no weight as an agent or an impresario. We'll not only get you more money, but when you're ready for personal appearances, we'll get you fabulous sums."

I told Borge, "When you're through with Crosby, I'll put you in the Waldorf Astoria for $5,000 a week and get you $7,500—or even more at the Capitol Theatre in New York. I will handle you personally."

His only reply was, "I don't like Ted Lessor."

On my return to Hollywood, I phoned Ted. "We have a seven-year contract, haven't we?" I asked. To my annoyance Lesser replied, "No! Borge would sign for only one year." I then said, "Why in hell didn't you tell me?" At that time Victor was so happy at the Kraft contract that he would have signed for any length of time I directed. So for the remaining three months of his contract, we split the 10 percent commission with the Music Corporation of America. There is no way you can hold an unhappy client! Contract or no, he just will not stay with you!

Two or three years later (I think the war was still on), the Music Corporation of America found a Socony Vacuum Radio Show for Benny Goodman and Victor Borge. I believe each received $7,500 for the show, and they had a fat budget because they used several personalities who I knew would not work for peanuts. I wasn't doing anything at that time and could have used the show and the money. But true to form I never heard from or received a call from Victor Borge. I was amazed on rereading the article in the *Post* to find that he did give credit to Harry Maizlish.

Whatever possessed Harry to call me, I will never know, but it was probably because, as he expressed it over the phone, he was at his wit's end and desperate.

Borge was the "wow" I knew he would be on the "Kraft Music Hall." In fact, as Borge tells it in the *Post* article, he was supposed to do twelve minutes, two appearances of six minutes each. "In three minutes," said Borge, "the place was bedlam. The studio telephones rang like a six-alarm fire when Bing hastily reshuffled the script. Bing himself was my best audience and he kept me out there for twenty-nine minutes. The NBC switchboard, they said, was jammed for the next four hours!" As Borge said it, "There were telegrams and phone calls from radio editors in every corner of the land. There were offers from other shows and agents were getting in line to sign me for personal appearances. All of them were asking, 'Who's this crazy Dane?' It was a $64,000 question and at least I had the right answer. I was numb with joy. I was on the Crosby show fifty-six times over an eighteen-month period. After the initial show the nation's radio editors voted me the Number Two Discovery of the year." Borge then proceeds to say, "There was only one shadow for me on this new sunny road. Rudy Vallée was stunned when he saw what was happening on the rival radio show and his sponsors were frothing because he let me go."

There are some things that are just incredible, inexplicable, and completely out of this world. I don't know how Borge could ever have felt that I was "stunned" by his success, when I knew exactly what would happen on the Crosby show *the moment I saw him perform at the Pirate's Den.* I knew because Borge had something that was truly, outstandingly great. But for some reason it is galling to Borge to admit that I was the only person who recognized his great gifts.

As the years rolled on Borge invaded every field of show business: The Exposition in Toronto, where they paid him a fantastic sum of $30,000 a week; appearances in stadiums throughout the country and in Europe. He was well on his way to at least his second or third million. By 1948 television began to loom importantly on the horizon; it was a medium made for Victor Borge, and his television shows were a delight. And for those shows, the monies paid him were fantastic, even for those days.

It finally remained for an obscure music publisher named Harry Squires to conceive the idea of the "one-man show" in the theater. He and Victor journeyed to Seattle, Washington, engaged the Metropolitan Theatre, and then Squires set out to pack the opening night with the elite of Seattle by personally phoning them and asking them to be Victor's guests. The opening night was a triumph and before the week was out Borge had grossed almost $30,000—which he loudly proclaimed on the back page of *Weekly Variety*.

Then in October of 1953 Squires decided they should engage the Golden Theatre in New York and present Victor in his one-man show as they had in Seattle. It so happened that Mrs. Vallée and I were staying at the Essex House in New York. We received a call from a young man who said that he was the owner of the Metropolitan Theatre in Seattle where Borge had tried out the one-man show and would like to come up to talk with me. During the course of our conversation, in which we discussed the possibility of my trying to do the same one-man show at the Metropolitan in Seattle, I asked him why he was in town. "I flew down to catch Victor Borge's opening tonight at the Golden Theatre," he explained. As he left our suite, I kiddingly said, "Ask Victor to put two seats in the box office for me and Mrs. Vallée." And, of course, *lying in my teeth*, I said, "I want to pay for them!"

That night I approached the box office. "You have two seats for Mr. and Mrs. Vallée?" I asked.

The ticket seller said, "Yes. That will be $6.50 each, please."

The crowning surprise to me came in 1964 when I was hosting a CBS-TV show called "On Broadway Tonight." One of our guests was Robert Goulet, for whom I have a great admiration—not only as a performer but as a man. Like all stars of today Goulet has his entourage of young men to assist him in every way possible in his performances all over the country. One of these was a very handsome young man who walked into my dressing room at the broadcast studio to acquaint me with the most outstanding revelation concerning Victor Borge I could ever have imagined. It appears this young man is one of the four sons of Harry Squires, and with great delight and much chuckling, he informed me that Victor Borge's Vibro Enterprise of selling Cornish hens had gone completely bankrupt and that Victor had lost over a million dollars in the Enterprise! (Borge called his enterprise Vibro, which, of course, came from his name Victor Borge.) Then this Squires' kin revealed something I heard with incredulous disbelief, but apparently it was a fact. On his father's deathbed the Sr. Squires told the four sons, "Borge owes me over $100,000 in commissions. If I die, forget it."

Many of the grocers and workmen who live near his beautiful

Victor Borge Sued For $750,000

NEW YORK, July 1 (UPI).—A suit for $750,000 has been started against comedian Victor Borge by his personal representative, Harry D. Squires, attorneys for Squires reported Friday.

The suit claims Borge failed to pay fees and expenses to Squires from 1953 to the present. Borge was served with papers in the suit Thursday, attorney Morton Miller said.

Borge admitted he had been served papers in the action, but refused to comment until he talked with his lawyers.

Borge Sued by the IRS

TOMS RIVER, N.J. (AP)—Federal Internal Revenue Service agents have filed a $338,007 tax lien against pianist-comedian Victor Borge and his wife, Sanna.

The lien, filed in the Ocean County Clerk's office, charges the Borges with failure to pay income taxes dating back to 1958, ranging in amounts from $23,271 in 1960 to $131,378 in 1967.

The lien was filed here because Borge docks his $90,000 yacht at the New Jersey Yacht Corp. in Point Pleasant.

estate in Greenwich, Connecticut, into which he has poured his fortune and not far from the docks where he moors his $80,000 yacht, have written his bills off the books.

Apparently Borge will never change. Borge escaped the clutches of the Nazis on the last boat leaving Denmark for the United States. He brought with him his wife Elsie and children. Elsie, who had stuck by him through his early days of travail and poverty, has now been replaced by a younger and more beautiful woman. I occasionally bump into Elsie, who lives in Santa Barbara and is happily married to a very charming man who is engaged in television, radio, and electronics. We both chuckle over the night when I took them to dinner at the Brands, when they hadn't eaten for a day and a half!

On page 126 in the March 23, 1957 issue of the *Post*, Borge reprints a copy of a letter that I sent to him shortly after Christmas in 1941. He had sent me a keg of scotch as a token of thanks, and as he says, I wrote him an acknowledging note just as the storm was breaking over his head. I don't know what storm he's talking about, unless he means the Crosby show, but here's a part of it:

My Dear Victor:

You shouldn't have done it but it was a very sweet gesture and every time we tap our lovely keg of scotch, it will remind me of a friendship that I hope will endure and grow stronger as the days go by. I've not yet had to face the eastern executives of my broadcast but when I do meet them, my reply will be a very simple one: I was thinking of your interests and I have no regrets for so doing!

As ever,
Rudy

Never

To say I have enjoyed or suffered through some bizarre and esoteric experiences during my career would be putting it mildly. I've done my share of impromptu performances and I've also had my share of unexpected catastrophes that nearly caused me to miss a scheduled engagement. These situations and the way a performer handles them can be critical to his continued success in show business, so if I had to give someone advice in this area, it would be simply this: No matter how unexpected the engagement, no matter how frustrating the obstacles encountered in trying to keep a previously scheduled engagement—never say die!

I can recall two experiences in particular where I was completely unprepared for the things that were going to happen to me, and I had no choice but to take my own advice. The first incident happened in 1949 and involved one of Hildegarde's temper tantrums; the other incident concerned a strange adventure in 1952 when I tried to keep an engagement on board ship, after we literally "missed the boat."

15

Say Die

I first knew Hildegarde when I had her on my radio show, the "Fleischmann Hour." Our Thursday night broadcast lasted for ten years on the NBC network, had an audience of over eighteen million listeners, and was considered the finest variety show of its time. Performers high and low vied with each other to guest on our show, for practically nothing. We were the Palace Theatre of the air and could help make a performer—as we did in the case of Edgar Bergen, who was totally unknown to the public at large —a great success in just a few broadcasts.

Hildegarde guested with us in the early thirties. I can never quite explain why I took a dislike to her, but I did, even though it was unjustified. I was not happy to present her; I did not like her work on our program, and the feeling of dislike continued. It remained for us to be on the same ship, the *Ile de France*, going to the coronation of King George in London in 1937, to become friends. On the last night out we cohosted a show on board ship to raise money for the widows and children of seamen who had lost their lives at sea. That night we became very good friends, a friendship that has persisted to this day. Later I was amazed to see the transformation in her style and the quality of her singing. It was almost a miracle what a voice teacher had done for her.

Not long after that, in 1938 and 1939, I performed for ten weeks in the famous Cocoanut Grove at the Ambassador Hotel in Los Angeles. With my band of eighteen pieces we provided music for dancing and three or four acts of my choosing, which we presented twice an evening. They were happy engagements— as happy as those at the Hollywood Restaurant in New York—so much so that John Barton Browne, the director of the room, begged me to continue for several more seasons. By this time I had had my fill of leading an orchestra and in 1939 I disbanded my group.

In 1949 I received a call from Archie Loveland, a former orchestra leader who had secured a position with the great William Morris agency in Beverly Hills. Archie called me and asked if I would like to play the Cocoanut Grove as a single, without my band. I immediately said I would be happy to do so. But as the weeks passed with no word from Loveland I realized that he had not been able to consummate the contract and was too embarrassed to tell me so.

There was an organization in Los Angeles dedicated to raising money for crippled children that, once a year on Halloween evening, took over the Ambassador Hotel's Cocoanut Grove to give a dinner dance to raise money for crippled children. A young secretary at RKO studios had written me every year, suggesting I purchase two tickets at $50 each, which I was very happy to do. However, in 1949 she called me and told me *she didn't want me to purchase tickets*, but asked if I would come to the Grove and draw some prizes. Naturally I replied that I would be most happy to do so.

At that time I was very involved with a beauteous dress designer named Mary Ann. She and I arrived at the Cocoanut Grove about 9:15 P.M. Before going to my table I went over to Eddie Oliver, a pianist who had worked at the Mocambo and some of Hollywood's best night spots. He had accompanied me before. "Here are some piano parts, Eddie," I told him, *"just in case they ask me to do anything."*

I don't know whether the Grove had erected a runway just for

Mary Ann Nyberg, who later married Arthur Knight, writer-critic

that evening or whether the runway was there for Hildegarde (as she was performing at the Grove). On Monday evening, her night off, the Grove was usually dark. The very elite group raising the money for the crippled children had evidently asked her to perform gratuitously or for a reduced fee. It is quite possible that she asked for remuneration. That might account for what happened.

We sat at a long table for ten. A gentleman to my right was quite inebriated when he leaned over to me and said, "Rudy, will ya sing the 'Whiffenpoof Song'?"

"Yes," I answered quietly. "You yell out for it later when I'm on the floor."

I surveyed the crowd. It was made up of the elite of Los Angeles. Most of the people were formally dressed and it was a crowd that should have instantly acclaimed Hildegarde. She had always appealed to the elite of New York; her engagements at the Persian Room and at the St. Regis Hotel were always successful. I assumed it would be the same here.

About 10:15, Hildegarde came on as we were just finishing

our dinner. She cast a glance of disapproval at me and I dropped my knife and fork as I knew she would resent my eating while she was performing. As Hildegarde began to perform, it was quite obvious that *something was radically wrong!* This audience, which should have been hers completely (she was in rare form when she began, in good voice), for some reason was not accepting her. She came to the highlight of her act, the presentation of a flower (usually a rose) to some elderly gentleman whom she had discovered in the audience (usually a man of elegant appearance, in his seventies or eighties). There is a bit of humor and yet a bit of pathos in the act and it usually goes over with tremendous warmth and applause. This time, for some reason, it fizzled out completely. Hildegarde had been performing midway in the front of the long runway; she was flounced back to the piano, took off her gloves, and began to play quite angrily, as the orchestra followed her playing. Abruptly she stood up and stomped off, then came back for one quick bow and was gone!

I had witnessed many thousands of performances—not only at the Brooklyn and New York Paramounts—but in theaters all over the country and in my Hollywood Restaurant engagements and elsewhere. I fully realized that the stage was now set *for anyone to take over!* I think the janitor at the Cocoanut Grove would have been a hit if he had merely come out sweeping!

Someone came out to announce the drawing for an automobile and several other prizes. Two women, encased in huge transparent pumpkins through which one could see all the tickets stacked inside, came out on roller skates. I was asked to come up and draw the tickets. The drawing of the prizes consumed a few minutes, and, just as I was about to return to my table, the tipsy neighbor on my right suddenly found his voice.

"Hey, Rudy," he yelled, "how about the 'Whiffenpoof Song'?"

I did the best double take of my career, as I looked in his direction, and in a voice feigning great surprise, I said, "Oh! Would you like to hear the 'Whiffenpoof Song'?"

As I said it again there was a tremendous hand from the audience. I then began a portion of my nightclub act that I was just beginning to formulate at that time—a routine about my age and my hair, which instantly brought the audience into my camp as I kidded myself. I then proceeded to sing "As Time Goes By";

another song, I think it was "Lydia, The Tattooed Lady"; and then "The Whiffenpoof Song"; with some political stories to follow. They gave me a standing ovation and I returned to my table.

The next day Archie Loveland phoned me and said that the Grove would like me to come in as a single. Thus I played the Cocoanut Grove at Easter time for four weeks with very happy results—thanks to Hildegarde, to whom I really owed the 10 percent commission!

Things didn't go quite so smoothly in 1952. In fact, no experience in my entire career combined as many assorted elements of complete misfortune, and yet ended in such a glorious triumph as that evening in Philadelphia.

I was managed then by the Music Corporation of America (MCA), which a national magazine called "The Star Spangled Octopus" (because of its stranglehold on the booking of talent in America). Its hotel, supper club, and nightclub department was staffed by young men just out of college. The young fellow who was arranging the details for this appearance was a fraternity brother in SAE, so I felt that if anything was loused up, it surely would not be intentional on his part. It was to be an affair in Philadelphia supposedly for a hospital on the evening of September 15, and would pay a rather tidy sum for an hour's work. It could be that the selection of Tommy Tucker and his orchestra was accidental, but Tommy also was a brother in SAE. Unfortunately, they were out of the city and would be in New York on the Saturday preceding the Monday night we were to appear together for this charity-hospital drive. At least, I so construed it. The fact that it all had something to do with a hospital was sufficient in my mind to blind me to any other details. I thought *it must be a charity affair*, though I couldn't reconcile the tidy sum they were paying me with raising money for the hospitals of Philadelphia. How wrong my supposition was to be, time would prove.

My fraternity brother informed me that the pianist of the Tommy Tucker band would be at my disposal for rehearsal on either Sunday or Monday at noon, but it would be impossible for the entire band to be present. I had long ago reconciled myself to doing a show with only a piano, and sometimes even without any accompaniment whatsoever. I knew that for the few musical numbers I would do, the pianist would be more than sufficient, or at least he could convey to the rest of the band my tempos, my adlibitums, or the liberties I would take with some parts of the various songs. Also, most of my forty or fifty minutes would be humorous and witty routines, which I had evolved and polished over the past four years.

My fraternity brother mentioned that a gentleman, who had been a fan of mine for many years, wanted to meet me at five o'clock in the Benjamin Franklin Hotel in Philadelphia. Then he added the fateful words, "before you go down to the boat." Had I reread a letter I received, I would have noted that the ship was to leave the dock at a particular moment. I thought I knew the city of Philadelphia and its rivers fairly well, and I had never seen any large boats of any type flying up and down the Schuylkill, so I assumed that the ship *was tied up at the dock*—permanently!

I had arranged for the Tommy Tucker pianist to meet me at the Essex House in New York at 2:30 on Monday afternoon, just preceding the performance, to run over three or four numbers. If I had plied him with a few questions about the performance time and place, I would have flown out of the apartment with our bags half-packed, especially in view of the fact that we had been having trouble with our car. But my wife, Eleanor, and I proceeded to pack our bags leisurely. By the time we were loaded and on our way it was approximately 4:15. Upon emerging from the Lincoln Tunnel the confusion of the signs, combined with my painful ignorance as to whether Philadelphia lay to the north or south, found us winding our way toward the George Washington Bridge, which is to say we were returning to New York instead of heading for our destination. This mistake not only consumed time, but wasted my finances as well.

We turned back and rolled along happily enough until I realized that something was wrong with our motor, when I looked back and discovered that our rear window was completely covered with oil. However, I knew that we could not stop, although by this time it was apparent that I would miss the five o'clock reunion with my fan. Approximately seventy minutes later we passed the sign that said "Camden Turnoff." I should have remembered that Camden is right across the river from Philadelphia; but I didn't, and I determined to continue on. We rolled on for at least thirty or forty minutes more, until I knew that something was wrong. Upon inquiry at the first booth we could find on the turnpike, I discovered that we were heading for Wilmington, Delaware—which made me the prize boob of the year. By now it was approximately 6:15.

In the hopes that my fan might still be waiting, as soon as we left the turnpike I tried to put a phone call through to explain my tardiness. But I gave up after holding the phone for a good ten minutes. Now my problem was to find the heart of the city of Philadelphia. We drove on carefully, as it started to rain. Meanwhile the oil gauge blinked alarmingly. It wasn't until the hour of 7:45 that, after many red lights and much traffic, we finally arrived in front of the Benjamin Franklin Hotel.

I jumped out, explained to the doorman that we wouldn't be more than a few minutes, and proceeded into the labyrinth of the hotel, fearing for the worst. My fears were more than justified, because I found an intelligent bell captain who showed me a brochure outlining the annual hospital convention schedule, the first day of which was to be celebrated by "the trip on the boat with Tommy Tucker and his orchestra, and only one entertainer for the evening." You guessed it, the entertainer was Hubert Prior Vallée! From nowhere came the manager who informed me that they had held the boat until 6:45, a half-hour beyond its scheduled departure, while they had paged me from the dock, the lobby of the hotel, and everywhere, wondering where I could be. Of course, to my mind there came the idea of a ship-to-shore telephone. I was assured by all present that this was an old ship and lacked the usual modern-day means of communication with the home pier.

Beyond that, no one seemed able to give me any information. My heart was down in my boots, not so much at the king's ransom that I was losing, but chiefly because I had a reputation of being a performer who always appeared, whether late or early— at least I had never disappointed an audience. Mrs. Vallée, sympathetic as always, did not upbraid me as well she might have, and for want of something to do, I pulled out my tuxedo jacket and pants, and with a small bag containing my shaving equipment and shoes, shirt and tie, I went back into the hotel to take advantage of the manager's offer to use his office if I wished to change or relax for a few minutes. I emerged from the hotel formally dressed and clean-shaven: "All dressed up and no place to go!" (Popular song, circa 1913.)

It occurred to me that when the ship came back to the dock perhaps I could persuade the captain and the sponsors of the trip to keep everyone on board while I performed at least for twenty or thirty minutes. But common sense told me that these persons, who had been on board probably since five o'clock or even earlier, would be bloody-well anxious to get off. There was another economical and maritime problem that presented itself. I knew that the crew aboard the ship might number several hundred persons, who at the conclusion of their duties and by union regulations were supposed to depart from the ship at a specified hour, or be entitled to overtime.

We drove to the docks and spotted the night watchman. "Is there any chance of reaching the Coast Guard?" I asked him. I felt that maybe my buddies, whom I had come to know in Philadelphia when we played there during the war days, might be willing to take me out to the big ship in a fast-moving Coast Guard cutter or a small speed boat.

This lone soul replied, "Naw, this ship is just like the *Queen Mary*—you just can't board 'er."

He pulled out some 8 × 10 glossy photographs of the ship, and upon seeing them I let out a whoop of joy, which was short-lived. Although the photographs revealed the fact that this leviathan *could* be boarded from a canoe, the fact remained that we didn't even have a plastic or rubber raft to go out and seek it!

Then Mrs. Vallée saved the day. She suddenly called me over to the window. "Look," she said, pointing to a little light that was affixed to something moving on the water, to the right of us. A small boat, powered by a motor, was coming into the dock next to our big shed. She and I looked at each other excitedly. The owner agreed to take us out, and we jumped into the boat, backed out of the dock, and were off!

It remained for a landlubber like me to figure out that since our little boat was running about five knots an hour less than the ship we were seeking, that when we did meet it, if by some unfortunate chance it did not perceive us in its path, we would, of course, have to play safe and make sure we were not directly in front of it; and unless we attracted attention to ourselves as it passed us, once it did recede into the night, even if we turned around and tried to follow it, we could never overtake it. We possessed a small flashlight, a large megaphone, and that was that.

I looked at my watch. We had been out approximately fifty-two minutes. At least one thing was in our favor—if we could somehow attract attention to ourselves and get on board, I would be able to do a fifty-minute show before we came into the dock. I was very deep in these thoughts when suddenly there she was! I blinked the flashlight and began yelling through the megaphone. The big ship was less than 100 yards away when a beam of light from the leviathan played upon us, and it was apparent that the big ship was coming to a stop. I grabbed my saxophone case as we moved in and soon we were being pulled over the railing.

We rushed up the stairs where the crowd was dancing to Tommy Tucker's band, and where Tommy Tucker's girl singer was performing. My heart was almost as low as it had been when we reached the Benjamin Franklin Hotel when it became apparent to me that the public address system on board would never enable me to perform so I might be heard. However, at least I was there, and I could go through the token motions of trying to entertain. Since we still had forty minutes to go before arriving at the dock, I would be able at least to fulfill my contractual obligations to the best of my ability.

I conferred with Tommy. I told him how I would like to be introduced, waved to the pianist, and as Tommy prepared to ask the crowd to sit down while I entertained them, a short, gray-haired man with glasses approached me—to deliver the coup de grace! He informed me that he was the chairman of the affair. As he talked I noticed a slight twitching in his left eye. He spoke meticulously, with a cold precision; he had a face that was stern and forbidding. He said in no uncertain terms that I was not to do more than three or four songs.

"You know that most of my routine is slightly risqué humor," I said.

"Yes," he replied, "I've heard about your show" (and now he was winking furiously) "and if you do one thing out of line, I'll stop the show." His jaw clamped together tightly and he turned on his heel, leaving me to wonder whether the wink meant that he was joking or not!

Already Tommy Tucker was introducing me. The next mo-

Doing an English number in a supper night club

ment I was facing an audience of about 500 persons, most of
whom had seated themselves on the floor, with a ring two or
three deep standing around the edge. Although I was in a dilemma, I decided once and for all to chance it. I began with an
opening routine I'd been using for the last three and one-half
years, one of the finest pieces of material that has ever come my
way. There is a certain point in this routine, approximately forty-
five seconds from its beginning, that tells me pretty much what
type of audience I am facing and what they want from me. I
reached this point, and was greeted with a roar of laughter that
shook the ship. This particular sally was hardly provocative
enough to bring our little man out with an authoritative wave
and a command for me to stop the show, and it encouraged me to
continue. As I reached the core of this particular routine, laugh
followed on laugh.

Before I knew it I was into my third and fourth comedy routines, then came the "Whiffenpoof Song," with political jokes,
another comedy number, then the "Vagabond Lover Medley."
Just as I finished "The Stein Song," I felt a lurch and a thud as we
hit the dock, and I knew we were in. As I looked at my watch, I
realized that for sixty minutes I had been able to bring roars of
laughter and appreciation from these disciples of Aesculapius
and Mercury, and a more enthusiastic audience I have never
faced. Those sixty minutes had redeemed what looked like a
completely lost cause!

As they rose to a standing ovation I became aware for the first
time that only when the audience was dancing did they block out
the speakers, making it seemingly impossible for the performer at
the microphone to be heard. But when they were seated, as they
were while I performed, the speakers were free to emit their
volume.

Then they were yelling for "My Time Is Your Time." I pulled
the key out of the air and began singing it, and they all joined
me. I think perhaps they tried to convey that they had some
appreciation of the travail and agony I had endured when we
"missed the boat," and were happy that we finally made it!

One-Punch

So many times reference has been made to my being a target for large, round, yellow Florida grapefruit on the stage of a theater in Boston, with many speculations as to how and why and whether it really ever happened, that I must once and for all set the story straight.

The plot begins in my freshman year at Yale, when in the fall of 1922 Yale decided that no longer would freshmen go either academic or scientific upon entrance, but rather would have a common freshman year and would decide which way to go at the end of that year. To head up this new idea they chose Dean Rosswell P. Angier, a Harvard man and a brilliant authority in psychology. He was a short man with a rather large head and very large eyes, and he wore pince-nez glasses.

As the time I transferred to Yale from the University of Maine mathematics was a requirement. So I was soon attending math classes; we got so far and then I was completely gone. I told Dean Angier about my problem. Mind you, there were 850 men in our class at Yale, and yet he took time out to counsel me, and counsel me wisely. I think he must have sensed that I was an

16

Vallée

artistic person and not inclined to any ability in mathematics. "I'll permit you to transfer to biology," he said, "and you can tutor next summer in mathematics and take it in your sophomore year —as it is a requisite for your graduating degree as a Bachelor of Philosophy." I went through my freshman year always under the cloud of the unpleasant thought of tutoring in mathematics during the summer and, worse still, having to take mathematics in the fall of 1923. But then I heard a rumor and asked Dean Angier about it. "Mr. Vallée," he said, "beginning with the class of 1926, mathematics is no longer required for Ph.B. degree." It is quite possible that he knew about this impending change and thus let me drop math my freshman year, knowing I would never have to take it.

In the spring of 1927 a fellow classmate, who played the piano, and who then disliked me intensely but later became one of my closest friends, informed me that we were to play a dance at the home of Dean Angier for his sons, who had been away at prep school, and for their friends—boys and girls also home from school. We were a small orchestra of four pieces. After about an hour of playing dance music for the kids, Dean Angier brought me a plate of ice cream. Being a very healthy person with a voracious appetite, and at times rather tactless (when I feel it is a natural thing to express myself honestly), I said to the dean, "Is this all we get?"

Evidently as he went back into the kitchen he was followed by his son, who noticed the father was flushed to his ears as he said to Mrs. Angier, "I guess we should have had something else for the orchestra. Rudy asked if this is all we have." Young Angier noticed the father's embarrassment and then and there vowed that some day he would get even with the person who caused it. As it was, in the fall of 1930, three years later, young Angier had installed himself as a freshman at Harvard. Evidently he learned that I was playing with my band at the Metropolitan Theatre in January 1931 and that I was singing a song called "Oh Give Me Something to Remember You By." He decided that he would, indeed, give me something that I would never forget!

Thus it was that he, with two cronies, brought several grapefruit into the theater and installed themselves in the front row of the balcony. This song was the last item of our act and it began with the entire orchestra playing it; then came a vocal from me, and followed by a chorus played by me on the saxophone, the rhythm behind me. I was half-way through my saxophone chorus when I heard the shattering sound of the crash cymbal. There was pandemonium in the audience and the two men who bring the big curtains together (the curtains were so heavy that it was impossible to bring them together without manual assistance) looked at me questioningly: "Shall we open them up again?"

I could only assume that my drummer, who never believed in the way I did things, was trying to get the band to play in the style of Benny Pollack, whose style he revered. I also assumed that Ray Toland had taken a vicious swipe at the crash cymbal for no reason at all. But as I turned and walked toward him, I saw that he held in his hand a large grapefruit—*practically cut in half*! This grapefruit, coming through the air, gaining momentum after it was hurled from the front row of the balcony by young Angier, fortunately missed me and struck the crash cymbal. Had it hit the saxophone where it curves into the mouth, it probably would have broken every tooth in my head, and maybe driven the mouthpiece into my spine, and severed it, killing me!

When I do this song in my nightclub act and tell this story, there are always ripples of amusement and, of course, on the surface it was amusing. There's little question but that the boy intended to hit me with it. Fortunately, his aim was bad. One year later, 1932—when I came to Boston with *George White's Scandals* on tour—this irresponsible boy came into my dressing room, laughing like a madman, still not realizing how close he came to maiming me for life or perhaps killing me. The night they threw the grapefruit the three boys were arrested and young Angier was suspended for a year. He had been involved in quite a few other escapades and pranks.

You have to remember the very keen rivalry between Yale and Harvard in order to appreciate the humor of this story: Someone asked the Harvard faculty if they suspended the boy because he threw the grapefruit. "No," they replied. "Because he *missed!*"

Less than a decade after the grapefruit incident I had another run-in with an agitator in the audience. We had reopened at the Cocoanut Grove in September 1939 to very good business. My assisting acts this time were the King's Men, who had been a part of the Whiteman complex, and two boys from the Middle West called "Mirth and Mack," who did impressions of the Marx Brothers, Groucho and Harpo. I had a very beautiful, dark-haired girl singer, and Bob Neller, a ventriloquist to end all ventriloquists! I had enlarged my band to eighteen pieces. My rendition of "Where To?" was the close of the show, which ran approximately forty-five or fifty minutes. It was a narration against a background of music. I did not sing any part of the number. Like "All Points West," a taxi driver is killed in a shoot-out between him and the officers who are chasing his cab in an effort to get hold of a criminal who is in the cab. Along the way the cab driver has to pick up a fop, a drunk, a very annoying and pompous senator, and a fellow who takes a gal in the cab with him to make love to her as they go through Central Park. Finally the criminal tells the cab driver to go like hell; that the cops are after him. In the end the cab driver is shot.

Then it happened. It was a Saturday night, and the Grove was jammed. I could see Governor Lehman of New York State, his wife, and a large party out on the dance floor, and Loretta Young at another corner. Ben Gage, the tall, six-foot-three announcer who married the beautiful MGM swimming star Esther Williams, was evidently hosting a large table that they had put in the middle of the dance floor since we were so crowded for room. Ben Gage invited me over to meet the eight or ten persons who were assembled there with him. I took no particular notice but at the end of the table was a short, dark-haired man with very large, black eyes. As we approached the time for our show I noticed that the big table had suddenly disappeared. My vanity was a little hurt as I had hoped they would be there to enjoy our show.

We had used on our "Fleischmann Hour" a few days before a young, suave, very handsome comedian who worked in tails and on roller skates. He resembled Robert Montgomery uncannily, almost seemed his double. He was in full regalia, tails and all. He asked me if I would put him on before we did our show, to let him do about eight or ten minutes to show his talents to John Barton Browne, who managed the Grove at the time and who had booked me for both of my ten-week engagements there. I liked this young comedian, and said, "I'd be most happy to do just that." With a fanfare from the orchestra, I introduced our young comedian. He was about two minutes into his act when suddenly from over to the right came a burst of profanity. I looked and there was the short man with the large, black eyes who had been at the Ben Gage table, now seated alone at a small table ringside. As the young comedian continued to try to capture the audience, this boor appeared to be in a drunken rage and finally made it impossible for the comedian to continue. Yet, no one did anything about it.

As we prepared to start our show I sent for Ralph and Sam, the two boys who worked for me, and instructed them to get behind that man, and if he did anything whatsoever in any way to hurt our show, *to carry him bodily from the room*! What followed was a nightmare. The two boys in their attempts to depict the Marx Brothers were heckled mercilessly by this character. He hurt Bob Neller's performance badly. I don't recall that he bothered the girl singer or the King's Men, but as I approached my pièce de résistance, "Where To?", which runs approximately five minutes, I pondered whether I should do it at all. If so, how could I avoid antagonizing him? I completely forgot that the cab driver picks up a drunk who threatens to have the driver arrested. I looked to the right at the lone drunk at the table. There were my two boys behind him; yet they had done nothing in spite of his outbursts of profanity and obscenities. I just couldn't figure it out, I couldn't understand it. But I didn't have time to go over and ask them why they had not removed him. Later I asked Ralph and Sam why they hadn't carried him off the floor. I should have realized—my show and I were sacrificed on the altar of greed and the degradation of greasing the palm. The assistant maitre d' had stood behind my boys and told them not to touch him because not only did this man, who was a cigar manufacturer, live in the Ambassador Hotel, but he tipped very liberally.

As I did the number and depicted each character, I faced either right or left as the cab driver talked to them or as the individual talked to the cab driver. If I had only zigged when I zagged, I would not have been facing the drunk at the table when I portrayed the drunk that the cab driver was about to pick up. As I went into the portion of "Where To?" where the drunk starts to insult the cab driver, I was looking directly to the right at the lone drunk. By now his fury knew no bounds and he let me have it with both barrels. Somehow I surmounted him in volume and got through that portion of "Where To?". The number moves on very swiftly to the final chase by the police and the criminal in the cab. I prayed and prayed that he would let me finish the final moment where the cab driver is dying and I've a green spotlight on me (indicative of death), that he wouldn't ruin the number completely. Fortunately, he was silent as the cab driver died. I finished the number, whipped my boys to their feet to bow with me to the audience, then I bowed back to the boys, then back again to the audience, then motioned for the boys to be seated. Without pause I strolled across the floor, put my hand under the chin of the drunk and pushed him and his chair back on the floor.

The audience rose to its feet, Governor Lehman came over and shook my hand, and Loretta Young kissed me!

Bill Cunningham used to tell a story about a much more violent encounter I had with another heckler. Bill, a brilliant, fearless operator-commentator-columnist of the *Boston Post*, is a man who flatters no one. He has always been friendly to me, and I believe that he honestly thinks it *did* happen as he described it to his daughter, to whom he introduced me at the Copley Plaza after my second show there in 1951. Bill described it in vivid detail, practically re-enacting the manner in which I once disposed of a heckler, depicting my vicious right, which floored the guy and left him lying there "out cold."

I wish I could justify Bill's enthusiastic and laudatory estimate of my prowess in the art of fisticuffs, but I have only once in my entire career ever connected with anyone, heckler or otherwise. In that case I only grazed the man's cheek, and it even turned out to be the wrong guy!

You have probably never known the sensation of standing with your back to an audience while directing a band in a soft waltz and feeling something strike your right ankle, turning and looking down only to see an empty Scotch bottle. The more infuriating feeling comes when you turn around and stare into a sea of impassive faces, registering complete apathy for the most part, with no indication of a willingness to point out the villain who had just thrown the bottle. It is this unique complicity of the herd, this apparent stick-togetherness that is so maddening. At least it would be a relief if you turned around and faced one-half of them giving you the bird, or if only a few showed some appreciation of the spot in which you find yourself. But no, there is a bored detachment on every face, as though nothing whatsoever had occurred.

It was this way in Toronto, Canada, on our second appearance at the Canadian National Exposition, one of the biggest events of the Dominion, which occurs each year in the fall at Toronto. I looked over at my public address system man who was operating our $8,000 amplifying system with his coffinlike box of controls in the audience. I saw that he pointed to a giant of a man, approximately six-foot-seven, who stood about three feet away from the control box. With my lips and face I mirrored the expression, "Are you sure?" Murray moved his head up and down and continued to point. There was no mistaking which man he meant, and as I approached this cyclops who looked slightly villainous with the moustache he was wearing, I glanced again at Murray for confirmation and again he indicated definitely that this was the individual.

As I neared the Canadian Man-Mountain Dean, I let fly a right that grazed his cheek. Had he lifted one of his huge arms and fists, he probably would have pulverized me, but he made no move whatsoever. He merely looked at me rather sadly, as he said, "I didn't do it." The amazing thing is that I knew instantly that he had not done it, and for a while I felt conscience-stricken. "I'm sorry," I apologized quickly.

I wended my way back to the band platform and continued to the end of the dance set. However, I was not entirely in error, as this young man was the scion of a charming, titled dowager with whom I'd had lunch the day before at her fabulous farm, which was only a hobby. Her income from one of the most successful gold mines in the world is so stupendous that she could run 100 farms like it, but hers was unique in that the cows sleep on varnished floors while beautiful recorded music is played throughout the day for all of the denizens of her entire rural estate—including the pigs.

I had not met the young man during the luncheon. He was apparently the black sheep of the family and may have resented my visit to his mother's estate, and so brought a group of his aristocratic snobs with him to our show and dance. He was with and directly in front of the individual who actually threw the bottle, and my boy Murray had seen him coming up as he had ducked while the other man behind him had thrown the bottle. Suffice it to say, the affair wound up with our young aristocrat becoming more annoyed as the moments went by, coming backstage for revenge only to face one Umba, an even bigger giant from Africa who tried to calm our boy. Umba finally moved the aristocratic nose over to the cheek, which was accomplished by the simple expedient of taking the aristocratic head under his arm and proceeding to effect this plastic surgery with one blow.

That was the only time I ever actually landed with my fists— though slightly. Oh, yes, I've studied boxing. In 1929, while I was at the Brooklyn Paramount, I was considered such a strong radio plug that Johnnie Green, one of the bantamweight contenders of that day, whose brother Buddy is a successful song writer, spent several hours in my dressing room at the Paramount attempting to teach me the manly art of self-protection. In other words, trading a pug for a plug of his brother's songs! Then, in 1938 in California, Bob Howard, who conditioned producers and directors and gave Cole Porter a new lease on life after Porter's tragic polo accident, also proceeded to condition me and to introduce me to the punching bag, inviting me to land a few on his chin.

Yale Collegian in Pittsburgh—1926

My Brooklyn Paramount instruction in no way justified my ever walking off the band platform as I did in Wilkes-Barre, Pennsylvania in 1930, but it would take the patience of a saint indeed to withstand the taunts and insults of a red, shiny-faced coal miner who stood there pouring it on for a little over an hour until the French-Irish in me decided that something had to be done about it. I walked off the stage toward him. Fortunately, somehow the crowd swarmed in, and our miner friend was removed from the place—a blessing for me as he would have probably knocked me into oblivion. There was one glorious satisfaction about the Wilkes-Barre event, however; it showed me what my band thought of me. As I turned, I discovered that my entire band, with the exception of the drummer and pianist, were in various spots behind me just in case anyone else pitched in and the fight became unfair.

The time I came closest to getting it was in 1933 in Raleigh, North Carolina—the Carolinas where we had so much trouble with an insolently impatient crowd that booed Alice Faye and me as we came on one hour after the band had been playing dance music, to begin our show—the Carolinas where one of our promoters decamped with the money due us, where the sleet and rain ruined two of our best dates, and where on a Sunday night with a splitting headache I found myself being constantly given the bird by a tall, professorial-looking character out on the floor. He had the most diabolical, leering smile I've ever seen on a man's face. Between my splitting headache and the unhappiness of our tour in that part of the country in general, this was too much. Again I was off the platform seeking my quarry. This character, however academic his features, clearly registered an intent to mayhem and murder as he stood there with his fist raised in the air waiting for me to get close enough. Fortunately, his actions had evidently been observed by two policemen, and between the crowd surging between us and the two coppers who came to our aid, our friend got the bum's rush.

It was at North Adams on a summer's evening that another one of those babies decided to be rude and obnoxious for minutes on end. This character remained in hiding in the crowd, and I had no recourse but to announce over the amplifying system that if he would kindly come up on the stage, I would proceed to knock his °°%/$&°° teeth down into his °°%/$&°° stomach. To my great surprise, this brought a roar of applause from the audience. They stopped dancing to watch for what they hoped would be a good melee. One-punch Vallée honestly hoped the character would come up, regardless of his size or ability, but later, plain old Rudy Vallée was frankly relieved when he didn't.

Living from

Crisis to

It was January 1961 when I received a telephone call from Bill Josephy, an agent who was with General Artists Corporation, originally Rockwell O'Keefe, which today is Creative Management Associates. Josephy asked me to meet him at the Polo Lounge at the Beverly Hills Hotel, where he said Cy Feuer wanted to talk about a Broadway musical.

I knew that Cy Feuer (correctly pronounced "Foyer") had teamed up with a former CBS page boy named Ernie Martin; together the two had gone to New York to seek their fortune as producers of musical shows. They had started off with an English import called *The Boyfriend*, with Julie Andrews. It had been a fair success and they had followed it up with another light success, *Where's Charley?* with Ray Bolger. They had finally come through, aided by Abe Burrows and the songwriter Frank Loesser, with a blockbuster, *Guys and Dolls*, which has made millions. Feuer told me that he and Ernie Martin were about to launch a new musical, to be called *How to Succeed in Business Without Really Trying*. He apologized for the length of the title.

"Don't apologize," I replied. "I think it's a very unique title."

17

Crisis with

How to Succeed

Then, punctuated by bursts of laughter, he proceeded to outline the story of *How to Succeed*. I was not terribly impressed. As Feuer concluded he mentioned something about my coming to New York but for some reason never really explained why I should go, nor did he detail who would take care of the expenses of the trip. He also should have told me that no one—but no one—ever went into a musical with which Frank Loesser was associated without first auditioning vocally for Loesser. This little Napoleon was indeed a martinet in every sense of the word, but a very gifted songwriter.

I told Feuer I would give the musical much thought and give my decision very shortly. The more I thought about it, the less I liked the idea of going to New York in a musical, as my previous experiences in two *George White's Scandals* had been miserable ones.

Josephy called me about a week later. "Have you arrived at a decision?" he asked.

"First I want to know if they'd be willing to release me after six months."

"No," Josephy answered. "They'd want you for at least a year."

"Forget it," I said.

I returned to searching for bookings here, there, and everywhere. In early March I was offered a two-week engagement in Orlando, Florida, at a small hotel for a very small fee, but it was something I thought I'd enjoy and I accepted it. During the course of the two weeks I received a wire from General Artists Corporation, New York, asking me if I would come to New York to discuss *How to Succeed in Business Without Really Trying.* Eventually they called me by phone.

I said, "If you'll pay my fare from Orlando to New York and then back to California, I'll come to New York."

They replied, "We'll pay your fare only from Orlando to New York."

"Forget it," I said.

After the engagement in Orlando I flew back to California. About this time I received a very lucrative offer to fly to White Sulphur Springs, where the American Broadcasting System was going to entertain all of the advertising executives in radio and television. Jimmy Durante, Dorothy Provine, and I were to be the three performing stars. Before leaving, I recalled a very happy engagement in London, Ontario in 1960. I phoned the owner of this small spot who said he'd be delighted to use me again and since it was only a hop, skip, and jump from White Sulphur Springs to London, Ontario, I tied the two together. On the Monday afternoon of rehearsal at this little club called the Iroquois, I received a phone call from Beverly Hills. It was Marty Baum. He had terminated his own agency (Baum, Newborn) to join General Artists Corporation. "Will you go to New York after you finish the engagement in London, Ontario?" he asked.

I lied and told him, "I have a recording date in Hollywood on Monday following my engagement in London, Ontario. I can't make it." Perhaps it was just as well I lied because if I had gone to New York, the chances are I would never have satisfied Frank Loesser, vocally, that is!

I went to bed on a Wednesday night and, as usual, told the operator not to ring me until I called her. The following morning about ten o'clock the phone rang. "What the hell, is the goddamned building on fire?" I grumbled.

The voice said, "Rudy. This is Cy Feuer. I'm down here with Act One. Will you read it?" Act One was written by Abe Burrows, who had written many radio scripts for me back in 1940.

I dressed and joined Feuer in the dining room of the Iroquois Hotel. Unknown to me, back in New York there had been a conversation between Cy Feuer and Abe Newborn. Abe Newborn with Marty Baum had formed an agency in 1955 called Baum-Newborn. They had engaged me to appear on the Gary Moore Show for $5,000, and I remembered them well because they asked me to repeat again a year later. Now they had both dissolved their own agency and had both become a part of General Artists, handling some of the personalities for the Cy Feuer-Ernie Martin show *How to Succeed in Business Without Really Trying.*

I was told later by Barron Polan, who formerly managed and married Jane Morgan, that it was he, Polan, who had convinced Cy Feuer I would be the ideal man for the part of J. B. Biggley. Somehow Polan had learned that there was a football song to be sung in the show and, remembering my success with "The Stein Song," felt that the song and the idea alone meant I should play the part.

Although London, Ontario, I am told, has more wealthy persons per capita than any other city in the world, the Iroquois Hotel, a little three-story building with eight or ten tiny bedrooms upstairs (which by Canadian law had to be there in order for them to be able to sell liquor in the dining room), was a very unpretentious building of gray concrete with no lobby and just a very unattractive, small door opening. As the two gentlemen approached this unattractive entrance, Cy Feuer said, "Well, if Rudy's playing places like this, we'll get him for nothing." When I had discussed the engagement earlier with Josephy over the telephone, after the Beverly Hills meeting, I had asked him what this engagement would pay, and he had replied "$1,500. A week of eight shows." When Feuer made the remark about getting me cheaper, Abe Newborn said, "No, he's been promised $1,500 and that's what it will be."

After reading Act One I asked Feuer and Newborn to join me in the manager's office. *I could detect the sweet smell of success.* Although I realized my part was not very long, I could see that it was very vital and important and that I would get quite a few laughs, because it was beautifully written as only Abe Burrows can write. They came into the office. "Yes, I'd love to be in it," I said with great enthusiasm.

Newborn reminded me that I would have to take *second bill-ing* to Robert Morse and also *second dressing room.* It showed how little he knew me. Unlike so many other performers who in their contracts specify the size of their billing, where it shall be placed relative to the order of the names, etc., I have never been concerned with where my name should be, how big the letters should be, or what dressing room I should have. I am only inter-ested in one thing: *Being in a hit show, with a hit team!* It was also mentioned that in addition to the two songs I was going to sing in the show there might be a third song. I little realized how important this third song was going to be and that it would al-most terminate my participation in the show itself.

We then shook hands, which of course was not a contract but at least it assured me I was going to do the show. Newborn asked Cy Feuer to leave the office and, as Feuer departed, he put one finger across the left lapel of his coat jacket. He did this surrepti-tiously, but I caught it. After Feuer closed the door, Newborn said to me, "Did you see that?" I laughed and said "Yes. And I know what it means." What Cy Feuer had intended to convey to Newborn by using one finger was, "Try to get him for $1,000." But Newborn reassured me laughingly that I would get my $1,500 as had been promised.

Both men flew back to New York and I flew home to Holly-wood to prepare for the trip East. I first played several nightclub engagements as we drove east. I then went to my 35th reunion at Yale, and finally had a memorable experience at the Lunt and Fontaine Theatre on 46th Street. Feuer and Martin had taken a lease on the theater, where *Sound of Music* was playing. Here I met Virginia Martin, Hugh Lambert (who was to be replaced by Bob Fosse), and several other members of the cast. And here I first began to get an insight into the character of Frank Loesser, who demanded that I show him how high I could sing and how low I could go vocally. Alcohol, especially in excess, is not kind to the vocal cords and I had been enjoying fabulous rum drinks for over twenty years. Since I was at that time sixty years old, age itself and the abuse my vocal cords had taken over the years hardly qualified me as the possessor of a glorious singing voice. I did my best to show Loesser my vocal prowess, but I could see he was not too pleased. We came to the matter of the third song, "A Secretary Is Not a Toy," which, I discovered later, was originally to be sung by Paul Reed in robust voice, a song that was to have a terribly important effect upon my being a permanent part of the show.

As I wrote Loesser from Philadelphia later on, I think he must have been drunk when he wrote this song, because, in my opinion, it is one of the worst melodies I have ever heard or tried to sing. "A Secretary Is Not a Toy" was to be sung to a young group of male executives who have been fooling around with some of the girl secretaries. I have never liked the melody of "Stardust," notwithstanding its tremendous universal success and acceptance, because of its extreme range and constant going down into the valley, ascending to mountains and down into the valley again. The melody of "A Secretary Is Not a Toy" made "The Star-Spangled Banner" and "Stardust" pale by comparison. I should have said to Loesser, "Stick this song up your ass. It's a lousy, stinking song, and I don't want any part of it!" But I suggested that he record the three songs I was to do on an acetate disc and let me take them with me to Bermuda so I might learn them to get his interpretation of them. He agreed and I took the record with me to Bermuda. Shortly after my return from Bermuda, it was time for rehearsals, which began on August 5, 1961 at the Variety Arts Studios in the Edison Hotel building, in what I called a "cut-rate funeral parlor."

Soon my disenchantment with Frank Loesser began to flower in full force. One evening he asked me to sing "A Secretary Is Not a Toy." I was joined by eight male voices in parts of the song. Quite frankly, I thought I did a fair job of it, inasmuch as the song was not written for my small voice in the first place, but was supposed to be sung by a very strong Lawrence Tibbett type of baritone voice with the trained quality of the Italian *bella voce*— which I possessed not at all. As I finished, I could see a slight disappointment on Loesser's face. I should have told him then and there: "Let me out of this song!"

Crisis No. 1: The Ouster Attempt

On the night of August 16 there were only two of us rehearsing: Virginia Martin and I. We were doing the dialogue lead-

ing up to where we sing a song called "A Heart of Gold." I
thought I was delivering the dialogue as well as it could be delivered and as sincerely and intelligently as possible when suddenly, *for the first time, Burrows snapped at me* and almost
belligerently criticized the way I was reading my lines. If I had
thought about it I would have realized that something was
wrong when two days before, as I went backstage at the 46th
Street Theatre just across the way, Ernie Martin was standing
inside the stage door, chewing gum as he always did. Ernie was a
six-foot-one, very tanned and handsome young fellow who, as I
said, had been a page boy at CBS before he teamed with Cy
Feuer to produce hit musicals. He had always been most cordial.
On this afternoon as I passed him I stopped for a few words with
him. "Ernie," I said, "we've got an *Of Thee I Sing, Guys and
Dolls*, and *My Fair Lady* all wrapped up in one in this musical,
and I'd like to invest in it." To my surprise, he barked at me, "I
don't want anybody in this show investing in it!" He chewed his
gum more rapidly, turned on his heel, and walked away from
me.

The next morning, August 17, the day dawned hot and sunny
and very muggy, with much humidity. We were rehearsing in the
"cut-rate funeral parlor" rooms and Abe Burrows had informed
me we had now secured the services of Bob Fosse, renowned for
his great success with *Pajama Game* and the "Steam Heat" number. Evidently Hugh Lambert had disappointed Frank Loesser
by the way he had directed the choreography of some of the
musical numbers. However, his staging of "Coffee Break" was
superb! Although he was not kicked out of the show, he no longer
had much of anything to do with the dancing. I was introduced
to Fosse.

Everyone in the upper echelon connected with the show was
there to see how he could stage "A Secretary Is Not a Toy."
Apparently that had been the stumbling block for his predecessor
as far as production of the number itself was concerned. We tried
every conceivable way of staging it. At one of the five-minute
breaks someone came over with some letters for me and I was
talking to this person, evidently with some animation. After the
person left, Fosse said to me, "If you could only give me some of
that animation you just gave that person, I'd be very happy."

Feeling I had given this lousy song all I could give it, I wondered at this remark! What the hell did he want, blood?

That afternoon, after lunch, Abe Newborn entered the room and suggested we go down to the Green Room of the Edison Hotel. We went there and sat at a table. Suddenly Newborn said to me, "They want you out of the show." If he had struck me across the face, he could not have surprised, bewildered, or hurt me more. They had chased me, phoned me, coaxed me, and wooed me for months, and now suddenly I was told I wasn't wanted in the show. Newborn continued, "And they're offering you $40,000 to get out of it."

I recovered my composure. "What's wrong?"

His startling reply was, "They don't think you're right for the part."

Now everything fell into place. I could understand Abe Burrows' annoyance with me the night before, and the truculence of Ernie Martin. Then my mind went back to an afternoon three days before when Frank Loesser took Virginia Martin and me into a small room in which there was a piano and asked us to sing "Heart of Gold." This song is perhaps as corny and lousy a song —from the standpoint of melody and lyrics—as could be imagined. If anyone had ever brought it to me to broadcast, I'd have thrown him out of my office. But for this show, in the way it was done by Virginia and me, it was a true gem. Of course, I had learned the song after just two or three hearings of the record Loesser had made for me.

There was one thing I did not know that was peculiar, almost ingrained in Frank Loesser, and that was his theory that in order to sing his songs properly, the singer must sing them over and over again, thousands and thousands of times. Virginia Martin and I sang the song through twice for Loesser. He then stated, "I want you to stay here until five o'clock singing this song." I couldn't believe my ears. "Frank," I said, "I won't sing it any better after the thousandth time than I will right now." He suddenly went into a rage. "I'm not going to have my show destroyed by your not singing my songs properly!" he said. Good God! You'd have thought I had a difficult aria to sing, one requiring much rehearsal, much direction, instead of this corny piece of junk. Of course, I didn't stay there and it is my best guess that from that moment on, I was doomed!

It was Charles Nelson Reilly who later on brought home to me why it was easy for Loesser to convince everyone I should go. Consider this: Loesser had just had a flop with Tony Perkins, a $280,000 flop called *Green Willows,* in which he tried to get Tony Perkins to sing. Abe Burrows had tried to salvage *Hail the Conquering Hero* with Tom Poston, a $550,000 flop. More importantly for Feuer and Martin, they had just had *Whoop-Up,* a $400,000 flop. Obviously, as Charles Nelson Reilly had said, "All these men were running scared!"

But Newborn reminded me, I had a contract for fifty-seven weeks, fifty-two in New York and five in Philadelphia at $1,500 a week; they would have to pay me for every week of that contract if I refused the $40,000 and did not actually participate in the show but did not get out of it. In fact, as it has been done before, they could order me to come every evening to the theater, sit below in the cellar, and leave after the show was over to justify receiving that money per week. I said to Abe, "So, we'll collect it each week."

"You can't do anything else," he said.

"So I'll do nothing else!"

We got up and I went upstairs to pick up my things and go home. As I entered one of the rooms I saw Burrows and Feuer talking. I went over to them. "What seems to be wrong, boys?" I asked.

Burrows said frankly, "Rudy, I don't think they'll hear you."

I replied, "I used to fill the Brooklyn Paramount Theatre, which had a capacity of 5,000 persons. They could hear me speak there without the megaphone when I made the announcements."

"That was different," he said.

"Let's go next door," I suggested. "Virginia Martin and I will read for you."

We went next door to the Lunt and Fontaine Theatre. Feuer and Burrows walked to the back of the theatre and Virginia and I read some of our dialogue. Feuer came up on the stage bubbling. "Yes, I think it'll work," he said excitedly.

Burrows argued: "*We rehearse eight to twelve hours a day in Philadelphia! You won't be able to take it.*" Suddenly he had me an octogenarian with one foot in the grave. Yet, I was the only person who, in three solid years, never missed one show!

I left, not knowing what the hell was going to happen. As I

went down to get a taxi, Red Ginzler, who made the exquisite musical arrangements for the show, was about to take a cab to go over to the apartment building in which we both lived on 56th Street. I got in with him. He had told me earlier that he was looking for a larger apartment in the same building. As we were riding along I told him he could have our place, since I was not going to be in the show. Apparently he'd learned this, because he was not surprised when I offered the apartment to him. At three o'clock in the morning I typed a letter to my wife, who had temporarily returned to California, telling her I was not going to be in the show, not to come East. I went to bed and slept a troubled sleep. I dropped the letter, Airmail Special, in the apartment building chute at three o'clock in the morning!

At noon the phone rang. It was Abe Newborn. As the bearer of very good tidings the great Newborn informed me that they were going to let me stay, and then added the most strange, incomprehensible, incredible statement he could have made: *"Maybe it happened for the best."* There have been friends who have wondered how I could have stayed in the show after knowing I was not wanted. But as for me, I dressed as usual, went over and rehearsed as usual, as though nothing had happened, though I knew full well why they had decided that I should stay. They had gambled that I would take the $40,000 and run. They didn't know me. They didn't know how sold I was on the show, how happy I was to be in it, how thrilled I was with my part, and that I wouldn't have left it for $100,000 or $200,000. Rather than pay me almost $100,000, they had decided to let me stay, figuring that somehow, some way, they'd get me out eventually.

We knocked off rehearsal at dinner time and I went back to the apartment and began mixing rum drinks. Suddenly, about one o'clock the phone rang. Eleanor had received my letter— mailed air mail, special delivery at three o'clock in the morning of August 18—*at 2 o'clock in the afternoon of the same day!* That was when the mails were really functioning! If I had ever had any doubts as to how much my Eleanor loves me, the phone call on the night of the eighteenth of August, 1961 forever dispelled any such notion. I finally stemmed the agony in her torrent of vocal tears and made her understand that I was *not* going to leave the show, that she should some East as originally planned.

The Saturday night before we left for Philadelphia we were

to have a runthrough of the entire show on the stage of the 46th Street Theatre. There was to be no scenery, no lighting, no spotlight, little or no furniture, just boxes and chairs, with only a piano in the pit and no goddamn interruptions by Bob Fosse with his fucking whistle—which he was constantly blowing to stop the action. But, and this is a very big but, for the first time *we were to have an audience*, an audience made up of the "angels" (the investors in the show) and their friends. Roughly, there must have been between three and four hundred persons in the theater, eager to see the show in which they had invested their monies. There were to be no stops and a regular fifteen-minute intermission.

Morse had not yet found himself. The first two or three places where he should have had a laugh or a giggle, very little happened. He was almost in tears, whereas the two or three things I had in the first fifteen or twenty minutes came off beautifully. I knew they couldn't miss, just as I had felt it that morning when I had read the script in London, Ontario. I knew these lines were just ideal for me, especially the phone call I make to my wife when she talks about promoting my nephew, and I say to her very explosively, "If I do that it'd be nepotism! Nepotism!! That's when your nephew is a goddamned fool!"

At intermission I passed Larry Kasha, who had been cueing me my lines just before the firing. As he passed me, he said, "I love you!" At the end of the show everyone but Frank Loesser came up on the stage. Abe Burrows, bless him, was big enough to say, "Rudy, how stupid could we be? You're the perfect man for this show. Take care of yourself! Drive carefully to Philadelphia! Don't get a cold! May I help you to your car?"

We moved on to Philadelphia and I knew every day as the show neared perfection that we had a real smash. The opening night was a triumph! We just swept that audience off its feet. It was marred, however, by one little incident that I must reveal. While we were rehearsing one afternoon in the "cut-rate funeral parlor" rooms, I had a scene with my nephew in the show, Charles Nelson Reilly, as we stood waiting for the elevator. I ask him what he is doing there, and he says that he's waiting for the elevator. I say, "Why don't you walk down?" He says, "It's thirty-five floors." Strangely enough, Burrows never realized that here was a spot for a really true-dynamite-laugh punch line. One afternoon as we were rehearsing this scene, and Reilly said, "It's thirty-five floors," I said, "Why don't you *fly* down?" Now that you have come to know Charles Nelson Reilly through his TV work, you can appreciate the picture of him flying down, considering his character and nature. As I said it that afternoon at rehearsal, Abe Burrows began pounding the piano, Sammy Smith was rolling on the floor, and even Reilly himself was laughing.

In Philadelphia I said to Abe Burrows, "Why can't I say, 'Why don't you fly down?'" He reminded me that Reilly had a problem. He knew it, we knew it, and it just couldn't be done. The opening night I decided to have a little fun but not tell anyone what was in my mind. And when we came to the line where Reilly says, "It's thirty-five floors," I said, "Why don't you jump?" Of course, the theater exploded into one of the biggest laughs of the evening! Since we had never done this before an audience, I was not aware of the fact that when Reilly said, "It's thirty-five floors," he would get a little laugh—not a big one, but a *little* laugh. That evening when he said, "It's thirty-five floors," just as his little laugh was starting, I killed it by saying "Why don't you jump?" At intermission Reilly came into my room and at first I thought he was kidding. But if I've ever seen an angry person, that was Charles Nelson Reilly incarnate! In fact, for a moment I thought he was going to commit mayhem. For two weeks he wouldn't speak to me, in spite of the fact that I told him I didn't have any idea that he was going to get a laugh there; that I never would have killed it. But it remained for Abe Burrows to tell me that if I ever did that again, he would throw me out of the show. "Because," he insisted, "you might have thrown Charlie for a complete loss." I promised Abe I wouldn't do it again.

As a sequel and a finish to this particular incident, about the eighth or ninth month of the show in New York we had what we called a "brush-up." As a company continues to perform the same material over and over again, after a while certain scenes seem to become stale and it requires a meeting in the afternoon for the director to point out the fact that these scenes are not being done as they were the first week. The brush-up takes care of these places that are beginning to suffer. At a brush-up about nine months after we had opened—as Burrows was about to dismiss us—he casually turned to me, and said, "Oh, yes, and when Charlie says, 'It's thirty-five floors,' say to him,

'Why don't you jump?' " Sammy Smith again rolled on the floor!

After opening night we picked up the papers in the lobby of the Warwick Hotel and took them to our room to read. I've often wondered what Robert Morse thought when he saw the reviews in Philadelphia or in New York, for that matter. Every word Abe Burrows had written for Robert Morse was the best of his life blood because he wanted this boy to be a sensation, as he *was* in the show. I regret that in a way I was responsible for Morse not receiving his just and proper due in the headlines of the reviews. Of course, he was the major portion of the reviews; they gave him every inch of credit he deserved. Their review of my part was also most favorable, most kind, and most eloquent. But whose picture do you think was on the page of the review that night—*both* reviews? Old Man Valloooo! You can't be around for forty years without somehow making an impact upon those who have enjoyed years of efforts to bring pleasure in entertainment.

Our first gross from Philadelphia was only $25,000. By the third week we were up to $75,000 and by the end of the fifth, $90,000. I knew without any question that we had a smash hit. Other shows trying out in Philadelphia at the same time were Noel Coward's *Sail Away* and George Gobel's ill-fated musical version of *Three Men on a Horse*, both of which folded very shortly after opening in New York.

About the third week of the show in Philadelphia Frank Loesser decided to throw a lavish party on a Sunday night at the Warwick Hotel in the room where they have their tremendous Sunday afternoon buffets. He invited everyone who had anything to do with the show. As the evening neared its end, about 2:30 in the morning, Loesser and I were both seated at a large table. He was completely ossified and *non compos mentis*, which explains his reaction to my question, one that had been burning in me ever since the afternoon of the firing. I leaned over, and asked: "Frank, were you the person who started my ouster from the show?" He turned and stared at me through noncomprehending owllike eyes and said nothing. Perhaps I should have been more charitable as Loesser knew even then that his time was running out. Unable to cut down on his five-pack-a-day smoking, he was destined to die of cancer of the lungs two years after our great hit finally closed.

One afternoon at intermission Mrs. Vallée was at the bar in

the Shubert Theater lobby when Frank Loesser came in and sat beside her. "Your husband is the most disciplined man in the show," he told her. That was hardly any compliment to me because by contrast to the antics in which Robert Morse indulges, I *had* to be the most disciplined!

A great many persons have asked me about Robert Morse and I can only say that he is a very talented man and a very difficult man. Fortunately, I think Bobby liked me. Because, had he not liked me, he could have made life miserable for me. Morse has practically no discipline at all. At any moment he might lean over and talk to one of the orchestra boys or he might suddenly get behind me and give me a "goose." You never knew what Morse was going to do. It is probably this unpredictability that made him such a formidable talent. We cemented our friendship. Now when he comes to the Coast, he often stays with us. Morse is a mixed-up person, but a very talented one.

We looked forward to our return to New York and two or three weeks of previews for theater parties that had bought the tickets for a charity. And then the opening night, October 14, 1961.

I had looked at my dressing room in the 46th Street Theater before we had left for Philadelphia and had discovered that it was not a dressing room but a broom closet! It was roughly seven feet wide and about fourteen feet long, with a toilet and washstand at the end. Compared with the spacious, elegant room Robert Morse had in the number one dressing room, mine was indeed a disgrace. Morse had a large room with the toilet adjoining it. The room was large enough for a piano and a big couch.

I didn't mind—*I was in a hit show* and as long as I had room to dress, that's all I required. I did, however, write Abe Newborn and instruct him to take out the shelf that runs in front of the mirrors and the lights at which four or five performers who might be using the room made themselves up. Since I use a sun-lamp and no makeup, I didn't need this shelf. In its place I was going to put a contour chair so I might lie there and watch TV in front of my television set (which would be a kittie-corner for me down at the end near the toilet). I asked Abe Newborn to have the room painted in a light green and the covering of the contour chair in the same color. The walls were a hideous yellow, discolored, peeling, and in need of fresh paint.

After we drove back to New York, I walked backstage into the theater to put my things in the dressing room before our first show. My heart fell! Nothing had been touched, nothing had been done as I had requested in my letter. I had always been grateful to Abe Newborn for the trip he made with Cy Feuer to London, Ontario. But after my writing to him very clearly and explicitly what I wanted done to my dressing room, I felt this was a complete and callous disregard of my request, and inasmuch as I was going to pay him 10 percent of every week's salary, I felt I was more than entitled to a prompt response to my wishes.

It remained for Eleanor to accomplish what I had been unable to do in a letter. One afternoon in New York, during our preview rehearsals, back in the twentieth row were Burrows, Fosse, Feuer, Martin, Larry Kasha, and, of course, Frank Loesser. Mrs. Vallée had come in with two friends from Long Island to watch the rehearsal and on learning of my disappointment about the dressing room, her emotion got the better of her. She walked down the aisle to where these gentlemen sat. With tears streaming down her face, she delivered her valedictory speech. "You boys don't know my husband at all! You don't understand him at all! If you'll just give him one percent, he'll give you back ninety percent. He asked to have his dressing room repainted and a contour chair put in. And what did you do? *Nothing.* You don't know my husband! You treat him like a bum! He's liable to walk out on that stage and completely ruin everything, completely screw it up the way he feels now! You've been cruel, cruel, cruel!" Then she ran up the aisle, crying. Cy Feuer came out to her later, and said, "Rudy is a very lucky man to have a wife who loves him as you do. Don't worry about it, everything will be done!" By the next afternoon the room had been painted, the chair was in, and everything was fine and dandy.

The opening night in New York dwarfed even Philadelphia. At the end of the show the applause rang long, loud, and clear. We all knew that here we had perhaps one of the greatest musical smash hits of all time! There was not one uncomplimentary review. A few critics felt that our musical was not particularly outstanding, that is, for tune-whistling hits. But they did realize that every song fitted every scene perfectly, and although they were not truly great hit songs, they were great for this show. Otherwise, nothing but raves, raves, raves! And you must remember that this was a title that just begged for a kick in the pants. How easy it would have been to say "How to Succeed Doesn't!" instead of Walter Kerr's headline, "How to Succeed Really Does." Again, the reviews in New York were most kind, particularly to me. Bill Glover's (of the Associated Press) headline was "Vallée and Comic." One reviewer called it "The Vallée Show." All of them were most cordial and usually carried a sketch or photograph of Old Pappy Vallée.

The rest of it is history. The show ran for roughly three and a half years. It opened on the night of October 14, 1961. On the night of October 14, 1963, two years later, Morse left the show to make motion pictures. I stayed on and Morse's part was taken over by Darryl Hickman, who had a better singing voice but who didn't give to the elfin part what Robert Morse gave to it—that impish part of the little bastard who walked over everyone to get to the top! About three or four months into the show Virginia Martin foolishly left us for a flop show called *Little Me*. She was replaced by Joy Claussen, who did a fine job of the part of Hedy La Rue. Paul Reed left us for another flop show, the musical version of *Miracle on 34th Street*, and Charles Nelson Reilly left us to join Carol Channing in her show. These defections, of course, hurt a little, although the Burrows book was so good and the songs so great that really nothing could hurt the show, because it remains one of the best musicals of its type, so fast-paced, so well directed by Burrows, with joke after joke after joke paying off so handsomely, and every song fulfilling its part in the show.

How to Succeed in Business Without Really Trying will go down in history, in my book at least, as one of the finest musicals of all time. It won the Pulitzer Prize, and for Robert Morse a Tony. I will be forever grateful to Cy Feuer for wanting Old Man Vallée as J. B. Biggley!

Crisis No. 2: The Film

After the humiliating and traumatic shock of the ouster attempt of August 17, 1961, if anyone had suggested that I would again have to endure the agony of wondering and suspense concerning the possibility of my not being cast for the role of J. B. Biggley in the motion picture version of *How to Succeed in Busi-*

ness Without Really Trying, I would have laughed at him! But there it was!!

I knew that the film rights would be purchased by any one of the few remaining giants of picture making and suddenly appeared the announcement that United Artists had decreed that the brothers Mirisch would bring Abe Burrows' Pulitzer Prize-winning writing to the silver screen!

Reflecting on their Academy Award-winning films, *The Apartment* and *Some Like It Hot*, I felt that our baby was in very good hands. But I failed to reckon with the vagaries of those who seem so wise and yet at times so stupid and unpredictable!

My first surprise was the amount of money that the Mirisch Brothers paid for the right to make the film. Warner Brothers had paid almost $5 million for the privilege of making *My Fair Lady*, but the Mirisch boys drove a hard bargain and paid less than $2 million! I resented the easy cost of a production which had won far more raves than did any other musical of that era, but hoped that the Mirisch Brothers would make it up in a film that would outdo the Feuer and Martin stage production!

The columns duly noted that Norman Jewison would produce and direct it. Remembering his superb creation of *The Russians Are Coming*, I felt that our movie would be in very good hands!

Note, that I said *our movie!!* There was no doubt in my mind but that regardless of their choice of casting, old man Vallée would be in there giving his nephew hell and trying to pacify his inamorata, Hedy La Rue! Of course, it went without saying that Robert Morse would be the first choice to re-create his role, which he abandoned after doing it for two years to make motion pictures.

But as the days wore on without a call, from the West Coast film agent of General Artists Corporation or my newly acquired personal manager, who was billeted in the East, a call saying that I was being signed for so many thousand dollars, I began to feel the premonition that all was not too well along the Potomac!

Suddenly the rumor mongers had it that Bing Crosby was going to land the plum which had been mine for three solid years on Broadway and umpteen weeks all over the country in summer and winter stock companies! Billy Gilbert's widow, "Lolly," who had come to regard us as "family," rose to the challenge by calling Crosby's secretary and proceeding to castigate this poor bewildered soul for her employer's having the audacity to even *think* of taking the role away from Rudy Vallée! I don't actually know whether or not Bing *was* ever considered but "Lolly" certainly gave his secretary a bad time as the hapless secretary didn't have the slightest idea of what the hell "Lolly" was talking about!

Another rumor, which was too wild to really be considered as factual, had them thinking of Mickey Rooney for the role of Biggley—a most unlikely choice from the physical aspects of The Mick, but as to his actual portrayal of the role, Mickey would have done it full justice as he is a truly gifted thespian!

But only recently did I get it on good authority that Milton Berle really figured that he *had it in the palm of his hand!* I cannot imagine Berle in the role of J. B. Biggley, as I have always felt that this creation of Burrows' fertile imagination was an Anglo-Saxon, Gentile, Protestant, WASPish, truculent, Ivy League, old-school-tie, Westchester socialite–blue blood, snob–aristocrat old fart curmudgeon. And Milton Berle, for all his talents, is none of these!

But I breathed a sigh of relief when it was announced that the picture would be produced and directed by David Swift. In fact, I shouted with joy when I read this announcement!

During the second year of my run of *How to Succeed* in New York, an agent named Jerry Bick had relayed an offer to me to do an important role in the Columbia Pictures production of *Good Neighbor Sam*, which would star Jack Lemmon. I was terribly flattered when David Swift not only phoned me from California, telling me how much he wanted me for the role, but that he was flying to New York to try to effect my release from the show for the three weeks it would take to film my part in the picture. In my dressing room, Swift further inflated my ego by telling me he wanted me so badly, it hurt!

The money was really "good" but when we asked Feuer and Martin for my three weeks off from the show to do the picture, our hopes were completely dashed and Swift flew back to seek another for the role. (It went to a most unlikely candidate, Edward G. Robinson, who was to portray a Scandinavian man, a tall and hulking giant dairy tycoon. Robinson somehow did not seem *physically* right for the role, but nevertheless he carried it off quite well!)

It remained for Swift, after reassuring me that I would "get" the role of Biggley, to simply inform the top brass at United Artists that they were to cut all this horseshit and that if they wanted him to direct the picture, then Rudy Vallée would be the *only choice for the role of J. B. Biggley!*

In memoriam, it really pained me to have to dole out $8,000 in commissions to two Shylocks who had absolutely nothing whatever to do with my landing the part in the United Artists film. But a contract is a contract and even though they knew they were taking money under false pretenses, they, of course, took it and ran to the bank.

When I worked in my first film for Preston Sturges, who gave me the best role of my film career in *The Palm Beach Story*, I vowed as did Eddie Bracken, to give my right arm if he ever needed it. Later on, when the fortunes of this giant film maker were at their lowest ebb, both Eddie and I were able to help him out of his sea of troubles for at least a short time. So did I now vow that if David Swift ever needed whatever assistance I could offer, he had only to ask for it!

Knowing Berle's colossal ego, I can imagine his consternation when he realized that he was not going to land this choice plum in a great film!

Crisis No. 3: Bless You, Jim Backus!

I had been out of the New York run of *How to Succeed* for almost a year when I received a call from a Glenn Jordan in Minneapolis, Minnesota. Evidently he was Mr. Big in the Minneapolis Civic Light Opera Company and was about to stage *How to Succeed* in that city.

The price was eminently satisfactory, but his demand that I give his production two weeks of rehearsal raised the hackles on my back, as I had made it a firm stipulation in the several other instances of offers to do the role in various parts of the country, that I needed actually *only one day's* rehearsal for a part that I had done for three solid years. But I would give them *four days!*

I work with only a few persons in the show and my lines can be fed to those who are learning it for the first time by someone else; once they have the lines, it is a simple matter of meshing our lines in two or three runs through. As proof of this, I cite the case of a week with a company that had been doing it in Canada but was now to do it in Albany. Due to the booking immediately following their week in another city, the only rehearsal was one runthrough the afternoon of the opening night in Albany. The rest of the cast knew their parts perfectly. We meshed beautifully during the afternoon runthrough and the opening night was a complete success!

Suddenly, Jordan switched from the subject of the number of days' rehearsal to a demand that I drop a line which is my first really solid laugh as I am on the phone, talking to my wife, who is trying to persuade me to promote her sister's son, my nephew, whom I detest. I snarl, "If I did that it would be nepotism! Nepotism!! That's when your nephew is a Goddamned fool!!"

Oh, I am well aware that this line shocks some of the more religious in the audience and on certain Wednesday matinees, when a large portion of the audience is made up of squeamish old biddies, usually on a junket from Atlanta, Georgia, I can sense their shocked gasps as I say, "is a Goddamned fool!!" Ah! but I love to shock 'em! I put all I can muster into the reading of that line.

When Jordan issued this ultimatum to me over the phone, I really blew my stack and simply said, "Fuck you!" and *hung up on him.*

I couldn't imagine then how I would regret my loss of temper, but live and learn and I assure you that I am not likely to ever again sin as I burned my bridges on that phone call!

My first realization that I had really pulled a boner was when Mr. Jordan staged *How to Succeed* in Kansas City and St. Louis. Of course he used Robert Morse, and of course Morse did not point out to Mr. Jordan that the latter should swallow his pride and hurt to achieve the best possible production of the show.

Obviously, the audience is interested in only one thing and that is to expect and demand the best show that Mr. Jordan can present to them. Petty jealousies and arguments do not concern the audience and this should have been paramount in everyone's mind, but human beings can be very easily hurt and not too ready to forgive and overlook a burst of temper, however justified.

No, I did not play those two cities as Willard Waterman, who had played the role of J. B. Biggley in our second road show company, was brought from Hollywood, where he had taken over the role of The Great Gildersleeve when Hal Peary, who had created it, had had a row with his sponsors!

I was quite busy that summer; so it did not perturb me too much. Still, I felt hurt that Morse had not put up some kind of a fight to have me by his side as I had been so happily for two years in New York. But now I was to really destroy myself *and ruin* my chances of ever expecting any quarter from Glenn Jordan.

I was startled to read that Glenn Jordan was being groomed for the top executive spot in The Los Angeles Civic Light Opera Association to replace Edwin Lester, who had guided the fortunes of the Civic Light Opera probably from its inception! I had dined at the home of one of my closest friends, the great composer Rudolph Friml, with Edwin Lester the only other guest of the evening. Over the years since that dinner in 1940, I had called Mr. Lester's office for special tickets and had always received the warmest courtesies. Thus, when I read the reviews of Mr. Jordan's maiden effort, which was really a bomb, I made a copy of these devastating reviews and mailed them to Edwin Lester, castigating him for his choice of successor to our Civic Light Opera. It never occurred to me that someday our Civic Light Opera Association might put on their own production of *How to Succeed.*

But the run of Robert Morse in David Merrick's stage play of the Mirisch film, *Some Like It Hot,* now titled *Sugar,* out here in Los Angeles, had been so successful that Morse was now importuned to not only perform, but to direct the production of *How to Succeed* during the summer months at the Music Center!

I had enjoyed *Sugar* twice in New York and had visited Morse in his dressing room on both occasions only to find him using the same young dresser (a star who makes many changes must have the assistance of a person who is trained in the art of dressing an actor) who had been my dresser during the last two years of my run in New York.

The New York run of *Sugar* had been only fairly successful as mixed reviews really crippled the production.

Morse on his previous visits to Hollywood for film and TV work had always called us and on the occasion when we did a

"Night Gallery" sequence in which, as a demented surgeon, I cut off his feet to make it impossible for him to leave my residence where I discover his gift of predicting the winners in the stock market and at the races, Morse occupied our guest room. But during the summer run of *Sugar* he failed to contact us at all and since we felt that we should not intrude upon him, we respected his wish to remain aloof, regardless of what provoked it.

As his engagement in *Sugar* was about to end, there suddenly appeared in Bill Edwards' column in *Daily Variety* the announcement that Robert Morse was to star in *How to Succeed* in the summer of 1975. I screamed at Edwards, "Didn't you ask if Rudy Vallée was going to be in the production?" to which Edwards embarrassedly replied that it just hadn't occurred to him to ask. I suggested that he do so, but of course he never did!

The *Sugar* production next went to San Francisco for a short run there.

Enter Joy Claussen, whom you have seen in all the "Aim" toothpaste commercials on television.

Joy performed as Hedy La Rue, my inamorata in the New York run of *How to Succeed*, for a little over two years and now, with her TV "Aim" millions had come out to the Coast to seek film and TV work. For some reason, David Swift had not chosen her for the film of *How to Succeed*, which was unfortunate as she does the role superbly and, being the same height as J. B. Biggley, she is thoroughly believable in the role and endows it with the humor the role demands. She had taken the loss of the film role very unhappily and refused to ever see it on its many TV showings.

She now had set her heart on getting the role at the Music Center, realizing that this was the best showcase for her talents. Her agent, on trying to interest Glenn Jordan in using her, had been put off with Jordan's laconic rejoinder, "I've never heard of her!"

Joy was now asking me if she should phone Robert Morse in San Francisco.

I laid out for her consideration, my hard-line thoughts on the making of a phone call to secure a favor or anything of that nature from the callee.

Reflect, if you will, just what you are doing when you phone anyone to ask for or to secure a concession from this person. You are choosing the time and place of battle and, more importantly, the weapons! Your adversary (because that is *exactly* what the person you are phoning *is*) may have just awakened with a miserable hangover or may have just emerged from the bathroom after a fruitless attempt on the toilet seat and is ready to bite nails. You can imagine the rebuff you are going to receive as you begin your plea to extract something from him! Even if you were calling to *give* him something, you are assuming that he is in a frame of mind to discuss the matter with you.

If he had been prepared for your call or had an inkling of your request he might have been more receptive to this unexpected call. Human beings do not like surprises, especially when they require that one make an effort to do something for someone else and which will benefit him not at all!

We had come to know Joy very well and my wife and Joy had become almost inseparable. When Joy had finally bought a home, we had helped her furnish it.

I now suggested that I should write Morse and ask his help in securing the role for Joy. In my letter, I said that we were not hurt by his failure to call us and that I knew that Jordan would not want me for the part of Biggley but Joy needed this role very badly and that anything he could do to help her get it would be a godsend to her.

Morse suddenly called me to explain that he was having problems with his marriage, which was why he hadn't called *anyone* during his stay in Los Angeles.

He then proceeded to try to convince me that although he was going to direct the production, that he had only 50 percent of the casting authority. Then he demolished me as he informed me that there were those in authority in the Civic Light Opera Board of Directors who considered Rudy Vallée too old for the part, also lacking the energy and power to project in the huge Dorothy Chandler Pavilion in which the Academy Awards have been held for the past two years.

Recall that once before on the afternoon of August 17, 1961, when after being informed that I was to be dropped from the New York production of *How to Succeed,* on asking Abe Burrows why, he had sadly informed me that the twelve hours a day of rehearsals when we went to Philadelphia would be too much for my decrepit and aging body and that I just wouldn't be able to "take it"! Yet, with one foot in the grave, I was the only member of the entire cast who never missed a show in three solid years! Now once again, the spectre of my age and loss of vitality were coming up to haunt me. Frankly, I have never been in better health and during a week in Kansas City, when playing the Muny Opera at night, I played five hours of steady tennis every afternoon in the hot Missouri sun! I am the last one to cry quits after two or three hours of tennis on weekends.

That Jordan might not wish to use me, I had already conceded, but how could I convince these oldsters that I was not one of them in spite of my age? However, Morse placated me slightly

With Robert Morse and Joy Claussen in the LosAngeles/San Francisco Civic Light Opera presentation of *How to Succeed* . . .

by informing me that all was not lost and that no decision would be made until March or April of 1975 and that he was still in there, rooting for me!

The crowning blow came when I was informed that a firm offer of $3,500 had been made to Jim Backus to play the part of Biggley! Yet, apparently he had not accepted it!

The offer to Backus was made by an agent whom I have known for many years and who has always tried to lay every girl I have ever known. I knew this agent well enough to have expected him to do what Cary Grant did when Jack Warner stupidly offered the part of Dr. Doolittle to Grant only to have Grant not only refuse the offer but rebuke Warner for not using the only person who should do the role he had created on Broadway—namely, Rex Harrison!

I resolved never to speak to this agent again, but when he called me about a college concert, after castigating him for his relaying the offer to Backus, he informed me that he had almost refused to offer it to Backus (and that it actually was $2,500 and not $3,500!) and when he had talked with Backus' wife (Backus was in the East) she had simply said that she wouldn't even tell Jim about it as he couldn't do it at all and rarely did stage shows!

This, of course, was my big break as now they had to find someone else for the role. There was talk of Dick Haymes. They auditioned Don de Fore, but it was still wide open.

I now resolved to try to heal the breach of friendship between Glenn Jordan and Rudy Vallée! I wrote a very simple letter in which I threw myself on the mercy of the court. I tried to bring home to him how miserable I would be in the agony of sitting on the "bench" and watching someone else doing the role in my hometown! Too many persons have echoed Abe Burrows' admission the night of our runthrough before those who had invested in it that they told him that I was the only person for the role and asked who was the genius who had chosen me for the part of J. B. Biggley! I pleaded with Jordan not to do this unthinkable wrong to me and said that I would crawl on my hands and knees to secure his forgiveness for my crude and unwarranted remark on the phone back in 1965. And as for rehearsals, I told him I would give him months of rehearsals and that neither billing nor money entered into it at all!

I can be grateful that Glenn Jordan is a fine, decent human being who does not carry a grudge forever and is willing to put an affront behind him as he did after receiving my letter. But there was still the objection to my securing the role from others of the Board. However, I now had two protagonists in my corner!

It was Edwin Lester who felt that Willard Waterman was the better choice, and my agent and I descended upon him and Jordan to try to settle it once and for all. Jordan had been suffering horribly with a fractured hip and on the afternoon of our meeting was not present. I discovered that Lester had been a fellow musician, pianist–orchestra leader, and song writer.

Suddenly Lester delivered an ultimatum which caused my heart to sink.

He declared that if he used any of the original cast that his fellow Angelinos (old-time Los Angeles aristocratic residents who make up the bulwark of the season subscribers to the Music Center offerings) would scream at him and rebuke him for using those tired old has-beens of the original New York Company! Yet in using Morse, who by now was fourteen years older, he was using one of these old "retreads," and later I discovered that Lester had offered the role of Rosemary to Michele Lee of the original company but she had simply refused it!

Near the end of our two-hour discussion, Lester seemed to be asleep as I detailed the story of the ouster in New York in 1961. I left with the feeling that I had accomplished absolutely nothing and that if Edwin Lester had his way, it would be Willard Waterman who did the role at the Music Center!

There followed several phone calls between Morse and me. I finally wrote a letter in which I tried to bring home to him very clearly that if he actually did use only newcomers to the roles, persons who had never done it anywhere at all, he was biting off one hell of a wad to put together this very intricate and difficult fast-paced show in three weeks and that he could only wonder on the opening night, whether some of these local thespians might not be wandering around the stage without the slightest idea of where they were supposed to go and what their lines were!

I closed my letter by pleading with him to grab the only person who can play the part of the head of the mail room in the first act and the chairman of the board in the second act. After

Another photograph from the Los Angeles/San Francisco Civic Light Opera version of *How to Succeed* . . .

doing it with a dozen or more actors who tried to accomplish this, I warned Bobby Morse that if Sammy Smith was available, he had best grab him—but fast! A week later, I read that Sammy Smith was signed! As I flew East to guest with Paul Williams on the Grammy Awards and to do a concert at Skidmore College in Saratoga Springs, New York, Morse finally delivered the decision which would determine my fate at the Music Center. If I would perform on the stage of the Dorothy Chandler Pavilion—read and sing and satisfy Glenn Jordan that I could be heard and have sufficient projection to reach the back of this big theater—I *might* win the role!

Thus, on March 10, together with Joy Claussen, I read the lines we have together and sang our song, "The Heart of Gold," which we each do separately and partly as a duet. We did it with microphones on our person (Joy could be heard a mile away, but she did it anyway) and then without any amplification as Mr. Lester doesn't like the use of microphones. I was told that they'd let me know either that night or the following morning.

My agent called me at six o'clock that night to tell me it looked very good and Morse called at midnight to happily say that not only was I to play Biggley, but Joy had also been accepted! Suffice to say, my favorite champagne flowed freely that night and the terrible strain of the preceding weeks was now over.

The show opened Tuesday night, the thirteenth of May, for seven weeks in Los Angeles and seven in San Francisco, beginning July 1.

At our first straight runthrough with no stopping we were observed by not only Glenn Jordan but Cy Feuer, who had first offered the part to me in the Polo Lounge of the Beverly Hills Hotel on the afternoon of January 6, 1961. Morse was smart enough to invite Feuer out to help him stage the show as Feuer is a very astute individual and was responsible for many of the best moments of the show.

Frankly, the runthrough was so well done that we could have opened days before if the stage hands had resolved all their lighting and scenery problems.

The rest of my story is really L'envoi, and although all of this may seem like a tempest in a teapot to many who have read this far, I assure you that it was something of deep and serious import to me and some of those whom I consider real and sincere friends!

To these good souls who have literally been keeping their fingers crossed and, sometimes, praying, that I would come out of this as I had the two previous unhappy experiences, I can only offer my deepest and heartfelt thanks. It is my hope that maybe after the opening, even as Abe Burrows spoke for those who had doubted my ability to carry off the role of J. B. Biggley during the rehearsals in New York, that maybe those of the Los Angeles Civic Light Opera who were skeptical and who honestly felt that I was over the hill and should have long ago been put out to pasture, may cry "mea culpa" and ask me to forgive their lack of faith in me and admit that there is life in the old dog, yet!

There are few more fields left to conquer but I assure you that I will never again burn my bridges as I did on the phone when I received a call from Glenn Jordan in Minneapolis, Minnesota.

PART III
OFFSTAGE

My Most

Unforgettable

He was eighty-two in the spring of 1949. One night my sister phoned to say that Dad had made a little cry from the bedroom and was gone.

Gone! I could hardly believe it! I would never forget him.

He had twinkling eyes set in a round, chubby, unlined face. He looked for all the world like a little, fat French priest. With a homburg perched jauntily on his head he went sauntering along, his left leg slightly bowed out, swinging the cane he occasionally used for support. With spats and the flowing black tie he always wore when not in the drugstore he looked somewhat like Winston Churchill. In fact, during the war while he visited me in New York, the casual passerby thought it *was* Churchill. Dad loved it!

I was supposed to be a great guy with the ladies, but if I could have been one-half the success he was I wouldn't have known some of the grief I have had in my lifetime. Dad was always covered with lipstick. Women—young and old—hung onto the stories he told. Lovers' toasts—happy tales—always

18

Character

preceded the drinks he mixed with the art of a druggist, which he was for forty years.

Dad was one of a family of twelve boys and one girl. The first Vallée—Dad loved to tell this—came over with Lafayette on his second trip to help the colonies. After the war he settled in Quebec, Canada. At the age of ninety he was one of the finest ice skaters in all of Canada. Dad's father was a tinsmith, although he looked more like Victor Hugo, or a preacher, with his crew cut, short beard, and the casual, quiet way he smoked a pipe. But the Vallée kids had to hustle and work.

Dad never went beyond the sixth grade and did very little studying on the side; so it's difficult to explain how during World War I he was one of the speakers the government asked to tour theaters in Maine and talk for four minutes (before the picture began) about liberty bonds.

My father had something the others didn't have. He could speak first in French—beautifully, flowingly, dramatically—and then in English, without a trace of an accent, except for his determination to call "cinch" "skinch," and his pronunciation of "four" as "fo"—something like a southerner. Both of these pronunciations used to drive Mother crazy!

After a short course in a pharmaceutical school, Dad's feet unerringly went to the drugstore. He spent the next forty years first as a clerk in Vermont and then as a partner in a small drugstore in Rumford Falls, Maine. Finally, for twenty-four years he was the proud proprietor of his own drugstore in Westbrook, Maine.

I think he always loved the theater. Whether I got my obsession for show business and the love of music from Dad, I don't know. He liked to tell how back in Vermont he had a little town band he pretended to direct, although only four of the fifteen members could actually play their horns. I can hazily recollect Dad getting them in front of the opera house to play at election time.

The raccoon coat denoted true opulence and success to collegians in the 1927 era—in the 30s, too, for that matter.

My Dad—Charles A. Vallée

I remember how, in Rumford, Maine, Dad Vallée would fill his drugstore window with bright shiny Lincoln pennies to give away to kids who went to the matinee on Saturday afternoons; and how he would gather up the stale candy that had collected in the drugstore show windows and had hardened in the sun. He put it into little sacks to make grab-bags for the kids on Saturday afternoon matinees. What deal he worked out with the theater management, I'll never know. Maybe he gave the candy away for the sheer fun of seeing the kids grab for it.

Dad was always a showman. He had the first fancy *white marble* soda fountain in that part of Maine. He had a way of taking a prosaic thing, such as a soda fountain, and making it glow with life. His description of it before its arrival in Westbrook had people watering at the mouth to see it. Dad loved to tell how he was the first to introduce the banana split—"Spleet," as he pronounced it. He didn't exaggerate; they sold like hotcakes.

We opened the store together every Sunday morning at 7:00, putting the Sunday newspapers together, sweeping out the store, bringing up the ice (chopping twenty pails of it to pack around the ice cream). Drunks would wander in off the street for their early bromo seltzers. Dad always had a kind word and some sort of consolation for them. In fact, like most druggists, he was the town confessor. People told him their troubles, even asked him to prescribe for them when they were ill.

Dad was smart enough, though, not to mix in their religious arguments and fights. Our town of Westbrook was populated on one side of the river by the French-Canadian Catholics, on the other by the predominantly Protestant Irish and Scotch mill workers and the Anglo-Saxon collegiate elite. Naturally, nationality and religion could become quite an issue in a small town like Westbrook.

He was a fine druggist. He religiously attended the annual Rexall conventions, always with Mother. For many years he was a joy and a delight to the brass hats of the growing Rexall Company. The head man of 7,000 Rexall stores, Louis K. Liggett, loved him. He often had Dad help handle the great crowds of participating druggists. Dad had an art of taking ordinary alcohol, mixing it with a harmless pink syrup, and making a drink that was later referred to as "white mule" or "liquid dynamite."

That's where Dad and I differed. He enjoyed being among people. He could have outdone Art Linkletter, Ralph Edwards, and all the other emcees. He liked to know people—their towns, their origins, their families, and what they thought. My mother was English-Irish, with plenty of reserve, which she handed down to me. Once I am among them I can enjoy people and be happy with them, but as a rule I don't seek them as Dad did.

Dad once stayed with me (1945, it was) in my present home in the Hollywood Hills. It's one of the most unusual homes in the world, and I thought he would be thrilled to see what his boy had finally been able to call "home." I was heartbroken when I learned indirectly that he had told his cronies at the Elk's Club: "By God, it's like Alcatraz!" I hadn't realized that I and the two boys who worked for me were so busy during the day that we left Dad stranded with no way of getting down the hill (he couldn't drive). Unknown to me, he was itching to get down to the Elk's Club to be with the boys, to wander around town, and to be among people.

I took Dad on a five-day junket that Warner Brothers lavishly arranged to plug the picture *Santa Fe*. A couple hundred of us went to Santa Fe, New Mexico on special trains and airplanes. There were comfortable hotel accommodations, excellent food and liquor, beautiful women, stars and noted personalities. And who do you think the hero of the occasion was? Dad! Whenever I met Charlie Einfeld, who handled the entire trip for Warner Brothers, or Arthur Unger, who published the *Daily Variety* in Hollywood, they always remarked about the wonderful trip we had on the Santa Fe junket, but whom do you think they asked about? "Where's that Dad of yours?"

It used to drive Mother crazy, but Dad apparently never had a care in the world. Actually he did, but for some reason he rarely showed it before Mother. I know he worried about the drugstore, and about us kids, and all the little things that happened to us I know sobered and saddened him. When I say sobered, I don't mean from drinking. Except for an occasional cigar and a very rare sip of wine or a bottle of beer, he was quite temperate! He had a constitution like iron, which he inherited from his great-grandfather—the one who skated at the age of ninety. Dad could put away two lobsters, dripping with butter, salted and seasoned until he started sneezing from the pepper, followed by a piece of apple pie with cheese, all washed down with a couple of bottles of beer, and go to bed and sleep as a babe.

The neighbors could set their clocks by Dad's departure to the drugstore, a fifth of a mile away, which he walked every day at one o'clock.

Dad's list of stories wasn't very long and his toasts were few in number, but he had a way of telling them as though it was for the first time, even to listeners who were hearing them for the umpteenth time. I always found myself joining in with Dad in the torrents of laughter with which he always finished his own stories and toasts. It wasn't at all necessary that he do it, but he used his toasts as a means of departing from his usual abstinence to enjoy the delights of several cocktails. He always got the crowd into the same mood.

He was brought up in a devout Catholic background. Without stopping to inquire what I might want to do, or for what I was most purposefully bent, Dad would have had me become a priest. Can you imagine the Vagabond Lover singing out the mass? Fortunately for me, Mother, who loved music and somehow sensed my innate desire to become a showman, put her foot down, and said, "No." I was left to my own natural bent. Even so, Dad was determined that I follow in his footsteps and take over in the drugstore. He didn't know how I hated it: the long drudgery; the chopping of twenty pails of ice in the morning, and twenty pails at night, lugging them up a flight of stairs to the soda fountain to be packed around the eight or more flavors of ice cream we sold; the endless and interminable opening of boxes and putting away of thousands of drug products and packages; the selling of a million and one items that a drugstore has to sell—from cigarettes to rolls of film. Dad loved all of this, because it brought him close to people.

He was a great believer in the art of French courtesy and charm. I can see him today as he would walk out from behind the fountain and approach a stout, apple-cheeked farm woman who was waiting for a streetcar. From out of the cold she would come into our drugstore, put down all her packages, which she had bought elsewhere, he knew (she wasn't going to spend a nickel with us), but with the air of Cyrano de Bergerac, Dad would pull out one of the chairs from behind a soda-fountain table near the window, and say, "Will madam be seated?" The red face of the farm woman would flush with pride and pleasure as she let herself drop into the seat. All the French savoir-faire, gallantry, and courtesy of centuries expressed itself in Charles Alphonse Valleé as his little fat figure bent over the 200-pound lady in the faded gingham dress, and said, "Will madam be seated?" Dad had quite a knack of saying things—beautiful little phrases—and I am happy I had him as my pattern. He had one little trick, though, which he would say with a smile after one of our mill workers would ask for a favor. He would exclaim, "With the greatest of *animosity!*" And the $1-a-day mill worker would beam, and say, "Oh, thank you, Mr. Vallée!"

Dad and I never got along in the drugstore, though I was one of the best clerks he had. I could handle three people while the average clerk was handling one. Of course, Dad knew he could trust me implicitly. Some of the clerks practically stole the store from under us. Dad knew as long as I was there when he was out for lunch or on his day off (which he seldom took), at least the clerks would be able to take less. Most storekeepers accept a certain amount of petty thievery, just as hotel and restaurant owners do with their silverware and napkins. Dad seemed to be singularly unfortunate. I know of at least two discoveries in the years I worked in the store of clerks who had practically given expensive items away, or had rung up half the price in the cash register and had put the other half in their pockets. Dad never prosecuted, and never seemed to hold a grudge when the offender was finally caught. We did a terrific business for a small drugstore in the 10,000-people town. Saturdays and Sundays eight to nine clerks was the rule rather than the exception. We stayed open until 10:30 and even later when streetcars brought in excursionists from nearby Riverton Amusement Park.

I think it broke Dad's heart when we quarreled and I walked out of the store, never to return as a steady clerk. It changed the whole course of my life, and I'm glad it happened. I inherited Dad's hot French temper, and he really let go with it when he thought there had been an injustice done, or when he sensed stupidity. I worked in the store only occasionally, during my off-school hours, on busy days, in the evenings, and on Sundays. Dad felt I should know where all the thousand-and-one trays of patent medicines should be. Instead of showing me where an item was, Dad delighted in standing a little distance away and trying to point it out to me verbally. When I failed to pick out the particular product I wanted from the maze of labels he would blow his top, and I would blow right back at him. This always bewildered a customer who didn't know quite what to make of the fuss he was causing. People came to know the Vallée tempers, and I guess we had quite a reputation in town for our give and take.

Dad was as generous a father as a boy will ever want to have. There wasn't anything I ever asked for that, if he could afford it, I didn't get. We ate like millionaires—the best of everything— and Dad, of course, always brought ice cream home for our Sunday lunch. Mother was a good cook, and a wonderful wife, and loved Dad dearly in spite of her impatience with his failure to worry.

It never occurred to Dad to sit down and ask me what I might want to do, or to discuss my schooling with me. I would have dropped dead had he ever asked me to sit down and discuss what I was studying. It would have been a great source of pleasure to me had he been so inclined. He loved his children very dearly, but he seemed to be unwilling to break down and give us the same warmth and charm he showered upon people outside the family. It's a strange contradiction, but it expressed itself on the morning that changed the entire course of my life.

The head clerk had put chocolate syrup in a lime juice jug. When out came the chocolate syrup instead of the lime juice, I blew up. Dad stuck up for the head clerk when I demanded to know who had done it. I stamped out of the store and went to the river for a swim to cool off.

Dad had bought me a Harley-Davidson motorcycle, which was to be my reward for working two and a half months during the summer vacation.

I then got a job setting up pins in a bowling alley until Dad blacklisted me there and in three other places where I tried to work. Finally, I got a job as a projectionist in our only film theater. There, fortunately, the manager (the brother-in-law of the head clerk who screwed up the lime juice), who, incidentally, was the first person I ever saw who wore a headpiece or toupée, told me that if I suited him Dad could go chase himself. I was living with a friend for the two weeks I worked in the theater. One night the chief of police (of our three-man police force) met me outside the theater and told me that Dad was reconciled to my working in the theater, and my mother wanted me home. After that Dad seemed to be sympathetic to the fact that I loved show business. He let me continue for fourteen months working in that theater, which led to another big new deluxe theater where the chief electrician turned over a saxophone he was renting. He beguiled me with the idea that I could play it when I went to see my girl on Sunday nights while she played the piano. That was the beginning of my career in show business.

Dad called me a cheap faker and ordered me out of the house when I tried to practice at noon. It disturbed his reading the newspaper after lunch. That didn't seem to deter him from proudly showing me off after dinner and asking me to play the saxophone with my sister at the piano for some traveling salesmen whom Dad had brought home for dinner. When I asked him for $80 to sil- verplate the brass saxophone I was renting, he refused—and again called me a cheap faker! In a way he was right. At that time I couldn't read music, and I was playing—as we popularly called it—"by ear."

I'll never forget that Sunday noon when he opened the *Port- land Evening Express* and saw the Strand Theater ad—the same

In front of the Star Theatre, Westbrook, Maine, talking with Fred Eugley, whom I went to work for in 1917. When I told him of my father's objections to my working outside the drugstore he said, "Screw your father! If you suit me you work here!" Fred was the brother-in-law of Aimée Boisaneau, who put the lime juice in the chocolate jug (or vice versa), which changed the course of my life. Fred had the first toupee I had ever seen. (Photo taken in 1930 during my three-day homecoming.)

theater where I had worked for a year as a projectionist and head usher. There was to be a saxophone soloist to accompany a Gloria Swanson picture as a feature on the bill: "Hubert Vallée, Saxophone Soloist." I peeked around behind the newspaper and saw two tears steal down his cheeks. After that, there was no question about plating the saxophone.

After my triumphant appearance at the Strand the world was mine! Fate and life have been good to me, but I hope I will have people feel about me as they felt about my father. Perhaps as I grow older I will come to like people as he did.

Dad was internationally loved. He toured with the Kiwanis Club and the Maine farmer delegation that went to Europe years ago. Wherever the group went, particularly in France, he was the hit of the day. He alone of the rest could speak two languages and he gave the benediction to the toasts in the beautiful way that only Charlie Vallée could.

Dad believed in not sparing the rod. I smarted many times under his broad razor strap during our trips to the attic after I had done something wrong, fancied or otherwise, in spite of Mother's tears and entreaties. These trips will remain with me to my dying day. Perhaps they had their value, I don't know. Whether it was Dad's strong hand or my experience in the navy in World War I—somewhere I learned the value of implicit obedience and respect for authority. It was hard for me when I saw Dad watching me perform in a nightclub or a radio show to imagine that he was once the stern father who used to whip the daylights out of me.

Later I could do no wrong. No radio show ever failed to come off for Dad. I finished some shows that I knew were far from being good ones, but Dad was always there waiting for me in the wings with a beatific light in his little blue eyes, and a big smile as he looked searchingly in my face for the truth. In *his* face and

Taken in Chasen's Restaurant, Beverly Hills (1939). *Left to right:* Wendy Barrie, Frank Morgan, Dad Vallée, myself, and W. C. Fields. A year later, the New York Leones of Mamma Leone's tried to establish a Hollywood Leone's on the Sunset Strip. On Thanksgiving Day, 1940, we who were pioneers of the New York Leone's hosted a dinner for fifty poor children, ages twelve to sixteen. Dad accompanied me then, too.

demeanor there was no question about how the show came off! It's all summed up in his little phrase—so reminiscent of Clarence Day's father: "By God! That was a good one, wasn't it?" "By God! That was a corker!" "By God! That was an elegant show, eh? Eh? Eh?" Dad believed that if words could make it so, it must have been!

His letters were a joy to read. He typed them himself and they had certain grammatical errors and some phrases I could hardly make out. He loved to tell me how he was taking care of his home garden (he canned his own vegetables), how his sweet peas were growing, and how his cold of the past week had kept him from getting down to the Elk's Club to join the boys.

At eighty-two years he was still a marvel. He was beginning to slow down just a little, but he would have been the last one to admit it and would resent anyone suggesting that he take it easy. He had never known a day of illness.

No fighter in the ring ever had a better second, or manager, who believed in him any more than Dad believed in me. With an inspiration like that, I must go on trying to entertain people and to take some of those qualities I inherited from him and put them to better use! He appeared on my radio show on several occasions. He loved to make these appearances, and in nightclubs he was hurt if I didn't call on him. He especially loved to come up on stage. He would clutch the microphone with both hands as though it would run away from him. In later life he wasn't the speaker he used to be. He no longer had the command of words of the agile mind of forty or fifty. I reminded him again and again when we'd get close to the time I was going to introduce him that it was "Heigh ho, everybody!" And the "H" of the "Heigh" should be heard. After Dad jauntily swung out to the floor and grabbed the microphone with trembling hands, it always came out "I owe, everybody!" Then the word "This," followed by a magnificent pause as he thought to impress his audience with the pride in his next statement, "is Rudy's Dad!" (He always trilled the "R.")

I knew what Dad was going to say, as he had memorized a little tribute to me. Clutching the microphone, he cried: "I owe everybody! This (with first finger right hand stabbing the air) is Rudy Vallée's Dad! (Big hand.) Beneath the complexity of his career, the splendor of his home and his fame, Rudy Vallée is still the same small-town boy who whilst manning my *sodee* fountain (I could never get him to remember that's "sod*ah*") was dreaming of greater things to come! When I came into this hall (I reminded him that it might be a theater, nightclub, or auditorium, but he always called it a hall), I became aware of your splendid city with its gracious buildings (I said, 'Dad, *graceful*, not *gracious*—buildings cannot be gracious!'), its progressive citizenrrrry, and last but not least (with a leer out of the corner of his eyes) its charming and beautiful ladies!" (Tremendous applause!)

I always worried for fear that some night when he was terribly tired he would forget parts of his little speech. Inasmuch as it was supposed to be an impromptu tribute to me, even though I knew what he was supposed to say, I couldn't prompt him! My fears were borne out one night at the Astor roof in New York in 1937. The boys in the band looked at me, and we nearly died when Dad began to falter halfway through the traditional discourse about the boy from Maine. It was an agonizing moment, but Dad pulled out of it, made up a new talk, and finished up in a blaze of glory!

When he visited me shortly after the war I was substituting for Ken Murray in his *Blackouts* while the latter was enjoying a much-needed rest. Following the Elder Lovelies, a group of ladies ranging in ages from fifty to seventy, I came on to make my little opening speech, and then came Dad, escorted by two of the Elder Lovelies. This particular appearance was at Christmas time, and Dad loved to tell a little story about Santa Claus. It's a cute story in poem form, with a little surprise and almost eyebrow-raising finish. Knowing that Dad was inclined to occasional lapses of memory, I suggested that he give me a copy of the poem so I could prompt him in case he forgot it any night. Without realizing it, I trod upon his great vanity. What? Need me to prompt him? He would forget it? Never in a million years! Well, of course, the inevitable happened. One night he got to the second stanza of the poem and—dead end! He was smart enough to go back and start all over again, figuring that the psychological billiard-ball reaction would eventually get him through. But again —dead end! He went back a third time, and by then it was becoming terribly embarrassing, not only to me but to the audi-

Dad with two of Ken Murray's Elder Lovelies in Murray's *Blackouts*

The Westbrook High School Orchestra, 1920 (Yours truly the second young man from the left, back row)

ence. Again he reached the same place and there was the awful impasse.

This time his son's wit saved the day. I leaned over, and said "Dad, how about the toast about the flea?"

"What?"

"How about the little toast about the flea?" I repeated.

He smiled, and cried, "Of course! Of course! Of course! Of course!"

This broke the tension and the crowd roared with laughter as Dad remembered his little toast. "Here's to the little bounding flea; it's hard to tell the sex, you see. It's hard to tell the *he* from the *she*, but *she* knows, and so does *he*." Off he went, triumphant over all adversity.

Dad Vallée never owed anyone anything. If he couldn't afford an item, he didn't buy it. He paid for everything when he got it, and sometimes before it came. He instilled that quality into all of us. He never said anything about it, but we just knew that anything the Vallées had, they owned! Even in my college days when I worked my way through Yale, I didn't buy a fur coat until I had the money to buy it. Las Vegas, the banks, and all the loan companies will hate me for this!

Dad, likewise, never gambled, either in a betting way or in an investment. Because there is so much of my father in me, I, too, have never wanted nor had the slightest desire to make even a light bet on a collegiate game or a horse race. It was probably Dad speaking in me when in 1929 the fellow who managed me at NBC (who prided himself on being a smart businessman and who sometimes spoke contemptuously of me as a "temperamental artist") informed me that we had $75,000 in the Manufacturer's Trust that we should invest, and I said, "I have no desire to see that money increased. I just want to know that it's there when I need it."

My manager fought with me to a fare-thee-well, pointing out that the best people in the world bought the blue chip, gilt-edged stocks and bonds. His final triumphant thought was, "If the stuff we buy goes bad, the country goes to the dogs."

"And," said the temperamental artist, "what is to prevent the country from going to the dogs?"

A few months later, in the fall of 1929, that's exactly what happened.

Hideaway

It was a two and a half-cent phone call from Don Dickerman that led me to build a nightclub in Greenwich Village that was to cost over $90,000 as a dead loss, but it was a penny postcard from Dickerman that eventually propelled me into building a $200,000 lodge in Maine, on an estate of 300 acres, with seven buildings, on the shores of one of the most beautiful lakes in the world.

During our summer tour of 1930 my hometown of Westbrook, Maine prevailed upon me to be the guest of honor for a three-day celebration with parades, dedications, a banquet and dance, and the naming of the square in front of my father's drugstore, "Rudy Vallée Square." I stole away from the festivities intending to rest one afternoon when a handsome fellow, who was courting my sister and working for the Curtis Wright Airplane Company in Portland, prevailed upon me to take my first ride in the air. It was a hydroplane, and the fact that we could land on water reminded me of a postcard Dickerman had sent me a few months before, describing a camp he had on a body of water known as Lake Kezar.

Within a matter of a few minutes I was talking to Dickerman,

in Maine

who informed me later that the tenuous wire that led to his little party-line crank phone through the woods had not brought him a call in three years.

"I think it's out of order," he told us. "Look for a bright blue float out on the lake and you'll find me."

We took off from Portland. Strangely enough, with little or no difficulty we located Lake Kezar and perceived Dickerman below, waving frantically. I stopped and drew a deep breath. I was entranced with the beauty of the lake, which the *National Geographic Magazine* says is one of the three most beautiful lakes in the world for ideal size and beauty of surrounding trees, vegetation, and mountains. In fact, I was so entranced I asked Dickerman to try to secure me a piece of land with the idea of building a small lodge for an occasional hibernation from my cares and activities in the big city.

Dickerman gave the matter immediate thought. "The only piece of property is one adjoining mine," he said. "It has a lake frontage of only about 200 yards. But," he added, "the owner won't sell unless the prospective buyer buys the entire 300 acres."

"The price?" I asked.

"About $8,000," Dickerman guessed.

The purchase was effected. Dickerman agreed we could extend *his* road a few hundred yards farther in order to reach the portion fronting the lake on which I was to build a dream castle—as Dickerman called it. However, when I decided not to have Dickerman build the edifice he envisioned, he suddenly decided that it would be impractical to extend his road; that the noise of our cars at night might disturb him or some of his guests. It was therefore necessary to construct a road one mile long through the heart of the woods to reach our lake frontage. At that time unemployment was at a high peak, and it was a simple matter to locate fifty or more unemployed French-Canadian boys in Westbrook, who worked in two groups over a period of six weeks, eventually meeting midway in much the same manner as men who build a tunnel from both sides under a river. It was a considerable bit of construction, and wound up costing us several thousand dollars, but it was a beautiful road, and one I knew was my own.

A Westbrook carpenter constructed a simple Cape Cod bungalow with warm gray shingles, three bedrooms, two baths, and a long living room of simple beam construction and pegged flooring, with a huge rock fireplace at one end. By the time the first building was finished I was appearing in *George White's Scandals* and at the Pennsylvania grill. On a Sunday morning I flew twenty of my close friends in two planes for our baptismal banquet in the new lodge, returning to New York on Monday morning.

During the summer of 1932 I purchased a fifteen-foot speedboat, several canoes, and outboard motors. I could hardly contain my excitement. This would be an ideal spot to entertain my band and company of entertainers with their wives each year. Construction was hastily begun on two other buildings named Lodges B and C, with the first one designated as Lodge A. We also decided to build a huge boathouse with a float in front of it, and upstairs a separate bar and pool room. Work proceeded rapidly. In September, after a long summer of one-nighters and theater engagements, we began the first of a series of nine pilgrimages that followed the same patterns every year.

During the course of the Thursday evening preceding our

usual trip to Maine, we would play a fantasy on the University of Maine "Stein Song" as it would be played by various composers somewhere in the middle of the program; then, as the program neared the closing two minutes, we would again reprieve the "Stein Song" while Graham McNamee announced our departure for the lodge. The last thirty seconds we played the "Stein Song" in several keys simultaneously, as our radio audience pictured the throwing of music into the air and general pandemonium, and I rushed from the studio to a waiting cab. I sped to Grand Central Station, where the State of Maine Express was held three or four minutes past its departing time to enable me to leave with it. Some of the boys in the band and their wives would be on the train with me; others in their own cars; and the rest, in a large chartered bus. They would drive through the night, arriving at Old Orchard Beach, where they would swim if the weather was propitious, and enjoy themselves on its long, sandy beach. Those of us on the train would arrive in Portland about 7:30 in the morning. A crew of ten women from the neighboring farmhouses would await us at the lodge, preparing the beds and making preparations for the food we would consume.

Friday night at Old Orchard Beach became a ritual, with the governor of Maine always on the stage next to Dad and Mother. The band began playing for dancing at 8:00. At 9:30 on the dot I would make a long, triumphant walk down the pier itself, a walk of about an eighth of a mile, saluting fans and friends of many years' acquaintance, and put on an hour show with the various personalities I had been presenting in theaters all summer. Quite by accident a Hollywood personality, Rosco Ates, happened to be with us the first summer; thereafter I made it a point to have a Hollywood personality from films as our guest each year. At the conclusion of the dance at one o'clock in the morning I would give autographs to those who requested them, while we packed our instruments and prepared for the seventy-mile trip to Lovell, Maine and Lake Kezar.

On arrival at the lodge all lights were on and fires roared in the fireplaces (each lodge had a fireplace). There were cold cuts, hot chicken à la king, sandwiches of every type, hot coffee, milk, champagne, and whatever you wished at our two bars. The staff of ten women waited up to see that everyone had everything he or she might want. We generally stayed up all that night, retiring early in the morning. At noon everyone was up for breakfast, and then fun out on the float, in the canoes, and in the water.

Individuals arose when they felt like getting up, and breakfast was served no matter what time of morning or afternoon it might be. Lunch was at 1:00, and dinner usually about 7:30 or 8:00 in the evening. We began a ritual in food, with leg of lamb on Saturday evening; charcoal-broiled steaks on Sunday evening, with cherries jubilee; roast beef on Monday; and chicken on Tuesday. On Sunday evenings the Stokowski album of *Scheherazade* furnished the background to our animated conversations and arguments during the course of our dinner at the roaring fireplaces. Wednesday noon a hot lunch was served as we departed for Worcester, Massachusetts, where we played the Bal-L'Air Dance Pavillion on the Worcester Turnpike. We drove through the night from Worcester, arriving in New York ready for our Thursday afternoon "Fleischmann" rehearsal. The profits from the Old Orchard and Worcester engagements were distributed among the band and the entertainers, so in a sense it was a vacation with pay. Mucho pay—each boy received at least $300 for the two nights!

If the weather was sunny and fair we arrived in New York tanned, happy, and rested. But if it rained during our visit, naturally with a group of thirty or forty people staying indoors, playing cards and pool, and imbibing perhaps a little too freely, tempers became frayed and we generally returned the worse for our trip. But we were fortunate that in our nine yearly visits we were rained out only twice.

The lodges continued to grow and improve like Topsy. I picked up ideas as I traveled throughout the country and incorporated them into the lodge itself. I realized that women don't like to rough it, and we secured the finest beds, mattresses, and softest sheets and pillow cases obtainable. A tile man was brought from Boston, and all the bathrooms were tiled in beautiful colors, with fixtures to match or contrast. A $3,000 Capehart phonograph played throughout the entire estate. Certain records were played on our arrival and also on our departure. Soft music during the day from well-chosen albums made the summer or fall afternoons and evenings romantic and more delightful. I discovered musical cigarette boxes that were made in Switzerland and would play popular tunes of my choosing. Each room was named

At Lake Kezar. Top left: Boathouse fronting water and one of the two crusiers. On the second floor of the boathouse were a separate bar and poolroom. Top right: Tennis court at the lake retreat. Bottom left and right: Views of the lake from near the boathouse.

after a song I had written, popularized, or introduced, and the cigarette box was painted to match the room and played the tune of that particular room. My room, of course, was "Vagabond Lover," and my bathroom of black fixtures with cherry-red plaster and tile was called "Lulu Belle" from the Lenore Ullric play. The room Alice Faye occupied in the summer of 1934 was called "Nasty Man." There were other rooms such as "Stein Song" and "Saxophobia" (in honor of my idol, Wiedoeft); then came "Deep Night" and "Sylvia." One bathroom in beautiful light and dark green tile played the theme tune from *East Is West*; another room in red, white, and blue played "The Star-Spangled Banner."

On weekends when I could get away from New York for three or four days, I and some close friends left on the State of Maine Express to enjoy a vacation. They awaited my fast taxi trip from the broadcast studio to the train, which was scheduled to leave at nine o'clock. The drawing room was filled with convivial beverages and food to while away the hours as we sped on into the night.

As the years went on we added bicycle boats, all sorts of

rubber floats, archery, and, since most of our guests liked to play tennis, a tennis court with a beautiful clubhouse with varicolored slate roof and a bar, so that after the cold chill of an October evening set in, hot buttered rum, hot toddies, and other drinks were the order of the evening. During the day, when a large group might be at the lodge, the pineapple frozen daiquiri was my specialty. Sometimes I made as many as two and three hundred of these masterpieces, using my Waring mixers, which Fred Waring himself had personally installed during his visit to the lodge.

For those who wished to gift me with something in appreciation for a lodge visit, I insisted that a brass-engraved plate be put on their gift. A red minipiano was the gift of Edgar Bergen and Charlie McCarthy, Class of 1936, the year Bergen first broadcast with us. Frances Langford and Dorothy Lamour gifted me with the pool table and a large bar, each gift with a brass plate denoting the year they had left my management or employ.

In the fall of 1935 Lodge A was enlarged to twice its size, with a new "Vagabond Lover" bedroom, my old one becoming "Betty Co-Ed." The big wood-beamed living room was now twice its size, a most delightful spot for those of us who wished to relax or play pool. The room with the bar and pool table adjoining was equally spacious.

It was in the fall of 1935 that Eddie Cantor became ill and asked me to come over from the lodge and pinch-hit for him on his cigarette program in New York. In appreciation of this he gifted me with a $5,000 Chris-Craft cruiser, thirty-one feet long, which (believe it or not) could accommodate thirty persons. Thereafter, our lunch became a nautical ritual, with a phonograph aboard playing the records of the broadcast the night before. There was also current for the Waring machine to make our daiquiris on board. Our Filipino chef prepared a hot lunch, and we cruised to the north end of the lake and sat in the cool of the trees listening to the radio broadcast records of the night before while the smaller Chris-Craft raced out with the ice cream that was hoisted on board to make our cherries jubilee. The canvas chairs on board had nautical design; the blankets a steering wheel design. On lovely moonlit nights we could cruise up and down the lake, wrapped in blankets, while the records played

Glenn Miller's "Moonlight Serenade" and other equally relaxing music. Our departure for lunch on the boat was always a traditional one, with a record from a Twentieth Century–Fox picture, the sound track of the music of forty of Alfred Newman's finest musicians. As we idled upstream, at a certain juncture where the music with a chorus of feminine voices soared upwards, I gunned the boat and it leapt forward from the dock. Our return was always musically cued by the playing of "Jealousie" by the Boston Pops Orchestra. The large Chris-Craft was called "Banjo Eyes" and had a gold-leaf caricature of Eddie Cantor's head as it appears in the Brown Derby in Hollywood, and underneath in gold was the boat insignia, "Banjo Eyes."

My sponsors furnished the coffee and Royal desserts, and the president of Philip Morris saw to it that his cigarettes were in abundance during our stay. The president of Planter's Peanuts gifted us with nuts of every type, and other friends and manufacturers saw to it that we were well supplied with the good things that made our visits more enjoyable. I would pick up as many as three or four hundred large Persian limes for our daiquiris on the Friday morning we arrived in Portland. A famous chef who excelled at making blackberry and black raspberry pies would

At the Maine lodge on my Chris-Craft cruiser with Francesca Sims. I found her in Al Jolson's *Hold On To Your Hats!* in Philadelphia (1935-36).

LODGE LOGIC AND YOUR ECCENTRIC HOST

Your host is eccentric and admits it! . . . He is just ODD enough to hope that his guests here will read this list of requests and then not carelessly leave rooms and things in a disarranged and untidy fashion . . . It is a great deal to expect an individual when through taking a shower, to put the used towel in the hamper and THEN TO REACH INTO THE CLOSET FOR A CLEAN ONE AND TO PUT IT ON THE TOWEL RACK FOR THE NEXT GUEST . . . But your host is just MAD enough to expect you to do just that! . . . WONDER OF WONDERS! . . . He hopes that he is fortunate enough in having guests who take a pride and joy in being neat.

Guests who are really concerned as to how they can save others from picking up after them . . . Of course, this is contrary to HUMAN NATURE and most people apparently are not brought up any longer to be thoughtful and neat . . . (at least, not when there are other persons to do it for them) . . . In this modern age of extreme laziness it is difficult just what final caution to leave . . . It used to be "Do as you would at HOME" . . . But after seeing how untidy some people are in their own homes that is a bad injunction!

—*PLEASE READ ON*

FIRST GENERAL RULE

Kindly put things back where and as you find them.

DON'T   over - eat.
over - drink.   (*You'll be ill and spoil your enjoyment*
over - exercise.   *of Lake Kezar and the Lodge if you do.*)

DON'T   throw lighted matches or cigarettes as you drive down through the road leading to the Lodge itself.

(OUR GREATEST FEAR AND TERROR IS FOREST FIRE — THE FOUR HOUSES WOULD GO UP LIKE TINDER BEFORE A ROLLING FOREST FIRE!)

DON'T   throw large pieces of paper or bulky things into the toilet bowls; they clog easily and plumbers must come 25 miles to undo the damage.

DON'T   leave your own toilet utensils and your own toothpaste in the wash basins in the bathroom.

DON'T   leave towels on the bathroom floor or in your room — put them in the hampers, that's what hampers are for. When thru using a face or bath towel please use them to clean the mirror or chromium bath fixtures — it only takes a little elbow grease and a clean mirror and gleaming fixtures will delight the next user.

Reproduced here and on succeeding pages are the contents of the book of rules I gave each guest at my Maine lodge.

DON'T operate the Capehart Phonograph. Our caretaker will be happy to put on new records for you. Please don't attempt to do so yourself as it is easy to put the machine out of order which means NO RECORDS and NO MUSIC.

DON'T go out on the water alone if you cannot swim, or if you swim only a little.

DON'T yell unduly when out on the Lake. When you may really need HELP you won't get it—you may have cried "wolf" too often.

Avoid sunburn; it can be painful and dangerous, and ruin your entire stay. Use the protective preparations available.

DON'T take the Chris Craft out without a pilot; the Lake is filled with reefs which, when struck, instantly ruin the propeller.

DON'T go out in canoes unless you are an expert swimmer.

REMEMBER NOT TO THROW LARGE PIECES OF PAPER OR BULKY THINGS INTO THE TOILET BOWLS.

Don't take cars away without permission. Please blow your horn at corners of road.

Help us to keep out sand and dirt by using the MATS outside the entrance doors.

When rain threatens, please help us by going to your room and closing the windows.

REMEMBER NOT TO THROW LARGE PIECES OF PAPER OR BULKY THINGS INTO THE TOILET BOWLS.

DON'T leave soap in the wash basin; put it in the holder, or, find a place on the rub for it.

If you notice that the supply of Kleenex or toilet paper in any particular bedroom or bathroom is getting low, please tell one of the servants that it may be replenished so that no one will find the supply completely gone.

Avoid talking loudly early in the morning and do not run motors on boats or play the phonograph, piano or organ, as noise travels easily through thin walls. *Someone might want to SLEEP!*

(Incidentally the organ is a very delicate instrument)

DON'T try massé shots on our pool table. It doesn't help the cloth.

REMEMBER NOT TO THROW LARGE PIECES OF PAPER OR BULKY THINGS INTO THE TOILET BOWLS.

Lodge Logic and Your Eccentric Host (continued)

Servants are brought primarily to cook, serve food, make beds, and keep the rooms clean.

THEY ARE NOT HERE TO:

1. Put caps and stoppers back on tubes of shaving or dental cream, bottles of liquid vaseline, mouth wash, etc.

2. Close cans of dental and other powders.

3. Wipe up surplus powders spilled on the wash basins.

4. Put towels back in hampers for YOU.

5. Pull back and chain up shower bath curtains after YOU shower.

6. Pick up YOUR cigarette ends, cigar ends, chewing gum paper, cellophane wrappers, etc.

7. Pick up strands of hair and hair pins.

In the evening if it seems to be growing colder, ask for electric heating pads or more blankets **BEFORE YOU RETIRE**—we have them, and you will avoid a nightmare of cold instead of sound sleep which you so desire.

ABOUT HOT WATER:

1. Don't waste hot water.

2. **CAUTION:** Be alert under the shower in case the water suddenly turns to live steam, thereby avoiding scalding!

3. **BE CAREFUL:** It is easy to slip in the rub when taking a standing shower.

AGAIN: Even when a Record becomes stuck—Don't attempt to play or operate the big Phonograph! PLEASE!

WALTER B. PITKIN says: "*Life Begins At Vacation Time.*"

These are his ideas on how to make your vacation successful:

"The supreme secret of vacationing is relaxation."

"At least twice a day *STRETCH!* Do it in bed—on the beach. *STRETCH* as the cat does—as the dog does—but *STRETCH!*"

"Try to take a siesta every afternoon. A slight nap will do you a world of good. Stay limp when awake whenever possible."

DON'T discuss the work you have been doing or unfinished business while up here at the Lodge. Talking shop will only recall all your worries and cares connected with your business. Choose other subjects. To avoid boredom indulge in your favorite hobbies if we have them here.

•

SO, TO SUM UP: Relax . . .
Stretch as the cat does, often and completely . . .
Walk and swim plenty . . .
Above all *don't shop* . . .

NOTE TO SOUVENIR COLLECTORS: The lighters are gifts to the Lodge from the boys in Rudy's band, each engraved. If you must have a souvenir, ask the caretaker for some thing. He will try to satisfy your request.

REITERATION: Don't take the speedboat out without asking.

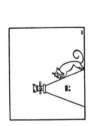

YE OLDE HOTEL CAUTION APPLIES
HERE: PLEASE TURN OUT LIGHTS
WHEN LEAVING A ROOM

▶

FINAL GENERAL RULE

Kindly put things back where and as you find them.

THANK YOU

▶

OF COURSE, GENTLE READER, THE
PRECEDING SUGGESTIONS WERE NOT
INTENDED FOR YOU; I AM SURE YOU WOULD
HAVE FOLLOWED THEM NATURALLY ANYWAY

Lodge Logic and Your Eccentric Host

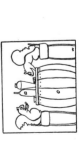

make up twenty or thirty of his best delicacies, which we would take along with us. I excavated a wine cellar underneath Lodge A. Here, I stored in racks some of the finest wines, particularly my favorite pink champagne, which not only my friends on weekends but through the year were free to enjoy to their hearts' content.

Only one who has seen the Maine countryside in October can appreciate the beauty of an Indian summer in Maine, when the leaves from the birch and maple trees create a riot of beautiful colors so breathtaking that when I show some of my motion picture shots, it is almost impossible to believe that these are actually true pictures. I have one shot of a red canoe with a red sail, which truly epitomized the song "Red Sails in the Sunset." On arrival I always arranged for an album of Rudolf Friml's records to be played, beginning with "Toujours l'Amour" while the guests were assigned to their rooms and luggage put away. On the sad days of departure the sound track from a Bing Crosby picture, with Bing singing "It's So Easy to Remember but So Hard to Forget," kept repeating while we loaded the luggage and said a reluctant good-bye to the lodge. Fishing was practically non-existent since the lake was not very well stocked, but there was a small nine-hole golf course nearby.

In 1933 I put in a pipe organ, and on one weekend I invited the inimitable team of Lee Simms and Ila Mae Bailey. It is one of the loveliest scenes in my memory—Lee Simms at the organ, and the rich voice of Ila Mae Bailey singing as she was dressing upstairs preparing to come down for dinner, as the twilight fell over the lake. The pipe organ, which I gifted to the Catholic church in Westbrook, gave way to a Hammond organ, and later on a Hammond Novachord. It was my delight and the delight of many of my friends to pick up odd gadgets and pieces of equipment as we traveled throughout the country. Each year the lodge became more and more a thing of beauty and practicality.

During the winter a lone caretaker stuck out the long, dreary months and plowed the road in the event I decided to come for a winter weekend of complete rest, study, and preparation for new shows. But it was the summer and fall months that made the lodge our dream place, and those who I felt might enjoy a visit were invited by a brochure that depicted on its cover the entrance, with two large field-rock gateposts, and with the simple statement "You are invited to the lodge" underneath the entrance, along with the story of how it had evolved and what it had to offer.

I was rarely in evidence, as I generally had much work to do with study, preparation, and research of songs, but when a bartender was needed, I was happy to perform my chores, and with a wealth of tennis racquets and an unlimited supply of tennis balls, when the gang boasted some good tennis players, the contest waxed fast and furious. Alice Faye paid for the re-covering of all our large umbrellas every two or three years; and though few ever paused long enough to sit underneath them on the metal furniture, they made a pretty and inviting picture.

I discovered that some persons are by nature careless, untidy, and thoughtless, not only of their own welfare and comfort, but of that of others. Thus evolved my set of rules, which were bound in birchbark covers, with gaily colored circles printed on them. This little treatise was entitled "Lodge Logic and Your Eccentric Host," with illustrations by my brother William. I stated simply, "Your host is eccentric, and admits it." Most of the above may seem rather captious and perhaps a little supercritical on my part. But having watched so many people suffer with a bad sunburn and observing that one thoughtless person could ruin everyone's sleep by playing the organ too early in the morning; having had to go myself and call the plumber—a distance of twenty-odd miles; and having observed that the lake was deep and things could happen that might result in a tragedy, I felt these suggestions necessary. Suffice it to say that during the ten years I owned the lodge there fortunately were no tragedies beyond a few family squabbles, a few bruises, and maybe a few cuts on hands or feet. All in all, I like to think that those who enjoyed my hospitality have, as I do, unforgettable memories of a few days of relaxation and enjoyment on the shores of the third most beautiful lake in the world.

In 1945, realizing that California was definitely my permanent home, and that the unoccupied lodge was rapidly deteriorating due to the difficulty of finding a caretaker, as well as being a drain on my income, I sold the establishment for a mere pittance, and have never permitted myself to cast a backward look.

The Evolution

I can see the look of absolute incredulity on the faces of those to whom I relate the fact that we purchase between twenty-five and thirty cases of American California champagne every fifty days. No one can believe it. Of course, it must be understood that we serve champagne in twenty-one-ounce goblets, usually pouring a third of the large bottle over six or more ice cubes; thus, one can easily see why we consume it so rapidly. Any visitor to our home, even perhaps the man to discuss the cleaning of the rugs, is immediately presented with a large goblet of champagne as he surveys the work to be done.

My indoctrination into the art and enjoyment of *spiritus frumenti*, or in plain language ethyl alcohol, was at the early age of twelve when I went up to the attic in our home in Westbrook, Maine and approached a fairly large cask containing claret wine, a lovely and delightful red wine of incomparable taste and quality. I was able to insert a rubber tubing into the cask, and by the process of siphoning I filled several quart bottles with this delightful wine which my father delivered to the Catholic church for the Ordinary of the mass. In the process I couldn't help but

# of a Wino

swallow a few mouthfuls "which I sneaked past a pair of agreeably surprised tonsils" (Fred Allen, 1926). Other than this occasional sortie into the field of claret wine, my soul and system were chaste —in keeping with Prohibition, which had afflicted Maine since the year 1909.

Even after my entrance as a freshman into the University of Maine in the fall of 1921, I did not participate in any of the light drinking in which some of the fraternity brothers indulged on certain occasions, especially at initiation. It was not until 1922 in my first freshman year at Yale that I bought my first bottle of bootleg Gordon's gin, label and all on the bottle, for a date with a rather plump but attractive young blonde waitress from Child's Restaurant in New Haven. I'm sure it was the first time I ever became intoxicated. As I recall, I drank almost to the point of becoming ill, but not quite.

I really feel that my true indoctrination into the art and enjoyment of mixed drinks began in 1934 with the repeal of Prohibition. About this time my lodge in Maine had grown to five buildings. Once a year, beginning in 1932, I took my entire band, their wives and sweethearts, and the four or five acts of my company to the lodge for a five-day whirlwind round of the best food and the best liquor. Perhaps one of the reasons that Mrs. Vallée and I get along so well in our drinking habits is that we both have always liked drinks that taste good. It has probably never occurred to the snobs and the elite who affect a great liking for the martini and scotch that not only are these drinks "acquired tastes" but they are also a caste badge and a declaration of the high estate of those who have indulged in these two particular drinks. The rest of us peasants prefer drinks that taste pleasant, even though they may leave us with a great hangover the next morning. Thus it was that I took to the lodge in Maine the ingredients for many mixed drinks, such as the old-fashioned, the Alexander, and the sidecar.

In 1934 I met a girl named Judy Stewart, whose dedication to Seagram's V.O. was really something. Because of this I became quite involved in the liquor industry itself. It all started in Cleveland a year later when I was playing the Palace Theater, doing four and five shows a day with my band and company of entertainers. On a vaudeville bill in 1926, we Yale Collegians followed Fred Allen and his lovely wife Portland Hoffa. For his routine he introduced various personalities, all of whom failed to appear after he announced them. As each act failed to show he reached into the footlights and picked up a telephone (the old-fashioned kind) and supposedly had a conversation with the person he had just introduced. After introducing Mrs. Tiller, Allen said, "What's that? You won't be with us tonight? What's the trouble? Oh, the still exploded! Blew you and your husband out into the street? What's that? It's the first time you've been out together in ten years? You think your husband is suffering from shock? Why, what's he doing? Oh, he's running up and down the streets in his union suit. Tell him to be very careful, Mrs. Tiller. Summer is over, winter draws on." I memorized Fred Allen's entire act and later used it with his permission!

One afternoon in Cleveland I was doing the Allen routine in our second show. After I read the line "The still exploded?", for some inexplicable reason I injected the line "That's what you get for trying to compete with Seagram's!" It got a little laugh—not a big one, but a little one. The next show I decided to try another line, and I said "That's what you get for trying to compete with

Old Crow!" Nothing! Practically no reaction at all! The fourth show of the evening I went back to the Seagram's V.O. with a resultant fairly strong reaction. The next day over came a case of assorted Seagram's liquors—the first of many.

It was the custom of the liquor industry in Los Angeles to have a yearly banquet, and in 1940 it was held at the Cocoanut Grove. Morey Cerf asked me if I would be the master of ceremonies for the event. That evening I met all of the heads of the various liquor firms in Los Angeles, became quite friendly with some of them, and since that time I have considered myself an ambassador for the liquor industry. Consequently it has been my good fortune to be the recipient of the best of liquors at the best prices.

In 1937 my attorney, Judge Hyman Bushel, and I made a trip to Havana for a six-day vacation fiesta. We stayed at the National Hotel and since rum was the popular drink of Cuba at that time, we visited not only Sloppy Joe's, where Sloppy Joe was supposed to have the finest daiquiris, but the Bacardi house, where Bacardi drinks float freely at no cost. I had definitely become daiquiri-conscious!

"I understand you like to make daiquiris!" Fred Waring once said to me.

"Yes, Fred," I replied, "ever since my trip to Cuba in 1937 I have become a real daiquiri enthusiast!"

"How would you like to have a mixer that makes four daiquiris at one crack and you don't have to use any sifter?" he inquired.

I don't think Fred knew that I was a "gadget kid" from way back and his words were catnip to me. "When can I see it?"

"I'm performing at the New York Paramount Theatre and I have one in my dressing room," he said.

Later, in his dressing room he demonstrated the machine. First he poured in a quantity of rum, some lime juice, some ice, and started the machine going. In a twinkling of an eye it was all liquid. Then Fred did something even more dramatic: He threw in four red cherries and the entire mixture turned a pink color.

"Wow!" said the gadget kid. "I've *got* to have one of those machines!"

"As soon as they come off the line," Fred said.

Soon I was giving them away like water. Fred shipped them

to me for $18 each, and it became my pleasure to gift my friends with them. In later years when Ellie, my wife, and I traveled we always carried a mixer and eight or nine gallons of rum of various types so we could make drinks between the shows and after the shows until four or five in the morning.

My band and I had first played America's ocean playground —Atlantic City, New Jersey—in the summer of 1930. There I also hosted or emceed at least six of the beauty pageants on the stage of the ballroom, and my orchestra accompanied the girls as they sang, played instruments, or danced. The early part of the week my band and I played dance music in the ballroom, alternating with another "name" band, usually the Casa Loma band under Glen Gray. It was on one of those dull nights in 1939 that I first became aware of a champagne I really liked. My previous attempts to enjoy the most popular of all French wines fell flat for the simple reason that the taste of the best French champagne, especially the very dry Brut, just did not please my palate. In my crude dressing room backstage in the Steel Pier ballroom I sat waiting for the Casa Loma band to finish their set. There, a comedian named Roy Sedley, who was part of my traveling company for five years, was to convert me to the enjoyment of pink champagne.

"Would you like to sample this pink champagne?" he asked.

"I don't like champagne," I told him. "It gives me a headache."

Sedley drew himself up. "This is not ordinary champagne," he declared. "It's pink champagne! Charles Boyer and Irene Dunne drank it in the very emotional picture *Love Affair!*"

At that I surrendered and reached for the paper cup. It was quite late, I was thirsty, and the delicious cool flavor of the pink champagne hit the spot. "How long has this been going on?" I asked. "Get some more, quickly!"

As they poured me to bed one night after an evening of drinking pink champagne at the Renault Tavern, I vaguely wondered how I would be able to keep a tennis appointment the next day. But when I awoke I found my head remarkably clear, and on the courts I played like a madman; I believe I won two out of three sets. So I said to myself, "That Renault pink champagne, that's for me!"

The French method of making champagne is to put the ingredients after a certain time in large wood vats; then, after fermentation they are poured into bottles where the champagne ferments naturally. When the bottles are stacked in the racks lying at an angle, all the impurities and sediment collect in the necks of the bottles. The neck of each bottle is eventually frozen and the small plug of frozen sediment is removed. It is this laborious process that makes the finest French champagne so expensive. I did not discover until later that the Renault champagnes were actually made the same way as are most American champagnes today—by the Charmac bulk process. This process ferments the grapes with the yeast in huge metal or glass tanks of many thousands of gallons per tank.

It was now 1939—time for me to entrain to California to work in a Warner Brothers picture, *Golddiggers in Paris.* During this time I became friends with Al Ames, who was working for the Roma Winery in Fresno.

One day Ames asked, "How'd you like to get some pink champagne as good if not better than Renault at a much lower price?"

I asked him what he meant by "lower," and he really flabbergasted me, when he replied "$9.80 a case." Of course, I bought Roma's Jean Bart (a famous French admiral) pink champagne by the fifties (cases, that is!).

Not long after that the Ben Roscoes joined me at my Sunset Strip home for dinner one night, and as we were drinking down at my bar Ben asked me casually if I had seen the *California State Liquor Journal.*

"Why do you ask?" I said.

"There's a picture of you pouring Renault pink champane in a New York restaurant," he announced.

I asked Ben to send me a copy of the photo. After I received it I mailed it to my attorney in New York, instructing him to bring action for $1,000 against Renault Wines for its unauthorized use of the picture in a promotional campaign. While I had not had too many legal actions brought against me, it was a good feeling to be able to sue someone else for a change! We finally settled for 100 cases of wine to be delivered wherever I specified and two cases of splits of Renault brandy and champagne, which was labeled "French 75."

During our stay in New York with *How to Succeed,* the landlord of our Arabian Nights apartment on East 56th Street decided to raise the rent, so I began looking for an apartment in the neighborhood. We found one just a block away with a front and back terrace. It offered a corner for a bar, a room that could be and did become a guest room, and my office, and two large terraces—the rear one a perfect place to walk our poodles.

We were still on the rum kick, but now that I had an office I began a regular daily routine of retiring late, arising late, then going into my office, where in front of my IBM typewriter was a large calendar and a pile of tickets for *How to Succeed.* I was now allowed to purchase six tickets for each show. These were very choice seats and were offered as an inducement to stay on for the second year. I purchased almost $1,000 in seats each month and marked on the calendar to whom the seats were to be assigned.

Big companies such as the eastern distributors of my favorite beer, Schlitz—which I drink on the rocks—were often visited by distributors or executives from Milwaukee and they wanted seats for the visiting firemen. Of course, they offered to pay for them, but the main thing was to get the seats. Thus, it was not uncommon for me to receive a call from the Schlitz headquarters in Brooklyn asking how my beer supply was, and when I said we could use a few cases, the next afternoon there would be a delivery of ten or twenty cases of that delicious hops. My old sponsor, Standard Brands, for whom I had broadcast on radio in the "Fleischmann Hour," was constantly taking me out to dinner and asking what I needed in Planter's peanuts, coffee, tea, and Schweppe's new creations in lemon- and orange-flavored sodas. Of course, they needed more tickets for out-of-town buyers of their products and I had just what they needed. It was a happy wedding!

My daily routine in those days began with a light breakfast. Then into the office to work on the mail, our financial matters, and whatnot until 4:30 or 5:00. After that I went to our bar, a masterful creation given us by our good friend Syd Spielman, who makes millions of refrigerators, usually in small sizes, for living rooms and home bars. This bar had the usual brass rail and cabinets for the bottles, but it also had a refrigerator and a sink with running hot and cold water. I had procured some comfortable bar stools from the Table Maker, and from five to six o'clock

I sat and watched television, consuming Planter's peanuts or some of the new dry-roasted mixed nuts (courtesy of Standard Brands) and religiously imbibing a fabulous dry sherry.

This sherry was first brought to my attention the day after I met my wife at Lake Tahoe. The famous chef and restauranteur, George Mardikian, had taken me to the Beringer Winery, which was managed in 1945 by a most efficient, kind, and gregarious man, Fred Abruzzini, who had been most generous. Among the twelve cases of wine we took away with us were two cases of Beringer's pale dry sherry. I did not particularly enjoy the taste of this sherry until one afternoon several years later—after I had married the girl I had met on the beach at Lake Tahoe and we had visited the Abruzzinis in their home near the wineries. It was a Sunday afternoon and as we sat in the small living room with the TV set on and the fireplace burning merrily, I had begun to sip Beringer pale dry sherry. The next thing I knew they were waking me up. I had been asleep for hours. I discovered that afternoon that, at least for me, sherry is the product of grapes most conducive to relaxation and blessed sleep. For three solid years while I was in *How to Succeed,* five out of six nights, my routine was always the same: By six o'clock I was ready for my afternoon nap. *The sherry insured instant sleep!*

The last two years of our stay in our 56th Street apartment I purchased from Kip's Bay Locker—a liquor store near the United Nations building—a case of Beringer's pale dry sherry once a month every month for those two years at the low price of $18.90, even though it was distilled 3,000 miles away!

As we went into 1964 I found myself drinking an inordinate amount of vodka. This may have been due to our weekends with friends in Long Island, where that was practically all they served. On tours of night spots and hotels after leaving the show I found it easier to carry a case or two of vodka and to pick up the mix to use with it. By the time we were making the film of *How to Succeed* I was drinking a quart of vodka a day! I began about five P.M. while watching TV and put a quart away. From five until two or three in the morning it made life much more bearable.

As we finished the shooting of the film of *How to Succeed,* I found myself looking heavier than I had ever been in my entire life, so I simply called a halt to the vodka routine and began the enjoyment of wines as a steady diet instead of the on and off imbibing of previous years when I had bought many cases of Renault pink champagne, which was made in New Jersey and which gave me many evenings of delightful quaffing of the grape.

I discovered a delightful red wine made in Silverton, Ohio by Meier's Wine Company and which was called mellow burgundy when in actuality it was not a burgundy at all but simply a Concord grape juice that had been beautifully fermented!

Just as I decided upon my new pathway to the enjoyment of wines, I first tasted Lejon extra dry champagne at a wedding reception and began the systematic purchase of about thirty cases every fifty days. We drank it like water and when the carpet man came to clean the carpet I could hear the popping of the cork as my lovely wife opened and served several glasses of this fine champagne.

A year or so later I stumbled upon Jacques Bonet, also a California champagne with a very distinctive taste which terminated our sojourn with Mr. Lejon.

Several hundred cases later, I was persuaded to try another California champagne that was fermented at the old Leland Stanford Winery at Mission San José but now owned by the Weibel family.

Although Weibel has several champagnes, I prefer their Stanford Governor's Cuvée to any other champagne regardless of its

Champagne delivery at Silvertip

origin or method of distillation. It is bottled in a distinctively shaped bottle not unlike that which contains benedictine and brandy, with a very long fine-quality gold foil seal. This is the first champagne to have the taste of a French champagne at one end and the American taste at the other!

I am so enamored of this wine that I have asked for and have been granted the privilege of being a salesman for it and thus, as the von Ribbentrop of the entertainment world, I watch for meetings at which are discussed premieres, dinners, banquets, or coming out parties, and functions of every variety in the hopes of making them see the light and serving my superb champagne at the soirée!

At the end of a long hard day, I can think of no happier or better way to close the day than sitting down in my big Niagara Cyclo Massage Chair (it's actually more of a throne than a chair) with several bottles of Stanford's governor's cuvée and plenty of ice cubes and watching my favorite TV programs.

But if I still find myself wide awake as the last station signs off for the early morning, I then open a bottle of sherry as it is really only sherry that knits the raveled sleeve of care and sends me off to a good sound sleep.

And for those of you who read this here and now, let me suggest that you hie yourself to your nearest liquor store and order several cases of Italian Swiss Colony's out-of-this-world, classic dry sherry. I have been searching for years to find this sherry, which has such a delightful nuttiness of flavor and exactly the right sherry taste for me. The cost? Only one dollar nineteen a bottle with a discount by the case.

I have put away *twelve cases* for my really old age and will probably buy twenty or thirty cases more before it disappears as all good things somehow always do.

I don't know why this should be, but I'm not taking any chances on the master who is responsible for this more heavenly sherry suddenly deciding not to brew any more of it, leaving you and me to scramble everywhere for what few bottles might be tucked away somewhere.

This sherry is really liquid gold and if you *are* partial to this strange but delicious aperitif, don't miss out on it, especially at this price!

So I say to all of you, dear readers, *bottoms up!*

The Girl at

It was 1945. Although we had defeated Germany, the war continued with the grim prospect of losing maybe two million American men in the taking of Japan. I was still a bandmaster in the Coast Guard, lieutenant senior grade. Someone in the liquor industry called and asked me if I would join a group who enjoyed playing tennis and go to San Francisco, all expenses paid by the liquor industry of San Francisco, to play tennis indoors and outdoors, and auction off balls and racquets to raise money to help defeat Japan. As I look back now, it seems so silly, because the most we could raise would be ten, fifteen, maybe twenty thousand dollars and, unknown to all of us—at least to most of us—the atomic bomb was only a few weeks away.

Inasmuch as my Coast Guard duties were light, I looked forward to this weekend, the last one in June. With two civilian friends, Charlie Wick and a fellow named Jack Bates who owned a couple of music stores in Los Angeles, we drove to San Francisco, arriving there Friday night, the weekend of June 30, for the tennis matches and auctions of Saturday and Sunday. Jack Kramer, who was in the Coast Guard with us at Wilmington and

21

King's Beach

Long Beach, evidently was able to secure permission to get away. Errol Flynn, Bruce Cabot—practically every celebrity who enjoyed playing tennis—was in our group of twenty to thirty tennis buffs who played indoors and outdoors at Candlelight Park, auditoriums, etc. After the sets were over we auctioned off balls and racquets and raised probably ten or fifteen thousand dollars by Sunday evening. Ten or fifteen thousand bucks! And the atomic bomb to save a million lives and billions of dollars just weeks away!!

They put us up at the St. Francis Hotel, one of San Francisco's fine, old, venerable hotels. During dinner Sunday night Charles Wick, a young Cleveland pianist, who came to Hollywood to get a job with Tommy Dorsey for a while and then moved into my home in the Hills to keep me company during the war, had, with my help, become an agent for the William Morris Agency. Wick suddenly suggested that we go to Cal-Neva.

"What the hell is Cal-Neva?" I asked.

He said, "It's a nightclub and gambling hotel at Lake Tahoe." I had heard of Lake Tahoe, but I had never heard of Cal-

289

Publicity shot—with me on radio program were guests Wayne Morris and Errol Flynn.

Neva. "Why do you want to go?" I asked.

"I've booked Emile Boreo there," Wick answered.

I had watched Emile Boreo perform with a group of White Russians twenty-three years before in New York in a show called *Chauve Souris*. In this show—a sort of musical revue—Boreo introduced the famous "Parade of the Wooden Soldiers," a song that had become a classic over the years. He also did various specialties, molding a felt hat much as Red Skelton does into various shapes as worn by different types of individuals. He was also adept in singing crazy songs and making peculiar sounds. Since the next day was July 1, I saw no reason why we should go back to Los Angeles but decided, rather, for the July 4 holiday to go up to this spot, which Charlie assured me was a beautiful one.

As we neared the gates of Cal-Neva there were two men

standing in front of the main building. One of them was Boreo and the other Bones Remmer, a fellow who looked like a red-faced lobster—at least his nose looked like a claw. We had arrived about 5:30 and the sun was sinking. As we drove in I heard Remmer say to Boreo, "Put him on! Get him to perform!"

I said, "Mr. Remmer, I'll be happy to perform for my good friend Emile."

After washing up and changing into fresh clothing we went into the main dining room of Cal-Neva, which is known for an unusual feature: There's a black line that goes across the middle of the dance floor. On the west side of the line you are in California; on the east side of the line you are in Nevada. The gambling, therefore, has to be on the east side of the black line; but when you are dancing you go from state to state. The three of us sat at our table and the moochers started muscling in for drinks

My bride in 1952

and a bite to eat, as the war was still on and food and liquor were hard to get.

As I watched Boreo perform I realized that he was a lost soul. His act, which at one time had some appeal, now seemed outdated and was definitely not going over. Wick went to the piano and accompanied me on three or four songs and I did a couple of jokes—I did my best to try to help the act. When the check came it was probably $70 or $80 due to the freeloaders who descended upon us. I paid it with a healthy tip. Yet, at the back of my mind was the annoying thought that Remmer had not even sent a cocktail to our table! That was the early show; then came the late show. Again I got out on the floor and performed, and again I paid a check—and again no cocktails from Remmer, who was in the room watching me work!

That was July 1. There was only one other place at Lake Tahoe and that was Cal-Vada, on the Nevada side, naturally. This was a place where mostly the hookers hung out. So the next two nights, having nowhere else to go, we found ourselves again in Cal-Neva, and again for both shows I got up and did my bit; again I paid the check, and again no cocktails or any complimentary food or anything else from Mr. Remmer. At the end of the last show on the night of July 3, I told Boreo very bluntly: "Don't ask me to perform any more, I've had it!" Naturally, he was a little upset, but I think he understood why I felt that way.

The day of July 4 dawned bright and sunny. A mile down from Cal-Neva is King's Beach, a little beach on the shores of Lake Tahoe, at that time one of the most beautiful lakes in the world; with towering mountains all around it. Today, of course, Lake Tahoe is considered one of the most attractive spots for vacations, and it has grown tremendously, particularly the south shore, where Harrah's and several other great gambling casino-hotels do turnaway business.

Charlie Wick, Jack Bates, and I hied ourselves over to King's Beach, changed into our bathing suits, and took a dip. Suddenly my eyes were riveted to a very attractive redhead who was swimming some distance from the shore on one of the floats that had been anchored there. With her was a young boy, approximately nine or ten years of age who, I theorized, could have been her son. Although she was still in high school, she was quite tall and

could have been a young mother. She bore a striking resemblance
to a girl with whom I had been deeply in love and who still was
very much in my system, although at that time I was going with
a beautiful blonde, a dress designer at Columbia Studios.

I decided to seek an acquaintanceship with this young lady,
swam out fairly close to her, around her, almost between her
legs—but she did not betray the least interest in me. In fact, I
don't think she was aware that I was anywhere near her. That
was par for the course for me as I've never attracted very much
attention. I generally have had to do the knocking at the door
and the awakening of interest. I dropped the idea of trying to
meet her in the water, swam back to the shore, and walked up to
a porch on the lefthand side of the exit, the only one from the
beach, where a Princeton couple were entertaining some of their
friends with a profusion of drinks. As I sat there drinking I kept a
wary eye on the redhead. Finally, after about an hour and a half
she emerged from the water with the young boy and started
down the road. I jumped off the porch and stopped her, assuming, of course, that she knew who I was. The whole beach was
agog, because I was the only celebrity there that day.

I've always been very easily hurt, and thus have always
avoided the trite phrase, "I'm Rudy Vallée," for fear the other
person might say, "So what?" But, "Would you like to go to Cal-
Neva this evening?" I ventured.

She was not disagreeable or mean in her refusal, but simply
said: "I don't go out with strangers."

Fearing that she might be somewhat skittish of a thrice-
married man (and most amazing of all, that day—July 4, 1945—
was the last day of my interlocutory decree of divorce from
Bettejane Greer), I said, "Why not bring your father and
mother?" But again she politely refused and bounded off with the
young boy. I rejoined my friends on the porch and then, about an
hour later, suddenly back she came. "Ah hah!" I said to myself,
"She has seen the error of her ways!" I jumped off the porch, and
again I asked her if she was sure she wouldn't like to go to Cal-
Neva. Again she politely refused. But this time I resolved to find
out her name. I said, "May I ask your name?"

"My name is Eleanor Norris," she replied.

And I said, "Your father's name?"

A 1949 restaging of Eleanor's turndown of my King's Beach invitation (July, 1945) to take her to Cal-Neva Lodge. The photograph was taken around the time we announced our engagement (summer of 1949). In the original incident, the boy was much shorter, of course.

"Harlie," she said.

"L-I-E or L-E-Y?" I asked.

"L-I-E."

"Where do you live?" I asked.

"Berkeley," she said.

That was all I needed to know. "Have you ever been to Hollywood?" I questioned.

"Yes."

I then said, "Next time you come down, I'd like to take you to the Beachcomber's."

"Oh, that would be delightful!" she exclaimed. With that she went back to her mother, and said to her: "Some Hollywood character asked me to go to Cal-Neva, and suggested that if I came to Hollywood, he'd take me to the Beachcomber's."

Her mother said, "You stay away from those Hollywood phonies!"

The afternoon over, back at Cal-Neva I went to Emile Boreo's room. "Emile," I said, "put me on tonight."

"But you said—"

"Forget what I said! Put me on tonight!"

I knew she must be there that night, as Cal-Neva was the only place to go. So I prepared to perform, in my Coast Guard uniform, as usual. That evening my eyes searched the room. She was nowhere to be seen! At intermission I drove to Cal-Vada; she wasn't there! I went to the bowling alley; she wasn't there! I drove to the Little Theatre, a mile away near King's Beach. I went through the theater in the dark, hoping I could find her. There was a full moon that night and I resolved to have this girl in my arms, to hold her close to me, and to kiss her. As I walked through the dark of the theater, having been an usher in my younger days, I looked with a trained eye for her. She was not on the main floor. There was a small balcony upstairs where the kids did all their necking. I looked there, hoping that I wouldn't find her in the arms of some boy. She wasn't there. I hied back to Cal-Neva and, again in my uniform, did my second show.

Unknown to me, she had watched me perform during the first show. While her parents were gambling she and the young boy had gone to the entrance of the room at Cal-Neva. The boy had stood on a chair and they had peeked through the curtains. As they had looked in, they could only see the back of me. She hadn't realized that the man in uniform was the same person who had asked her to go to Cal-Neva that evening!

Between shows I called George Mardikian, who owned the Omar Khayyam in San Francisco. While we were doing the tennis tournaments in San Francisco I had phoned him to ask him if he would take me to the Louis Martini Winery after the finish of our stint. He had said he'd be happy to do so, and take me to two other wineries as well. Now, here at Cal-Neva I called him to tell him that something had happened and that I would not be able to join him on the morning of July 5 as we had originally planned, but that I would phone him as we neared our meeting place in Napa County.

On the morning of the fifth we drove to King's Beach and I waited for the redhead to appear. It was a very blustery, windy day, with few persons on the beach. By four o'clock it was quite apparent that she wasn't going to show. So I phoned George and told him we were leaving Lake Tahoe and that I'd probably be able to get to the rendezvous in three or four hours. By the time I met him it was about 8:30 and Madame Delatour of Beaulieu, one of the finest wineries, had retired. We went on then to Berringer Brothers Winery, where Fred Abruzzini, a true pioneer in the art of the growing of grapes and a genius in the art of winemaking, presided. We loaded ourselves with ten or twelve cases of the best Berringer Brothers' wines and drove on to Louis Martini's. Fortunately, we had two cars and were able to load in another ten cases of the best of Louis Martini. We then drove on to San Francisco, where we had a midnight dinner at the Omar Khayyam.

Shortly after our return to Los Angeles I received a call from the navy asking me if I would go to Camp Parks, the big Seabee base outside of San Francisco, where some twenty or thirty thousand men were being trained to do the hard work that the Seabees do for the navy. They had a forty-piece band and I was asked to conduct it and do a few songs.

I had looked up the address of Harlie Norris in the Berkeley phone book and wrote a letter to Miss Eleanor Norris at 119 El Camino Real, Berkeley, California, inviting her to bring her parents to catch my show at Camp Parks, also to be my guests for dinner on the night before the show. Eleanor came home from the Orinda Country Club to find her mother and her older sister very excited. The envelope containing the letter had my name on the back of it. Her mother's face glowed when she said, "You've received a letter from Rudy Vallée!"

Eleanor said, "I don't know Rudy Vallée. I've never met him."

"Open it!" her mother commanded. Eleanor opened the letter and read my invitation. "You stupid nitwit!" her mother cried. "That was the man from Hollywood who asked you to go to Cal-Neva. What's the matter with you?"

Eleanor simply said, "I don't even remember what he looks like."

Down they went to the rumpus room where the old movie magazines were kept, and found a picture of me, one taken during the filming of *Palm Beach Story*, in which I hold my pince-nez glasses before my eyes and make a rather pompous face.

"Ugh!" Eleanor said. "I'm not going out with him!"

Her mother said, "You certainly *are*!"

"But," said Eleanor, "I have a date with a boy from St. Mary's Pre-Flight School this evening!"

"Well," her mother said, "we'll give him some money for beer and he can go out with the boys, and after Rudy Vallée goes home you can have your date with him."

My pianist and I flew over in a special navy plane. I found I had a station wagon driven by a chief petty officer and another one if I needed it. On the night before the show I picked up the Norrises at their residence and drove into San Francisco to the Omar Khayyam.

George Mardikian gave us what he calls "The Rudy Vallée Corner." He outdid himself. The repast began with the famous "Omar's Delight," a cocktail that is made from Southern Comfort and is *really* a delight, and continued with the "Soup of the Armenian Kings." Mardikian broke the huge Armenian matzo type of bread, followed by many hors d'oeuvres and apple, pineapple, and banana fritters, which he no longer makes except on special occasions—with the dessert climax "Ak Me Kedev"!

Because I was a little helpful in creating his restaurant in San Francisco there is only one photograph as you come down the stairs into the Omar Khayyam and that is an 11 × 14-inch photograph of "Yours Truly." It has been stolen three times and replaced three times. "The Rudy Vallée Corner," which he refused one night to Barbara Hutton when she wanted it, still remains.

After dinner we went to the Mark Hopkins where I was later to perform after I had married Eleanor. Eleanor was wearing a little, white, flimsy type of dress that young persons wear at graduation time, and as we were dancing I saw another woman in a satin sheath dress with four-inch heels—very sexy. "Eleanor," I said, "I hope you'll wear something like that for me sometime."

When she and her mother were in the ladies' room later, Eleanor said, "I think the guy's crazy," and she told her mother what I had said about the dress. When we arrived back at the Norris residence we went inside to have a drink and Mrs. Norris began plying me with questions. Because it takes me almost an hour to tell a simple story, owing to my tendency to digress, the hour finally reached two o'clock!

Aunt Kate and Eleanor's girl friend were stuck upstairs where they had gone to the ladies' room, and the two boys from St. Mary's Pre-Flight School were in the kitchen getting drunk on beer. I finally departed about 2:30, and hoped that Eleanor would at least still have some sort of romance with her date from St. Mary's.

The next night we all drove in two station wagons to Camp Parks, where I did my show with the Camp Parks Band. Upstairs in the officers' club afterwards, while we were having a few drinks, I asked Mr. Norris if I might take Eleanor to Trader Vic's *alone*. Father Norris had liked me from the moment we met. I didn't realize that Eleanor was standing behind me and could hear me make this request.

Mr. Norris said affably, "Yes, oh yes!"

Behind him stood Eleanor, shaking her head, "No, oh *no!*"

As Eleanor and I climbed in the station wagon, the chief petty officer, being very wise, turned up the rear-view mirror, meaning, "Go to it, kid; she's all yours!"

Eleanor didn't know I had a fetish for long nails. Painted long fingernails aroused me and made me very excited sexually, just as a tight-fitting satin dress and five-inch heels likewise excited me. Eleanor had the bad habit of picking at her nails and they were usually very short. Her older sister Betty for some reason had said to her that night, "You can't go out with Rudy Vallée with nails like that!" So she stuck on some ten-cent store nails that were long and very attractive. I took her hand as we sat in the car. "What beautiful nails!" I said. She was afraid that at any moment one of the nails might pop off and hit the roof of the car.

I gently put my arm around her and pulled her toward me. She remonstrated, but very sweetly, by saying, "No, I don't think you should," and like a nitwit—I didn't!

We arrived at Trader Vic's. I had known Vic Bergeron in 1938 when he was only Vic Bergeron with his little $6,000 bar called "Hinky-Dinks," where, ironically, no food was served. A year later it was to become "Trader Vic's," the precursor of a long chain of Trader Vic's all over the world. That evening Vic outdid himself, but this time I insisted on paying for our dinner. Finally, I stood up and sadly, almost defiantly, said, "Miss Norris, it's been a delightful evening. Your station wagon awaits you outside." And I took off. I was so goddamned mad! Here I'd taken the girl out two nights and wasn't even rewarded with a kiss. I really wanted to say, "Go to hell!" but didn't, and that was that!

The following Christmas I sent Eleanor's mother a large box of O'Brien's candies made in Fresno, California. About that time

Eleanor was in the University of Nevada at Reno and it annoyed her a little bit that I had sent something to her mother but nothing to her. At that time I was going with the beautiful blonde dress designer from Columbia Pictures.

In the summer of 1946 the blonde and I and Benny Krueger, another saxophone idol, who was now working for me conducting my orchestra in radio, decided to take a trip to Reno, driving first to Yosemite, then to Reno, and on to Lake Tahoe for July 4. I phoned Mrs. Norris. "I'll be in Tahoe on the fourth," I said. "Where do you think we should stay?"

"I'd suggest Brockway Tavern," she said, "about a half-mile down from Cal-Neva."

The three of us had a good trip and a delightful evening at Yosemite, where they still rolled a fire-ball over the falls at nine o'clock. Arriving in Reno, we enjoyed a couple of days there, and then on July 4 went to Lake Tahoe and Brockway Tavern. I was asked if I would entertain the evening of the fourth in the main ballroom of Brockway Tavern. Benny Krueger was then able to play a little piano, not very much—but enough to accompany me in three or four numbers.

Before the show began Mr. and Mrs. Norris came in and, hiding behind them, Eleanor. I ran around and tapped her, and she popped up, very embarrassed at being alone without a date. I introduced her to my beautiful one and Mr. Krueger, and Mrs. Norris suggested that we come by their cottage at Lake Tahoe for cocktails.

The next afternoon the blonde and I dropped over to the Norris' cottage, and while there I found myself in need of certain things.

"We can go to Tahoe Tavern, where you can buy them," Eleanor said.

This was a spot about five miles west of Lake Tahoe. Eleanor must have had an ulterior motive in suggesting that we go there, as she knew there would be several boys who always hung around the tavern and who, of course, would greet her, thus showing me that she knew a lot of boys. Sure enough! As we arrived there were at least four or five young, attractive swains, and they yelled, "Hey, Norris, hey, Eleanor!" She was in seventh heaven.

On the drive back, with Mary Ann snuggled next to me and Eleanor on the outside, Mary Ann slyly suggested, "Let's drop Eleanor off and go back to our room."

Eleanor rushed in to her mother after we dropped her off, crying, "Mother! Mother! They're sleeping together!"

Her mother, a very wise and understanding woman, said, "Well, dear, you must understand these things. They live differently from the way we do and you mustn't misjudge them."

YOO-HOO!   R.S.V.P.

Mary Ann

Sketch mailed to me by Mary Ann after one of our slight tiffs (1948 or early 1949)

I was very fond of Mary Ann. She was a talented person, both as an artist and a designer, and she was a very attractive person who wore extremely sexy clothes and wore them beautifully. In the enjoyment of sex she left nothing to be desired. Had she not trapped me I would probably have married her, because I had come to the point of wanting to be with her constantly. Twice she suggested that we not see each other any more because as she put it, "We're getting nowhere." Each time after a week or so she would call and suggest we should begin again. The third time, after she made this statement on the telephone, when I came into my office the next day at the little studio where I was making films for television, there on the floor of my office was every gift I had ever given her. I could only conclude from this that she had found a new "sugar daddy" and that our romance was definitely over. I learned later that she was sitting by the phone waiting and hoping I would call, but the return of the gifts could mean only one thing to me, and I didn't want to call and be turned down.

Subsequently there was a Coast Guard dance being given at Long Beach for a lot of us who had been in service there. Not being able to find the right girl to take with me, I phoned Eleanor and asked her if her mother would let her come down for the dance. Quite surprisingly, her mother said yes—if she could find a chaperone. She thought a friend of Edgar Bergen's wife would probably be very happy to chaperone Eleanor during her stay there.

That night I discovered that Eleanor was a very passionate girl. Not that anything actually happened, but in my arms she was a ball of fire. And the feeling of her body against mine and her kisses made me well aware of what lay in store for me if I were to marry her.

It was now 1949 and I was playing the Cocoanut Grove as a single without my band. I received a call from Mrs. Norris asking me if I could get them a guest card at the Tennis Club and the Racquet Club in Palm Springs, where I had a beautiful home that I had purchased in 1946 and to which I had taken Mary Ann many times. A guest card at both clubs was an easy matter for me as I had become a lifetime member of both clubs—a lifetime member with no dues. This was because I had secured entertainment for both clubs over the period of several years, and both Charlie Farrell and the Tennis Club had given me a life membership and made me their entertainment director.

I invited Eleanor and her mother to come to the Cocoanut Grove to catch my performance. They sat directly in front of me on a second tier. Eleanor was wearing a little middy outfit with a flat navy cap. Seated in back of them was Manny Pine, a friend of mine from New York who was managing two Jewish girl singers, the Barry Sisters. Pine, a dead ringer for Akim Tamiroff, had been staying with me at my home in the Hollywood Hills and was going to Palm Springs with me two days later after I terminated my engagement at the Cocoanut Grove. He had with him two girls from my office, one of whom was my secretary and the other a pseudo office girl whom I had met when she was working at the Douglas Aircraft plant and whom I had taken out on several dates.

Eleanor told me later that she and her mother had had no idea who the three persons behind them were but she had overheard Manny Pine say in the tones of a New York gangster, "You want to marry Rudy Vallée? I'll arrange that! That's a cinch; I'll arrange it!" Eleanor and her mother had looked at each other in frozen horror. Good God, was this how marriages were made? And who could this person be who was going to see that Rudy Vallée married a girl who was seated behind them?

Two days later Manny and I drove to Palm Springs to my home. It was now early June and Palm Springs was practically deserted. Eleanor and her mother were there for the week. We took them to the Tennis Club. There were only about three couples dancing on the floor. Manny danced with Eleanor's mother and I with Eleanor. Again, as we danced, the sex urge in me was aroused to fever pitch and I think she knew it.

One evening Rudolph Friml happened to be enjoying the Springs. He called me and came over with his Chinese wife not only to play for a while at the piano but also to go out for dinner with us. Walter Gross, one of the world's greatest all-round pianists and composer of "Tenderly," was there, too, and he made an evening at the piano a musical delight. The evening after, Walter and Mrs. Norris left, and Eleanor and I were alone in my house. She and I decided to get into the pool about two o'clock in the morning. As we swam around in the water our bodies were suddenly close together in rapturous delight. I think it was that evening we fell deeply in love with each other and that I decided this was the girl I wanted to marry.

About four o'clock in the morning I felt I should take Eleanor back to where she and her mother were staying. As we drove to her mother's place, unknown to us her mother was circling around to come to my place to see what in the hell we were doing. Just as we drove up in front of her mother's place her mother drove up in her car and got out. She was embarrassed to tears, as I said, "Mother, here is your daughter—*just as you gave her to me.*" Mrs. Norris burst into laughter, in which Ellie and I joined.

The next day they were to depart for home. It happened to be an afternoon when I had agreed to entertain some lovely young beauties who were there as a part of the Desert Circus and "An Evening at the Tennis Club," at which all the young girls would parade in a beauty contest. As I talked to Eleanor about the possibility of getting married, this time in the cold, sober dawn of the day, she wouldn't give me a definite yes, but said, "I'll talk to my folks about it."

She and her mother were about ten minutes from my house, headed north, when Eleanor decided to come back to see me again. As she came back she found my bar crowded with these eight or ten beautiful young things and excused her return by saying that she was looking for a ring that she had lost somewhere in the house the night before. Seeing all the girls, she was furious, absolutely furious, and determined more than ever that we should wed.

I subsequently made several trips to Berkeley to see her with my longing for her increasing all the time. One night, resplendent in my black and white shoes, white trousers, and sport jacket, and in my blue Buick station wagon, I drove to the house and knocked at the door. Eleanor opened it, crying: "I can't see you again ever. I just can't see you ever again!" and closed the door. Well, of course, I was flabbergasted and deeply hurt. I retreated to the Clairemont Hotel two blocks away. I phoned her and to my surprise she agreed to go with me to Trader Vic's, where— after several of his fabulous rum drinks—we both began to get maudlin and misty-eyed. Later we leaned against the rainpipe outside her house until six in the morning, smooching. But when

I phoned the next day she was not at the house; she had gone to stay elsewhere. However, sweet conspirator Aunt Kate told me where she was and how I could reach her.

I called her and told her I was going to Lake Tahoe to perform. She knew about this and, strangely enough, her folks on that very day were also going there for the annual summer enjoyment of their cottage. I had a feeling that once at Lake Tahoe, I might be able to break down the resistance of the father and mother. In my previous talks with her parents, particularly the father, I had found that they were very fond of me.

"Rudy," her father said, "there isn't anyone in the world of whom we think more. But we're dreadfully afraid for Eleanor and fear for the difference in your ages. It has nothing to do with the failure of your past marriages, but it's just that you're much older."

But happily, somehow at Lake Tahoe all the opposition evaporated, and I called Winchell to give him the good news. Sanford Adler, owner of Cal-Neva at that time, gave us a fabulous wedding announcement party in the room where I was working. We invited our friends from Berkeley, Napa County, and San Francisco, and it was a delightful evening. And as Eleanor and I twirled on the floor our passions were mounting all the time.

Adler had given me a beautiful cottage overlooking the lake while I was performing there. I had brought with me a case of brandy and a case of crème de menthe, and a cake of ice was sent to my room every evening. I then made the most delightful stingers, which we drank until four or five in the morning as we lay there·entwined in each other's arms. It was sexual torment as we wanted so much to consummate it, but I had promised Eleanor I would acquiesce to her wish that we wait until our wedding night. Nevertheless, they were beautiful, rapturous moments.

We discovered that it was extremely difficult to obtain permission from the Catholic Church for our marriage. Eleanor's father was a Protestant, her mother Catholic. And, as is usually the case, Eleanor was a stronger Catholic, a more violent one, than if *both* her parents had been Catholic. The Church looked askance at the fact that I had been divorced from Bettejane Greer. Eleanor's mother was a very determined woman, very strong-minded. She had made a comparative success selling real estate and she pursued with fanatical zeal the attempt to get permission from the Church. Finally, by hook or crook, she did secure it, and we were married by a little old priest who had been a boxer, a pugilist in the fight ring, a real character out of *Going My Way*, who didn't give a damn whether I'd ever been divorced or not.

Eleanor all her life had always wanted a real wedding with all the trimmings—her father and me in white tie and tails with top hat, a lot of ushers, maids of honor, and a beautiful satin gown—and to have the wedding in a church, of course, with communion the night before and a big blowout at the Orinda Country Club afterwards, with champagne corks popping all over the place, a delicious dinner, music, and dancing. She was always proud to boast that during the reception at the club—in the excitement and the imbibing of much champagne—as she leaned back her veil caught on fire from the candles behind her, and I smothered the burning veil with my own bare hands. Fortunately, no harm was done to either of us.

Then came the trip to Pebble Beach, where her father had arranged a room for us for our wedding night. It was a perfect evening, perfect but for one thing—that evening, that day, it had to happen: the flag was up. Eleanor had her period! As I sat in the living room of the Norris home waiting for her to come down from the room upstairs her Aunt Kate informed me that Eleanor felt it would be best for me to stay at a hotel that night.

"You tell her to get the hell down here or I'll go upstairs and *get* her!" I retorted.

In about ten minutes Eleanor came down wearing what most women would consider a very beautiful long dress of coarse material in purple color. But my fetish is for tight-fitting, sheath gowns of a smooth, satin material, with four-inch heels, and long nails.

I looked at this monstrosity in purple. "What the hell are you made up for, Halloween eve?" I asked.

Eleanor burst into tears and ran up the stairs.

I turned to Aunt Kate. "You get her the hell down here or, believe me, I *will* go up!"

Eleanor finally came down with her bags; we got in the car and drove down to Pebble Beach. Her father had arranged a lovely hot meal for us when we arrived at the inn and I had brought with me a bottle of Napoleon brandy, almost 200 years

The Vallées on tour, 1958 or thereabouts

old. And, believe it or not, we desecrated that bottle by using it to make stingers. After that, *period or not, we broke the ice!*

Many of Eleanor's friends had said "You won't make it. It won't last. It just isn't going to be." We were married September 3, 1949, and today, still together, we look forward to all the days ahead.

Eleanor has had a life that few women have ever known. When I first talked to her parents about marrying her, I told them, "One thing I can tell you for sure, life with me will never be dull! In fact," I told her mother, "some day Eleanor is going to bring out one of my ventriloquial figures (I have three of them), and she'll be wearing a short French skirt with long French hose and five-inch heels." Mother Morris said, "That'll be the day!" In 1950, at Walter Reed Hospital in Washington where I was performing for the patients while playing the Shoreham Hotel, I was using my Negro dummy, and Eleanor, in a long green satin outfit with very high heels, brought the dummy out to me!

Eleanor Norris has matured into a lovely woman. The best in her ancestry has really flowered in this girl. The Irish in her has always given her tremendous emotion and great depth of feeling. But it was from her father that she inherited the great compassion, the great sympathy she has for everyone she meets, especially someone in trouble—the underdog. She always, but always, answers the telephone with gay warmth and a happy quality in her voice, so unlike the cold, terse, hostile tones one often hears.

It is her great depth of emotion that propels me to kid her when I say that Eleanor would cry at gas station openings! But over the years we have both come to feel the same emotions at the same time. As we watched the picture *Love Story*, we reached for our handkerchiefs at the same precise moments. And as we watch television and motion pictures, invariably with our hands entwined, we feel the need to brush away that tear at the same precise moment. We have never had any children, mainly because I preferred not to have them. Eleanor realizes now that it is just as well that we didn't, because in the hectic days of our early marriage, with so much travel, we would have had to neglect them and would practically never have seen them at all. The many poodles we have had over the past years have been our children. We've loved them very dearly. Many a morning when we awaken and Eleanor picks up her dog Peppy or maybe my little Mimi, and cradles it in her arms and kisses it tenderly, she shows me what an affectionate and tender mother she would have been.

Her great affection is for everyone she knows, which I can sum up with the old vaudeville chestnut—*everybody* loves *Eleanor* and Eleanor would like to *love* everybody, but she doesn't *know* everybody!

Silvertip:

Castle

The summer of 1941 found me becoming more and more dissatisfied with my first home, back of Ciro's on the Sunset Strip. Up to this time I had laughed at those who insisted that a pool was a necessity in Hollywood. It was the first time I had ever really spent an entire summer in Southern California, and although the nights are cool and delightful, the days, while not irritatingly warm, lend themselves perfectly to the pleasure of swimming in a pool.

I therefore assigned my tennis-playing and real estate friend, C. Ralph Sentney, to do the impossible. First I asked him to look for a house that would be near the radio studios of Hollywood and the motion picture studios in that area. Next, it must be high, with a sweeping view and the lights of either Hollywood or the San Fernando Valley. It should have at least an acre or an acre and a half of property, large enough for dogs to roam and exercise. I wanted four bedrooms and four baths, and a rock fireplace that would actually burn wood. A small spot in which motion pictures might be projected would be equally desirable, and if some portion of the house had a built-in bar, that, too, would be

in the Hills

most desirable. But above all it must have a pool, and, if possible, a tennis court. My final admonition to Sentney was to "find somebody in trouble."

After inspecting twenty-three homes, I came to the conclusion that it was as difficult to find the ideal house as it was to find the ideal employee. As we examined house after house there were always one or two things missing. It didn't have a pool, though it had a court. If it had a pool, the court was lacking. There were either too many bedrooms or not enough. Most of the houses were either in Beverly Hills or near Santa Monica, which made it a thirty- or forty-minute trip to the broadcasting studios. Only one or two good buys came very close to my specifications.

I was being conducted on these tours of inspection by a tall, wavy-haired, attractive, young Greek god who worked for Sentney. He was a boy who had probably made a try at pictures and wound up selling real estate while he bided his time for the right part and the right opportunity. He phoned me one morning after I had spent an evening drinking pink champagne at the Pirate's Den, and assured me that he had found just what I wanted. I climbed into my car and followed him up Laurel Canyon and headed east on Mulholland Drive. About this time the throbbing in my head was becoming unbearable and as we rounded curve after curve I decided to toot my horn and bring him to a stop and tell him to forget about it, that we would look at it on another day. Perhaps I had a subconscious divination of what awaited around the next bend. At least I continued driving, and forty seconds later I saw it perched high on the peak of a mountain tip.

It was built in 1930 by Ann Harding and her husband Harry Bannister on the site of what was once a reservoir. Whereas I find it possible to describe my place in Maine as "The Lodge," here in the Hollywood hills, "Silvertip," the name I have given to the Harding estate, defies all descriptive powers. However, I can tell you that it has a view of each point on the compass. On the north it stretches for miles to the base of the Sierra Nevadas and San Fernando Valley; Warner Brothers, Universal, and CBS Studio Center studios are a stone's throw from us; Lockheed Airport and Aircraft plants are directly north; and from the patio on the south side lies Hollywood, with its myriads of twinkling lights, frustrations, broken hearts, and pulsating success. With little visual effort on a normal day devoid of haze or smog, one can see the oil wells of Long Beach, and as corny as it sounds, Catalina Island stands out like a cameo, even to the uninitiated. There is an imposing set of iron gates that swing from two huge brownstone posts, a gatehouse that leads into the estate. There are fruit trees, avocados, peaches, limes, lemons, grapefruit, and oranges, and a lovely high summer house with flowers to delight the eyes of those who admire beautiful flowers, and then the house itself.

Paul Whiteman, on visiting me for dinner one evening, noted the thickness of the walls and the massive beams in the living room. He confidently predicted to me that no earthquake, not anything, would ever do any damage to the house; that it would last forever! There is a massive sunken living room; a rock fireplace actually fourteen feet wide and ten feet high; a beautiful rotunda with red tile steps leading down a circular staircase to an entrance hall; a dining room with a small fireplace and exquisite Italian furniture and table and chairs that came with the house; the large window that looks down on Warner Brothers Studios and the vast expanse of the San Fernando Valley; a secret staircase to a sunporch upstairs, from which beds pull out of the wall, with radio and phonograph installation already in; another long hallway carpeted in lush red carpet; a children's playroom I converted into a library; an attractive bedroom on the right; and a tremendously large master bedroom and large tiled bathroom. At the end of this hallway are long glass doors set in wrought iron, the construction obviously by master craftsmen, doors that would be impossible to have made today.

The floor below houses another bedroom and bath; the hallway that was used as a gymnasium; a beautiful open porch that overlooks the swimming pool, and that I have enclosed and now use as an office; flagstone steps descending to two small bathhouses near the pool; and further steps to take one from the three-car garage to another building affixed to the side of a great gradual slope, a building that is four stories in height and the roof of which is (believe it or not) a championship tennis court. The obvious query that leaps to the mouth of the person who sees the tennis court for the first time is "What happens if one

A few of many songs, some dating back to the early days of radio, familiar to bandsmen of the 1920s and 30s

Our home, Silvertip

hits a tennis ball too high?" In the first place the strong metal fence that goes around all sides of this roof is very high and strongly constructed—a fence that would rarely permit a ball to go out, and of such strength it would be impossible for any player, running as hard as he might, ever to have any fear of going through it and dropping from the considerable height on the north side of this roof. I may point out a dozen times that the *roof* of this building is a championship tennis court, but no one ever seems to grasp the full significance of what I have just explained until they see the first long corridor underneath the roof itself. As the door is entered a blue and white enameled sign says, "Rue de Vallée." This street sign was given to me years ago by a fan who picked it up in Paris. (The name "Vallée." is a rather common one in France. There are probably hundreds of Vallées, even more La Vallées, and a great many de la Vallées. Some may recall that the ex-wife of Maurice Chevalier was Yvonne Vallée.)

In this long corridor are eighteen wall panels of semicircular design, each panel being illuminated by a light bracket that hangs overhead. It was here, evidently, that Ann Harding had hung 8 × 10 glossy pictures of various scenes from her motion pictures. Fortunately, she left the hooks and the lights, and thus provided a perfect resting place for the several hundred framed copies of songs, pictures of personalities, announcements, cards, and clippings, which for years had hung from the walls of our New York offices. A widely syndicated feature-story writer, Aileen Mosby, who took the forty-cent tour through the house, either had not too good a memory or deliberately sought to give the impression that most of the pictures portrayed my likeness. Actually, one-third of them are of neutral subjects or personalities other than myself, but contained therein are the "Stein Song" piano copies as they appeared in the countries of France, Germany, Canada, Australia, China, England, and the United States; there are the gastronomic panels with the photographs of recipes from my good friend George Mardikian of the Omar Khayyam Restaurant in San Francisco and the redoubtable Trader Vic's, and a rum formula that was an exclusive gift to me from Don the Beachcomber, whose rum creations are without parallel anywhere in the world. There are the Yale panels; the military panels; the panels containing photographs of my trips to London and Paris; the *How to Succeed* panel with ten scrapbooks; the protégé panels with just a few photographs of those whom it has been my privilege to guide in their climb to success. Today the large scrapbooks number 281. Scattered here and there are other songs; pictures of various parts of the lake regions of Maine; pictures of my pet canines; announcements, such as the card that described our opening bill at the Palace in 1929. All in all, it is a fascinating gallery if you are interested in show business and have some liking for one Rudy Vallée. Frank Sinatra put it another way, however, as he and I left this particular corridor one day: "You would never guess who lived here!"

Underneath the roof next to the corridor just described is a sound-proofed theater with a stage at one end and a projection room at the other. The theater is capable of holding 125 people very comfortably, and the quality of sound projection leaves nothing to be desired. Miss Harding probably presented plays, as there are dressing rooms backstage, one of which we have converted into a ladies' powder room with poodle wallpaper design; another houses a refrigerator, electric range, and sink, with a tremendous array of southern California pottery in various pastel colors, featuring a fourteen-inch plate on which an entire meal can be served for gastronomic enjoyment. Backstage in a special panel are the thirty-odd color shots pressed into wood panels, showing my lodge in Maine in all its pristine and colorful glory. Then, back of the stage, is a large knotty-pine playroom in which ninety people can move about without the least constriction. In this room is a rock fireplace equally as large as the one in the main house, and a bar at which fifteen or twenty people can foregather most comfortably. The room has a carpet that will never wear out, and large, luxurious davenports. The farewell "Fleischmann" program gift, the Capehart phonograph in Swedish blonde oak, reposes in one corner of this attractive room.

Near the stairs that lead to another long corridor—originally an open porch that has now been enclosed—is what I call the "Christmas Room." On the walls of this room are large red panels with gold frames, and on the redwood panels are Christmas cards from persons in show business (some alive, some deceased)—persons whom I've known over the last forty-five years; in some cases, ten or fifteen cards are from the same individuals, such as the Ozzie Nelsons, and each successive card, of course, shows the family growing larger in numbers, and the children in size. There are cards of personalities in every field of the entertainment world, a collection that, if greeting cards were rated the same as a rare and unusual collection of stamps, would make these panels worth a fortune.

Underneath the theater-playroom are two more floors that house all of the recordings I have made over the last forty-seven years, and row after row of orchestrations of music, valued at more than $2 million. Then on the opposite wall are stored cases of liquors, spirits of every description, and from racks of Philippine wood hang a collection of wines containing over 2,000 bottles, every California vintner being represented by two bottles of his choicest wine, and every type of red and white wine the palate might conceive. Stored here also are electrical equipment; musical instruments, including the saxophones of Rudy Wiedoeft and Benny Krueger; a collection of luggage for travel that alone would fill one-half of the average luggage store; a collection of furniture, particularly beds, that will eventually find their way into the newly built homes of some of our friends who can use them; and beneath this floor is a tremendous storage place in which we keep things not likely to be used, except at rare intervals throughout the years.

Outside, just above the tennis court, is a pool. Slightly smaller than the conventional standard size, it is more than adequate for our summer enjoyment. At the west end of the pool is a flagstone barbecue fireplace, with a speaker that works from the large Capehart in the living room, and a sink and storage space for food, cans, and supplies for parties that we enjoy on warm summer evenings into the late fall.

A few feet down from the barbecue, at the west end of the long theater and playroom building, but separate, is a miniature house, with a tiny fireplace, kitchen, and everything that would delight the heart of a small child. There are so many evidences that much thought was put into this fabulous estate with respect to the comfort and safety of the child that Ann Harding and Harry Bannister hoped to rear in this setting.

The sloping lawns, the trees, all the foliage and shrubbery, would really require the services of two gardeners, but two women fans keep everything in excellent appearance and tidy condition.

My greatest pride and joy is escorting our guests through the large beamed living room with its large rock fireplace, through metal French doors to a patio built in natural rock; huge boulders, approximately ten or twelve feet high, support the sheltering beamed roof, which projects from the house right down to these massive boulders. The view through the boulders, particularly at night, is exactly what one might expect to find in the Burma Bowl of the Himalayas.

There are days when Silvertip is bathed in sunlight and the view of the mountains in the distance is so impressive, I almost have to pinch myself to make sure that a punk kid from Maine who played a fair saxophone, and who sang in an untrained, slightly nasal voice, should have acquired such a breath-taking castle. It is a spot that never fails to thrill even Europeans and hard-boiled Easterners who never dreamed that anything quite so beautifully situated and artfully conceived and executed might exist in this part of the world, or any place, for that matter! I've said many times, if Hitler had taken over the United States, he would have said: "This is my Berchtesgaden. Out! Vallée, out! *Raus mit dem!*"

I caution the person who is driving over to see the home for the first time: Be very careful—if you turn right instead of left at any point you may wind up nowhere. But 20th Century-Fox's Harry Brand said it best: "The road to Rudy Vallée's place is littered with the bones of people who tried to find it!"

The reason it is so difficult to find our place is that the names of nearby streets are so confusing. The short street that leads to our gate had been renamed six times before someone gave it the very unlikely name of Pyramid Place. Running almost parallel to Pyramid Place is Pyramid Drive, 500 yards away. On his visits to our home on Christmas Eve, Mayor Sam Yorty would invariably chew me out for not having changed the name of our street because his chauffeur always drove him to Pyramid Drive which ends in a cul de sac (which in "fractured French" means "ice bag"). (That's a joke, son!) Yorty pleaded with us to change the name of our street to Rue de Vallée, as he had seen the genuine French street sign at our place.

So, being on the traffic commission and knowing the fellows who arrange for changes in the names of our streets, I filled out all the necessary documents and secured the approval of nine out of the twelve neighbors who would be affected by the change and prepared to pay a few dollars for the little sign at the top of Montcalm Avenue which directs you or tells you that you are now on Pyramid Place, the sign that now would read, Rue de Vallée.

Robert Stevenson, our councilman, was involved in a charge of gambling conspiracy; so to take the "heat" off his legal battle, he suddenly became the champion of the people and thundered that my desire to change the name of a small portion of a street would cost the city millions of dollars!

When Stevenson frustrated the move to change Pyramid Place to Rue de Vallée, he unwittingly gave me publicity I could not have bought for two million dollars. The fourth estate throughout the world rose to the bait of a famous crooner desiring to have a street named after himself and they played it up in big headlines all over the world. The fifty states gave it substantial space, but in the Paris *Herald Tribune*, the *London Globe*, and even in Tokyo newspapers, the shame of this famous entertainer wishing himself immortality—streetwise, that is—really made the news a worldwide proposition! I have three large scrapbooks filled with clippings and photos of every size and data.

So to the ghost of Robert Stevenson, my thanks for your outrage, however inspired, as it has brought me a renewed interest from the public and tremendous sympathy from even a few enemies who felt that if Sinatra and others could have highways and byways named in their honor, why not a veteran of show business who has brought some pleasure to millions all over the world!

Index